Help or Harm

Help or Harm

The Human Security Effects of International NGOs

Amanda Murdie

Stanford University Press
Stanford, California

Stanford University Press
Stanford, California

Printed in the United States of America on acid-free, archival-quality paper

Library of Congress Cataloging-in-Publication Data

Murdie, Amanda, author.
 Help or harm : the human security effects of international NGOs / Amanda Murdie.
  pages cm
 Includes bibliographical references and index.
 ISBN 978-0-8047-9197-7 (cloth : alk. paper)
 1. Non-governmental organizations. 2. Human security. I. Title.
 JZ4841.M87 2014
 361.7′7—dc23

                                                          2014010111

ISBN 978-0-8047-9247-9 (electronic)

Typeset by Newgen in 10/14 Minion

Contents

An appendix on proof of equilibria is posted at http://www.amandamurdie.org/
help-or-harm.html.

Acknowledgments

THE DEBT OF GRATITUDE I owe others for their assistance in this project can never be repaid. I can only hope to acknowledge them here and "pay it forward" in my personal dealings with others.

At Emory University, David R. Davis suggested that I read Margaret Keck and Kathyrn Sikkink's *Activists Beyond Borders: Advocacy Networks in International Politics*. The book absolutely changed my life. Not only did it introduce me to a wonderful literature about how international non-governmental organizations (INGOs) work, but it provided me with a research focus that today, almost ten years later, I still consider both intellectually stimulating and personally important. I do not know Margaret Keck or Kathyrn Sikkink personally, but it would be wrong for me not to thank them first for their work.

This project's roots require me to thank the entire faculty at Emory University. John Boli, Cliff Carrubba, David R. Davis, and Dani Reiter went above and beyond in providing mentoring, necessary critiques, and quiet encouragement throughout my time at Emory. Many others in the department, especially Carrie Wickham and Michael Giles, talked over the project with me from the very beginning. I was lucky enough to be at Emory during an explosion of great talent, and I am thankful for each of my colleagues there for sharing their time and expertise with me. Of particular note, Amy Liu and Tavishi Bhasin have both listened to me ramble about this project for far too long. Rob O'Reilly, director of the Emory Electronic Data Center, was critical in my development as a scholar, and I am so grateful for his perspective along the way.

I have been blessed as well with great and supportive universities where I worked on this project as a faculty member. Kansas State University provided an excellent start to my career, and I am thankful for all my colleagues there, especially Sam Bell, Jeffrey Pickering, and Dale Herspring. Starting my first faculty position at the same time and place as Sam has been a stroke of luck that I am forever grateful for. The University of Missouri has also been fantastic: I thank all my colleagues who have walked to get coffee with me while I fretted over some part of the manuscript. I am honored to be surrounded by such talent. I'm especially thankful for the support that Cooper Drury and John Petrocik have given me.

So many people have read, commented on, and discussed portions of this project with me and have greatly improved the quality of the final project. Of course, any errors left in the project are my own, and I'm sure I'm leaving out very important contributors, so I apologize in advance. I am especially grateful for the comments and discussions on INGOs with my coauthors Victor Asal, Colin Barry, Kevin Brown, Patricia Blocksome, K. Chad Clay, David Cingranelli, Dursun Peksen, Michael Flynn, Alex Hicks, Jakub Kakietek, Craig Stapley, Sarah Stroup, Johannes Urpelainen, and Sean Webeck. Elizabeth Bloodgood, Sarah Bush, Steve Krasner, Hans Peter Schmidt, Thomas Risse, Mike Ward, and Wendy Wong have also provided great feedback on this book and related works. Doug Bond at Virtual Research Associates has been a great help as well. I've presented this work at many universities and conferences, and I am also so grateful for all of the suggestions and critiques, even the critiques that had some bite to them! I appreciate the advice and comments of my reviewers and my editor Geoffrey Burn at Stanford University Press.

My final debt of gratitude is owed to my family. My grandparents-in-law, David and Clara Murdie, never once questioned how silly it was for their grandson to support me in this crazy life. My brother and his family also provided great support. My own parents, David and Marty Hilley, deserve so many thanks for continually reminding me to focus only on what really matters, even if it means stepping aside from research. To my children, Tenacity and Serenity Murdie: you are my best friends and my proudest accomplishments. I don't think I would have worked half as hard on anything in my life if I didn't know you both were watching.

The biggest debt I owe can never be repaid. Of all the serendipitous things in my life, at 18, I met a very self-assured individual who believed that we could do more than our backgrounds. To my husband, Avery Murdie: I didn't dream big until I met you and could not have accomplished *any* of my dreams without you.

Help or Harm

1 INTRODUCTION

THOUSANDS OF NON-GOVERNMENTAL ORGANIZATIONS (NGOS), most of them international in scope, have descended upon post-Taliban Afghanistan. The vast majority of these organizations are interested in improving human security, working to provide important health and development services, and promoting rights for repressed populations in the country. Despite their lofty goals, the people of Afghanistan are not impressed. According to a 2008 and 2009 survey by the United Nations Office of Drugs and Crime, 54 percent of people in Afghanistan think NGOs within Afghanistan are corrupt. Organizations of all sizes and creed have been accused of taking funds from the international community and not using that money to help the people of Afghanistan. Some organizations have been found guilty of their accused crimes. Many Afghans have run on political platforms concerning the ineffectiveness of the NGO sector. As the joke goes, the NGO community in Afghanistan is so bad that "first there was Communism, then there was Talibanism, and now there is NGOism" (Mojumdar 2006; see also Cohen, Kupcu, and Khanna 2008).

Similar attitudes exist in Haiti, where, in the few years since the devastating 2010 earthquake and hurricane, the small state has quickly lived up to its designation of the "republic of NGOs." Per capita, more non-governmental organizations, most of them international in scope and focus, are in Haiti than anywhere else in the world. Many of these organizations are extremely well funded, working to provide basic sanitation, education, and health services to help rebuild Haiti. However, resentment is high: graffiti in Port-au-Prince labels organizations "thieves," "liars," and "corrupt," listing organizations by name and then saying in Haitian Creole that "all [are] complicit in the misery"

(Valbrun 2012). Locals often see the organizations as simply interested in filling their own coffers, buying expensive flats and SUVs in Haiti, and then, according to Birrell (2012), "heading off early to the beaches for the weekend."

Despite these negative reviews, some international non-governmental organizations are making a difference in basic service provision, both within Afghanistan and Haiti and elsewhere. Examples of successful outputs are widespread; for example, the organization Cooperative for Assistance and Relief Everywhere (CARE) International reported that between late 2001 and 2003, one of its key projects in Afghanistan irrigated 2700 hectares of land, protected another 600 from flood erosion, and built 1600 cubic meters of water drawing points (CARE 2003).

Similarly, non-governmental organizations working with the United Nations Office for the Coordination of Humanitarian Affairs in Haiti have removed "2 million cubic meters of rubble" and are "providing safe drinking water to 1.2 million people daily" (Valbrun 2010).

In many locales, there are examples of successful project outputs by non-governmental organizations, often with overall increases in service provision within the country. For example, vaccination drives by international non-governmental organizations have been tremendously successful. Organizations have even managed to hold vaccination days for children in the midst of civil wars, with both sides calling a "cease-fire" in order to attend vaccination clinics in the countries of Sudan, the Democratic Republic of Congo, and Sierra Leone, among others (Hotez 2001). As a result of the work of these organizations, often in concert with donor agencies and private foundations, cases of polio, a debilitating and often deadly disease that targets children, have been reduced by a whopping 99 percent since 1988. India, once the "epicenter of the polio epidemic," was actually polio free in 2011 (Pruthi 2012). As another example, international non-governmental organizations in Timor in the early 2000s were tremendously successful in providing health services after conflict; organizations there also helped empower the public health sector during reconstruction starting in 2003 (Alonso and Brugha 2006). Similarly, in 2001, organizations in Bangladesh created a government partnership for tuberculosis treatment, increasing access to key medicines for infected populations (Ullah et al. 2006).

Beyond basic service provision for human security, the success of international non-governmental organizations on human rights promotion, as another key area of human security, also appears mixed, with tremendous success by some organizations in some countries on certain issues and catastrophic failure by other organizations in other situations. Another example is the work of organizations in North Africa. Even two decades before organizations aided in orchestrating some of the peaceful protests and advocacy associated with the Arab Spring of 2011, human rights international non-governmental organizations in Morocco had worked to limit government repression, including the use of torture during interrogations. The work of human rights organizations even led to the closure of the infamous Tazmamart secret prison (Granzer 1999). Organizations pressured regime leaders directly and brought powerful international actors, including United States and French foreign policy leaders, into the advocacy network, providing background reports on Moroccan practices and empowering diaspora groups to take up the cause.

At the same time international non-governmental organizations in Morocco were stopping government abuses of physical integrity rights, however, organizations were having very limited success at stopping the practice of female genital cutting in the whole North African region. This was an issue that many organizations thought they could quickly outlaw and eradicate. Governments had very little interest in the practice, roles of women in society were quickly expanding, and many international resources were devoted to the cause. To a large degree, all of this work by international non-governmental organizations was for naught: a huge cultural war was created by the international efforts, framing advocacy related to the eradication of female genital cutting as paternalistic and "postcolonial imperialism" (Boyle 2005, 1). The efforts even led some domestic advocates to wonder why the practice of genital cutting was being pushed for eradication by international non-governmental organizations from Western countries, where the use of breast implants, seen as another form of genital mutilation, was widespread (Wilson 2002; Lake 2012). International advocacy on the issue created a backlash: more adult women in Burkina Faso and Yemen had undergone genital cutting in 2005 than in 1998 (WHO 2010). Most of the survey data on the issue finds that women in the region generally support the practice, even after the highly publicized eradication campaign of the 1990s (Wagner 2011). Among Moroccans, where female genital cutting was not historically practiced, there is now even anecdotal evidence of its use, even by those who have emigrated out of the region.

Beyond Morocco, it is even more difficult to ascertain when and where organizations are successful in improving human rights practices. International non-governmental organizations have been credited with everything from the end of apartheid in South Africa (Heinrich 2001) to the drastic human rights improvements in Guatemala after their civil war in the late 1990s and, to a lesser extent, Mexico in the mid-1990s (Ropp and Sikkink 1999; Godoy 2002). And yet, continued human rights advocacy by international non-governmental organizations over the use of the death penalty in China has fallen on deaf ears; similar calls for the end of abusive practices in Russia and Syria have also been wholeheartedly ignored by regime leaders.

What explains when and where international non-governmental organizations will be successful at improving human security? Why were organizations focused on development and health largely successful in India, Timor, and Bangladesh but not in Haiti and Afghanistan, where far more attention and international donor funds were directed? Within Haiti and Afghanistan, why are some organizations successful and others not? For organizations involved in promoting human rights, what determines when success happens? Why were organizations successful at getting the government of Morocco to change the fundamental ways it controlled the population (torture, political imprisonment) but similar organizations were not successful at getting individuals to stop a private practice (female genital cutting) that, prior to the 1990s in the region, was arguably already on the decline? Further, why did a little prodding by INGOs work to change human rights practices in Guatemala and Mexico but continued criticism has not been successful in China? In short, under what conditions should we expect international non-governmental organizations to matter for human security?

This book offers a comprehensive framework for understanding the effects of international non-governmental organizations (international NGOs or INGOs) on human security, briefly defined as a set of outcomes ensuring that an individual enjoys freedom from "want" and "fear" (UNDP 1994; Paris 2001). Many INGOs work tirelessly on issues of human security. As the examples above show, INGOs are active in all countries in the world, doing everything from providing vaccinations and basic sanitation in rural areas to pressuring world leaders in the United Nations to end political disappearances. Within the INGO world, organizations that work on issues of human security can be typically thought of as either primarily focused on service provision, like development or health organizations, or focused on advocacy, like organizations that focus on changing a government's human rights practices. In human security language, organizations that focus on service provision would be working to ensure that individuals were free from "want." Organizations working to promote human rights would be working to promote freedom from "fear."[1]

Since the 1980s, the number of international non-governmental organizations that are active in the world has increased significantly. These organizations, such as the well-known Amnesty International or Oxfam organizations, have increased their world presence drastically since the end of the Cold War, often setting up multiple permanent offices and expanding their volunteer bases within countries. In the last 20 years, for example, over 50 countries have seen the number of INGOs that are active within their borders increase over 500 percent; some countries saw the number of INGOs increase over 20-fold (Landman 2005; UIA 2008/2009).

This tremendous growth in INGOs has been coupled with drastic increases in the amount of aid and media attention these organizations receive. In fact, "some now estimate that more aid to developing countries is funneled through the NGO sector than the United Nations or the World Bank" (Brown et al. 2008, 25). INGOs have been heralded in the popular media for their work; multiple organizations, including Amnesty International, International Committee of the Red Cross, and Médecins Sans Frontières (Doctors Without Borders), have won Nobel Peace Prizes.

As the sector grew, many saw INGOs as an "emerging second superpower," capable of assisting in the fulfillment of human security when previous state and intergovernmental efforts had failed (Moore 2003). In her 1997 *Foreign Affairs* article, Jessica Matthews sums up the general praise directed at the whole NGO world in the midst of this tremendous growth period:

> At a time of accelerating change, NGOs are quicker than governments to respond to new demands and opportunities. Internationally, in both the poorest and richest countries, NGOs, when adequately funded, can outperform government in the delivery of many public services. Their growth, along with that of the other elements of civil society, can strengthen the fabric of the many still-fragile democracies. And they are better than governments at dealing with problems that grow slowly and affect society through their cumulative effect on individuals—the "soft" threats of environmental degradation, denial of human rights, population growth, poverty, and lack of development that may already be causing more deaths in conflict than are traditional acts of aggression. (63)

Despite all this praise and growth, surprisingly, very little is known about the actual effects of INGOs across countries. Even outside of the academic literature, INGO workers themselves wonder about the effects of their efforts:

> Counting marketable achievements such as how many leaflets were distributed, or the quantity of funds raised, prevents us from reflecting on what changes have been achieved, or the strength of our resistance to corporates or government, or, more realistically, from analysing our effectiveness long-term in a struggle against power that isn't meant to come with quarterly "successes." (Francie 2011, 60)

Now, to be sure, most organizations have ways to measure their individual organizational output. Interviews with INGO leaders of United States–based organizations have revealed that INGOs do care about "whether or not we are sort of getting the tasks achieved that we set for ourselves" but that the individual organizations "can't determine the outcomes. . . . We don't necessarily know how many people it will affect" (Mitchell 2010, 6).

Going beyond the work of one organization or one joint movement, the academic literature has not yet provided definitive answers on whether the overall INGO sector actually delivers "outcomes" for the citizenry in locations where INGOs are active. We have not cross-nationally examined what conditions make positive outcomes more likely. A cursory look at the top journals in international relations reveals that we, as academics, have spent far more time debating the effectiveness of intergovernmental organizations, like the United Nations or the European Union, than the effectiveness of INGOs.

Despite the overwhelmingly large number of INGOs, academic inquiry is especially lacking for organizations involved in service delivery, which have been almost completely omitted from both the theoretical and empirical literature on INGOs. The literature has focused primarily on advocacy INGOs, like human rights organizations, and has often attributed the issues and dynamics in the advocacy realm to service organizations. Despite this focus on advocacy INGOs, there has actually been more growth in the number of service INGOs, such as those providing economic development or health services in developing countries (Cameron 2000).

THE THEORETICAL DEBATE

Much larger than just the empirical question of whether INGOs matter, there exists a huge theoretical divide in international relations over how INGOs are viewed and what, if any, impact these organizations could have in the international system. Most of this divide is between the classic theoretical schools of realism and constructivism. On one hand, realism has very little space for

INGOs and nonstate actors in general (Ahmed and Potter 2006). According to realism, the international system today is dominated by states and, as Kenneth Waltz (1979) classically puts it, "So long as the major states are the major actors, the structure of international politics is defined in terms of them" (94). The focus in realism is on state interactions in an anarchic system. As Hocking and Smith (1990) point out, consistent with realism, states are critical actors in international relations because they possess sovereignty, recognition, and control over territory and population. None of these things are benchmarks of INGOs, of course, which are actually often advocating for changes in ways states control their population through force (i.e., the protection of human rights). Like realist notions of the role of intergovernmental organizations, realism sees INGOs as instruments of states, working to carry out the policies of state actors (Geeraerts 1995). As such, INGOs could be influential, perhaps, on service provision that would be in line with what major states want, providing development assistance and basic service provision in a country that is a strategic partner of the INGO's home state. INGOs would be unable, however, to push state actors to change their behavior on issues that went against the desires of the regime in power. If a country does not want to stop torturing its citizens, no amount of INGO pressure would be enough to make it do that.

Within the international relations theory of constructivism, where the theoretical focus is on social change, however, INGOs have quite a large role (Finnemore and Sikkink 2001). Most of the canonical literature on INGOs, including Margaret Keck and Kathryn Sikkink's 1998 *Activists Beyond Borders: Advocacy Networks in International Relations*, sees INGOs as critical actors in larger advocacy movements. INGOs serve as key entrepreneurs in normative development and then spread new norms to both state and nonstate actors, using a variety of political tactics (Finnemore and Sikkink 1998). Unlike other actors, according to this canonical constructivist framework, INGOs, as key actors in larger advocacy movements, are assumed to be motivated by "values rather than material concerns" (Keck and Sikkink 1998, 2). The tremendous potential for INGOs to be advocates for policy and behavior change rests on this idea that INGOs are "principled," motivated to help a domestic population with their struggles against an obdurate regime (Keck and Sikkink 1998; De-Mars 2005; Kelly 2005). Risse (2010) refers to this motivation as one of "shared values" (285). Because of their principled motivations, INGOs are able to garner the support of the domestic community where they are working and the international community writ large, including foundations, third-party states, clergy, and parts of intergovernmental organizations. With the combination of both this support "from below" and "from above," INGOs are able to induce improvements in human security (Brysk 1993). Worth noting, this idea of motivations in the canonical literature does not imply that INGOs are "stupid" or "not strategic" but that these actors are distinctly positioned in the world polity for social change because of their principled, shared values (Risse 2010, 287).

Both of these theoretical schools—realism and constructivism—offer large-scale predictions of whether INGOs will matter for outcomes in human security. In short, realism sees little potential for INGOs, especially if we are focusing on a human security outcome that is against the interests of the state. Constructivists, conversely, see huge potential in INGOs, as part of larger advocacy movements, to influence world politics. Some of the constructivist literature, including the canonical Keck and Sikkink (1998) and the 1999 edited volume *The Power of Human Rights: International Norms and Domestic Change*, by Thomas Risse, Stephen Ropp, and Kathryn Sikkink, even offer predictions concerning where improvement is most likely. Many of these conditional relationships, however, have not been empirically examined, especially if looking beyond the success of a single campaign (Risse 2002).

BEYOND THE IVORY TOWER: DEMONS AND ANGELS

Within both realism and constructivism, however, little attention is made to differences *among* INGOs. In both of these theoretical literatures, INGOs are typically a monolithic group with similar motivations. Further, the key causal stories through which INGOs are said to influence world politics, mainly coming from the constructivist literature mentioned above, focus almost solely on advocacy organizations. When extensions are made to service INGOs, across theoretical lenses, it is typically implicitly assumed that the same dynamics apply to both service and advocacy organizations (Cooley and Ron 2002; Prakash and Gugerty 2010).

Looking beyond the ivory tower of academia, however, it is clear that not all INGOs are equal: the underlying motivations of these organizations appear to differ. Some INGOs are very obviously acting as if motivated by principles or "shared values." Others, like the unfortunate examples of particular organizations in Haiti or Afghanistan, do not appear to be motivated by any principles or values in line with their mission statements. As one INGO specializing in ending genocide so dramatically put it, "Not all NGOs are angels. Some are demons" (AEGIS 2012). Scores of organizations, particularly those in service delivery, have been heavily critiqued for their rent-seeking, taking funds from the international community and not investing them in local service provision. For example, in reference to INGOs in Somalia in the early 2000s, Berhan (2002) said the following:

> Many people may believe that honestly concerned individuals and groups establish NGOs. But in most cases the situation clearly shows that selfish and greedy individuals use the system to create and benefit from NGOs.

Even within the United States, such accusations of rent-seeking abound. A recent article entitled "Above the Law: America's Worst Charities" highlights how the organization Kids Wish Network "spends less than 3 cents on the dollar helping kids," and many "are little more than fronts for fund-raising companies" (Hundley and Taggert 2013). In an article in the *Jakarta Post*, Puji Pujiono, a past official of the UN Office for the Coordination of Humanitarian Affairs in Indonesia, summed up the issue of service INGO rent-seeking as follows:

> It is common for me to see [INGOs] benefit from disaster recovery projects: another project, another new flashy car for each of them. (Sawitri 2006)

A similar, although somewhat distinct, issue emerges concerning whether advocacy organizations are behaving incongruously with the "shared values" that underlie extant theoretical understandings of INGOs and, in many cases, the very mission statements of the organizations themselves. Within many accounts of advocacy organizational behavior, some organizations are advocating for policies or practices that are in line with the desires of at least a small portion of the domestic population they are professed to be working on behalf of. Some, however, instead of working in line with their mission statement and our common academic understanding of the shared values and principles that are supposed to motivate INGOs, are only advocating for the often extreme policies that their international donors or foreign stakeholders want. It is argued that this is what occurred when some INGOs advocated for the full eradication of female genital cutting in North Africa during a time when even domestic women's rights groups in the region were advocating only for age restrictions and the medicalization of the practice (Boyle 2002).

The issue is not isolated to just that case; many critiques of advocacy INGOs in non-Western countries begin with questions about underlying motives. In a newspaper article cleverly entitled "Western Humanitarianism or Neo-Slavery," Amii Omara-Otunnu (2007) wrote, "It is doubtful that Western humanitarian work in Africa can have enduring positive impact unless Euro-Americans discard paternalistic racist attitude towards Africans," and organizations can "simply be Trojan horses for all sorts of forces and ulterior motives." Similarly, an op-ed piece by Joseph Mudingu (2006) in the Rwandan newspaper *New Times* began:

> The term *Non-Governmental [Organizations]* is actually a misnomer. The NGOs are financed and directed by the various imperialist agencies, the imperialist governments, and the comprador regimes. They act as the liaison between the people and the governments. They are the vehicles through which the exploiters seek to influence the opinions of "civil society."

This idea of very personalistic, organizational, or funder-driven values trumping "shared values" with the domestic population on whose behalf organizations supposedly work has not been completely lacking in the academic literature. James Petras and Henry Veltmeyer (2001), Lisa Sundstrom (2006), Susantha Goonatilake (2006), and Elizabeth Ferris (2011), for example, all have written books on the topic. Clifford Bob's (2005) award-winning book *The Marketing of Rebellion* makes the argument that INGOs, as organizations all interested in longevity and appeasing international donors, often make decisions based not on need or community desire but on what fits with their personalistic agenda. Much of this literature, however, has really "thrown out the baby with the bathwater," equating the motivational lack of congruence with local community desires of some organizations with the motivations of all INGOs. This is unfortunate, as Sam Vaknin reported in a 2005 United Press International story:

> Some NGOs . . . genuinely contribute to enhancing welfare, to the mitigation of hunger, the furtherance of human and civil rights, or the curbing of disease. Others . . . are sometimes ideologically biased, or religiously committed and, often, at the service of special interests. Conflicts of interest and unethical behavior abound. (1)

Thus, according to Vaknin, not all INGOs share the same motivations: there are heterogeneous types of INGOs that act as if they have very different underlying motivations. This basic idea applies both to service organizations, where organizations often show their lack of "shared values" by using donor funds on things other than service delivery, and advocacy organizations, where a lack of shared values really appears when organizations do not take into account the desires of the local population they supposedly are trying to help. This simple idea, extracted from a multitude of on-the-ground, eyewitness reports from within the INGO community, has been largely avoided in the academic literature.[2] However, in trying to understand when INGOs will aid in human security, acknowledging these on-the-ground issues leads me to ask a slightly updated research question: *How does the real possibility of INGOs with different motivations condition their overall effectiveness in areas of human security?*

In answering this question, this book extends the canonical theoretical literature on INGOs by relaxing the frequent assumption that all INGOs are motivated with "shared values" or "principles." Not all INGOs have to share the same motivations to help a domestic population achieve what it isn't able to on its own. Relaxing this assumption takes the debate away from one of classic versus revisionist ideas of INGO motivations.[3] The issue isn't whether INGOs are really "altruistic" but that INGOs differ in their underlying motivations. Some INGOs likely have motivations that are in line with the traditional notions of "shared values" and principles. Others, however, have motivations that seem to reflect both on-the-ground critiques and the revisionist literature: they are motivated, quite generally, by the personalistic rents that come from their work, appearing in the form of lined pockets or working only to please some foreign stakeholders. No work has examined how this key bifurcation in organizational motivations could condition the overall success of the INGO sector on human security outcomes. In line with the mountains of anecdotal stories out of places like Haiti, North Africa, and Afghanistan, however, examining this idea in a systematic way is critical for understanding whether and how the INGO sector can help millions in human security hot spots around the world.

CENTRAL ARGUMENTS OF THIS BOOK

At its heart, the first argument this book proposes is painfully simple: INGOs will be more likely to matter on issues of human security when and where those with "shared values" or principled motivations are likely to flourish. For both service and advocacy organizations, on issues and in states where both a domestic population and the larger international community know they are likely facing an organization with motivations that are of some value to them, we should see INGOs get the necessary support of these critical actors, leading to a likely increased human security outcome on the ground as a result of the INGO sector. This argument holds even when we acknowledge the ways that motivations and interactions differ for service compared to advocacy INGOs.

This first argument, although simple, illustrates the precarious nature of improving human security. When chaos reigns after civil wars or humanitarian disasters, it is likely that many development INGOs, for example, could be just in the region to fill their own pockets and not interested in providing services. In these times, fear of supporting an organization that does not actually intend to use funds efficiently to provide services may limit overall support of all INGOs, thwarting the potential for the whole INGO sector to actually provide services that will improve human security. Many development and humanitarian organizations in Haiti and Afghanistan have definitely worried about whether the reports and stories critical to certain organizations could limit their abilities to both get funding and work with the local populations they so desperately want to help (Mojumdar 2006).

When focusing on human rights advocacy, this simple argument also provides insights into how certain issues that appear to be more "hot-button" issues internationally, like the eradication of female genital cutting, may not be successful domestically, while other issues with less international media attention, like the releasing of political prisoners or improving prison conditions, may still manage to be positively influenced by human rights INGOs. When an issue involves organizations with preferences that appear less like "shared values" with the domestic population and more like advocacy on behalf of some foreign stakeholder, all advocacy INGOs may be negatively affected. This provides an important extension to arguments about how international pressure shapes issue emergence; just because an advocacy issue makes the international agenda does not mean that the advocacy will actually translate into marked improvements in human security on the ground (Carpenter 2007). Organizations with motives contrary to what the domestic population actually wants may limit domestic support at the end of the day, severely curtailing the success of the overall movement. Organizational advocates in Nigeria, for example, have expressed such concerns. Domestic groups there are often leery of supporting any Western human rights INGO for fear they may inadvertently support an INGO with an imperialist agenda for rights that runs strongly counter to local cultural norms (Okafor 2006).

What happens, then, when an organization is not in a situation where "shared values" types of INGOs are flourishing? Could a few bad apples really cause the whole barrel of INGOs to be thrown out? When it comes to organizations that are interested in human security in Haiti or Afghanistan or in women's rights in Morocco, what can they do to improve their chances of getting the support necessary for human security improvements? How do they ensure that they aren't lumped in with the bad apples? More than just academic conjecture, the possibility of the few without "shared values" making work difficult for the whole INGO sector is very real. The few bad apples can try to make themselves look like good apples. Many of the United States' nonprofits that were identified as the country's "worst charities" tried to "mimic" others in the sector (Hundley and Taggart 2013). As an official with CARE reported, "Unfortunately for NGOs, critics do not make this distinction" between those working for and with the domestic population and those that are just interested in some sort of personalist agenda (Mojumdar 2006). This can create "hostility" toward the whole humanitarian sector, leading many to "lump" them all together as troublesome, unsuccessful, and unwanted actors (Mojumdar 2006).

This book's second major theme examines ways in which INGOs send signals about their underlying motivations to the larger domestic and international populations, who can be uninformed but important for the work of the INGO sector. INGOs often try to make their "brand" known: they attend public conferences, sign statements about their intentions, hire locals and put them in positions of power, and release their financial statements to the broader community in attempts to appear transparent about their underlying motivations (Gourevitch and Lake 2012). These signals, when credible, can help the INGO get the support it needs, leading to a more likely human security effect on the ground. However, for advocacy organizations, where the international and domestic communities often want very different things, these signals can solidify an organization's stance on a divided issue, sometimes limiting its support either domestically or internationally. This is the second basic argument of this book: signals sent by INGOs can and do matter. It focuses on one key signal in particular: consultative status with the United Nations (UN) Economic, Social, and Cultural (ECOSOC) Council. This status provides organizations with an entrée to all aspects of the UN; it is the only way an organization can formally interact at the United Nations. To acquire this status, an organization must provide financial information and participate in a review process, where the organization's policy and ideological positions on certain issues are often addressed. This fascinating process has not been examined thoroughly and provides an inside glimpse into how an intergovernmental organization (the UN) can be used to differentiate INGOs for both international and domestic audiences.

In considering the actions INGOs take to communicate their underlying motivations as "signals," this book draws on a broad and vibrant literature on signaling in international relations, which is just beginning to examine signals made by nonstate actors, including INGOs (Jervis 1970; Fearon 1997; Mansfield, Milner, and Rosendorff 2003; Fang 2008; Weeks 2008; Chapman 2011). It also connects these actions to similar actions by domestic nonprofits and to research on how these programs develop in the nonprofit literature (Reinhardt 2009; Gugerty and Prakash 2010).

This signaling framework provides a rich theoretical story with many empirical implications. Importantly, the previous signaling literature in international relations has focused on how signals sent by actors condition the behavior of others and thus impact many different political outcomes, including war, foreign direct investment, and diplomacy (Jervis 1970; Mansfield et al. 2003; Sartori 2003; Chapman 2009). By examining how INGOs' signals impact other actors' behaviors, a more theoretically satisfying account of INGOs' conditional impact on eventual human security outcomes is constructed.

The third central theme of this book concerns the domestic-level characteristics that (1) make international and domestic support of INGOs likely and (2) provide the structural and institutional preconditions that help INGO operations. This theme draws heavily on the dynamics of heterogeneous types of INGOs and their signaling behavior. By itself, however, it also provides insights into how INGO influences on human security outcomes can be conditioned by factors of development, geography, and domestic political structures within the country in which the INGO is trying to work. In short, some locations are just "easier" cases for the INGO sector than others. Understanding what makes a country ripe for INGO success is important; international donors often evaluate service INGO success and make future funding decisions based on the grade the INGO received. If the organization, however, is simply in an area where success is that much more difficult, this information needs to be taken into account. For human rights advocacy, knowing which states are more vulnerable to the pressure of human rights INGOs is also important; these states may be able to start processes that could diffuse and influence their whole neighborhood (Bell, Clay, and Murdie 2012).

This book's approach to the study of INGOs is novel in a number of ways. First, as mentioned, unlike much of the previous literature on INGOs within international relations, I extend my theoretical focus to include both advocacy and service INGOs. The main goal of advocacy INGOs, such as Amnesty International or Greenpeace, is getting a targeted actor to adopt a policy or behavior in line with the position of the INGO (Ahmed and Potter 2006). Common advocacy INGO missions would involve human rights or environmental outcomes. Conversely, service INGOs, such as CARE or Oxfam, focus mainly on goods provision. Service INGOs include organizations that focus on health or development-related service provision, such as handing out contraceptives or digging wells in developing countries. Because I am particularly interested in improvements in human security outcomes, I restrict the focus here to human rights INGOs as a subsegment of advocacy organizations and to development INGOs as a key component of service INGOs. The theoretical argument, however, can also apply to other issue areas where INGOs often work.

In addressing both advocacy and service INGOs, this book provides an encompassing theoretical framework for understanding INGOs that also accounts for different dynamics for advocacy as opposed to service organizations; this distinction has not been explicit in many of the canonical and recent revisionist works on INGOs. For example, while both the international and domestic community may agree that they would like to avoid supporting a service organization that wants to use funds to fill its own coffers, the international community may want to support an organization *because* it has a personalistic agenda that runs counter to the values of the domestic population where the advocacy is taking place.

This book's theoretical argument is grounded in game-theoretic formal models, something that is not typically seen in INGO studies. These models help us to rigorously and logically think about how INGOs with heterogeneous underlying motivations influence their interactions with other actors critical for advocacy and service provision and, as a result, condition the organizations' impact on human security outcomes. In addition to providing a framework for understanding many extant empirical regularities, solutions to the formal models provide a variety of novel and testable implications concerning when issues related to nonprincipled organizations will likely limit overall INGO success and the usefulness of signals sent by INGOs.

Unlike most other books on INGOs, I examine the implications of my theoretical framework quantitatively on a sample of over 100 countries without perfect human security situations since the end of the Cold War. To test these implications quantitatively, I use a novel dataset on the activities, presence, and funding of over 1000 human rights and development INGOs and back up my large-scale findings with much case study and anecdotal research. These case study vignettes serve as "reality checks" to the game-theoretic logic and empirical findings of the book. I find that INGOs can have powerful effects on human rights and development outcomes. However, very generally, I find that the effect of these organizations is not monolithic; differences in organizational characteristics that reflect underlying motivations, issue focus, and state peculiarities condition when and where this vibrant and growing force of INGOs will be effective contributors to human security outcomes. This study, therefore, provides the first comprehensive quantitative tests of the impact of large numbers of issue-specific INGOs on a variety of human security outcomes and, more importantly, the first cross-national empirical examination of the factors that condition the impact of INGOs.

OVERVIEW OF THIS BOOK

Chapter 2, after spending a little bit of time on definitional issues, outlines the existing theoretical understanding of INGOs and their effects on human security. It then discusses the mechanisms through which INGOs are supposed to improve human security, distinguishing the work of service INGOs from the work of advocacy INGOs. I present both the traditional assumptions of INGO motivations from within international relations and the revisionist work and practitioner reports that question these assumptions. I discuss the book's baseline ideas about how the underlying motivations of INGOs differ and how both the international and domestic communities that work with the organizations are often uninformed about these motivations. The signaling approach in international relations is introduced and linked to behaviors by INGOs. This discussion serves as the motivations for the book's theoretical argument.

Chapter 3 presents the theoretical argument of the book, drawing on a series of game-theoretic models that are available in the appendices. I begin by outlining the basic tensions in INGO work in the human security sector and identifying the actors that often interact with INGOs. I then explicitly relax the assumption that all INGOs share the same underlying motivations and present the idea that organizations can send signals about their underlying motivations in an effort to gain support. This framework provides many scenarios for when and where INGOs are able to get the support they need for human security outcomes. The chapter addresses these scenarios and provides the testable hypotheses that flow from this framework. Due to differences in how underlying motivations appear for service as opposed to advocacy INGOs, I present the implications of the theoretical model separately for these two types of organizations. Even though the theory is based on game-theoretic models, this chapter is presented in very nontechnical terms, accessible to both an academic and a practitioner audience. Moreover, as discussed in the chapter, many of the empirical implications from the game-theoretic models are consistent with both practitioner and scholarly understandings of INGOs, a fact that provides a basic "reality check" to formal approach.

Chapters 4 and 5 provide empirical tests of the implications of the theoretical argument. As mentioned, the approach here is novel: most research on INGOs is qualitative, but I provide quantitative, large-scale tests of the conditional effectiveness of INGOs. Chapter 4, focusing on human security service outcomes related to freedom from "want," examines development INGOs and their impact on development outcomes in lesser development countries. In line with the theoretical framework, the results indicate that development INGOs can be powerful conduits for service delivery. However, in areas where development INGOs with very personalistic rent-seeking motivations are likely to flourish, the ability of the sector to function in ways that help improve human security outcomes drastically diminishes. In these situations, the overall effect of INGOs on service delivery can even be negative. However, when we focus on only organizations that "signal" their underlying motivations to provide services efficiently, we do see that certain INGOs can still have a positive impact on service delivery related to human security. This result holds even when we account for the structural preconditions that might make organizations more likely to send these signals in the first place. Other results in this chapter illustrate how certain geographic and economic conditions within a state can impede the ability of development INGOs to carry out human security projects and how certain controversial issues of development assistance are affected by development INGOs only when the domestic population is in favor of those services. These large-scale results are supported with case study anecdotes from East Africa, South America, and East Asia.

Chapter 5, focusing on advocacy related to the freedom from "fear," turns the empirical focus to human rights INGOs and their abilities to influence a variety of human rights outcomes within a country. The first portion of the chapter discusses how issue-focus matters: the domestic population of the state where the advocacy is taking place must be on board if broad human rights improvements can be made as a result of the effort. When we focus only on those issues where there is some broad-based support from the domestic population, a variety of structural conditions within the state, including its pre-existing regime type and vulnerability to the international community, make human rights improvement more likely. And, like before, organizations that send signals of their motivations are sometimes better able to get effective human rights improvement on the ground. Sometimes, however, these signals can isolate certain communities and reinforce stakeholder arrangements, making the advocacy world somewhat different than its service-provision counterparts. These dynamics, which are supported in the large-scale tests, are reiterated with case study anecdotes on human rights improvements in Mexico, China, and North Africa.

The empirical chapters utilize advanced statistical methods and novel events-based data on the activities of INGOs on human security outcomes. Throughout, however, I try to make the empirical chapters approachable to a large and diverse audience.

The book concludes by extending the argument back to the larger debates about how INGOs function in a state-centric world. INGOs can be powerful actors on a variety of human security issues, even issues that get at the basic arrangements between a regime and its population. This book thus adds to the broader "second image reversed" literature, which has previously focused exclusively on the effects of intergovernmental organizations on domestic politics (Reiter 2001; Pevehouse 2005; Gleditsch and Ward 2006). By focusing on international *non*-governmental organizations and their impact on domestic politics, I extend the scope of this literature to new actors at the same level of analysis.

However, unlike some utopian ideal of INGOs as an end-all for human security concerns, the effect of these organizations is not monolithic; differences in organizational characteristics that reflect underlying motivations, issue-focus, and state peculiarities condition when and where this vibrant and growing force of INGOs will be effective contributors to human security outcomes. Organizations differ in their underlying motivations, and, once this is understood, state and society actions to control unwanted behavior while supporting organizations that do signal their domestically minded "shared values" would be helpful for improving the whole INGO sector. The book concludes with some practical advice on this front.

2 INGOS IN WORLD POLITICS

INGOS ARE NOTHING NEW to world politics. In fact, INGOs were active in eighteenth- and nineteenth-century antislavery campaigns and in the suffrage movement before the 1900s (Keck and Sikkink 1998; Florini 2004). However, as mentioned before, the sheer numbers, attention, and funds directed at INGOs are new (Boli and Thomas 1999; Florini 2004; Ahmed and Potter 2006). Though research in international relations was silent on the growth and potential influence of INGOs for many years, since the 1990s, INGO research within the discipline has boomed. This increase in the attention paid to INGOs has been coupled with increased cross-disciplinary research, including research from the fields of business, sociology, anthropology, and education (Jabine and Claude 1992; Feldman 1997; Keck and Sikkink 1998; Schafer 1999; Risse et al. 1999; Mundy and Murphy 2001; Welch 2001).

The goal of this chapter is to motivate the theoretical innovations made in this book. To do so, I first define the INGO sector and outline the existing theoretical literature on INGOs, paying special attention to the dominant theoretical framework on INGOs from within international relations and the empirical tests of the implications of this framework. After addressing this literature, I discuss both scholarly and practitioner critiques, many of which focus on how the underlying motivations of INGOs differ from the principled ideal that has dominated most work in the area. After outlining these critiques, I address how INGOs themselves have responded to concerns about their organization's underlying motivations, and then I outline the cross-disciplinary literature that examines the INGOs' actions or signals. This framework provides the building blocks necessary for developing an accurate theory of the conditional effectiveness of INGOs on human security outcomes.

DEFINING THE INGO WORLD

International non-governmental organizations go by many names, and in general they focus on many different outcomes. Before discussing their motivations, actions, and effects, it is important to focus on the characteristics that define INGOs as a cohesive group and separate them from other actors in world politics. I utilize a very inclusive definition of INGOs, reflective of the ways in which organizations are defined at the United Nations (UN).

To begin—although this may sound redundant—INGOs are organizations, and as such, they are made up of groups of actors, typically individuals, that purposely structure their interactions to reflect some basic rules (Judge 1994; Martens 2002). Most formalize these rules in charters or mission statements, and many have a formal headquarter location. By defining INGOs as "formal institutions," I am separating the INGO realm from the overarching ideas of social movements, which often are unorganized and lack a formal office structure or recorded mission (Martens 2002, 281). Amnesty International or Human Rights Watch would fit this criterion of the definition of an INGO; the general human rights movement, however, would not. As Smith and Wiest (2012) make clear, INGOs can be generated by a social movement; an organization can start as a very loose grouping of individuals or groups that then formalize their organizational structure, becoming an INGO. This definition also makes INGOs distinct from transnational advocacy networks, which are defined as being composed of groups of INGOs and other advocacy actors, like clergy, parts of social movements, and local dissidents, but that, as a whole, still lack a unified organizational structure (Keck and Sikkink 1998).

Further, I define INGOs as organizations that are not states or controlled by states. INGOs can have contacts in government agencies; many, albeit most, receive some sort of funding from state actors or from agents of state actors. However, to be classified as a non-governmental organization means that the organization does not have a decision structure that is controlled by a state. This is similar to the definition first adopted in 1950 by the United Nations Economic and Social Council (ECOSOC):

> *Any international organization which is not established by intergovernmental agreement shall be considered as a non-governmental organization for the purpose of these arrangements.* (Resolution 288 (X) of February 27, 1950, Section 7)[1]

According to this definition, if the organization is not created by a government or by government agreements, it is an NGO. As the *Yearbook of International Organization*, the standard source book for international organizations of all types, points out, UN ECOSOC later reiterated the idea that governments could be part of NGOs, only not in any way that "interfere[s] with the free expression of views of the organization" (ECOSOC Resolution 1996/31 of June 25, 1968).

At the onset, the distinction between governments and NGOs seems rather elementary; of course, governments cannot control any organization labeled "*non*-governmental." In reality, however, this explicit distinction is necessary: many organizations have been accused of being controlled by governments, and many governments have been accused of creating organizations that resemble NGOs in order to either attract donor monies or to subterfuge critiques of the government with their own counter-advocacy in support of the regime. These organizations are often termed GONGOs (Gordenker and Weiss 1995). In a *Washington Post* article, Moisés Naím (2007) defined GONGOs as follows:

> GONGOs are government-organized non-governmental organizations. Behind this contradictory and almost laughable tongue twister lies an important and growing global trend that deserves more scrutiny: governments are funding and controlling non-governmental organizations (NGOs), often stealthily.

For example, in 2006, Russia was accused of creating the very professional-sounding organization International Council for Democratic Institutions and State Sovereignty, with the goal of influencing foreign policy opinions about independence for a small region of Moldova, which Russia had supported ("Disinformation," *The Economist*, August 3, 2006). By setting up this organization, the Russian government desired, at the very least, to spread a message counter to what was existing in the general civil dialogue at the time. A similar situation occurred in Uzbekistan, where, as Sievers (2003) points out, "GONGOs exist to absorb funds and soften the democratizing impacts of civil society.... Most of the 2300 NGOs [United Nations Development Programme] cites as having been created in Uzbekistan since 1991 are either [Islamic neighborhood organizations] or GONGOs" (108). GONGOs are also very active in China, where the Chinese government has often been accused of setting up organizations that appear legitimate but that work to spread propaganda of the state. McBeath and Leng (2006), for example, estimate that 350 GONGOs with an environmental focus were active in China in 2005. Although this book, by its very definition, seeks to separate out GONGOs from INGOs, the topic of government sponsorship definitely deserves further inquiry and is largely consistent with the overall theme of this book that these organizations are by no means a monolithic force.

Gordenker and Weiss (1995, 1997) provide two additional categories for INGOs that may seem to bend the boundaries of the defined governmental/ non-governmental distinction. For both of the Gordenker and Weiss (1995, 1997) categories, I follow their practice and include these organizations as INGOs by definition. First, Gordenker and Weiss (1995) outline QUANGOs, quasi-NGOs. These organizations "receive the bulk of their resources from public coffers" (361). As I outline in the next chapter, although donor funds may make some organizations more likely to be internationally aligned or rent-seeking, not all organizations that focus on public funds are so motivated. For those organizations that need large amounts of money for public works programs, it may make sense for the organization to work on collecting public contracts instead of small donations. INGOs from the Global North typically have different historical legacies as to whether such public resources are desired (Stroup 2012). In short, although, as Gordenker and Weiss (1995, 1997) point out, governments different in whether their funds are primarily private or public, this distinction does not determine their inclusion into the INGO category. Further, this distinction does not automatically equate to my later theoretical distinction among organizations: that of whether or not the organization is primarily motivated by personal gain.

The additional category of organization that appears to bend the governmental/non-governmental distinction outlined in Gordenker and Weiss is that of a "donor-organized organization"—one where an IGO or a state has set up an independent organization for its needs. Of course, like with QUANGOs, I include this organization as an INGO. It is not governed by the organizing donor. Gordenker and Weiss do the same thing. Like before, this type of organization could still be working for primarily personal gain or in line with what the domestic population wants.

The third defining characteristic of INGOs is their stated not-for-profit status. Again, as mentioned in the introduction, this does not mean that organizations do not operate in ways that provide them with private benefits, often termed *rents*. Instead, this simply means that INGOs, by their very definition, are separated from other nonstate actors, like multinational corporations or crime syndicates, in that they are not explicitly money-making organizations. Organizations often are professional, providing salaries to their formal employees instead of just relying on volunteers. Organizations are also worried about their longevity and may participate in very formal marketing campaigns. This, however, does not negate the fact that these organizations do not function among both domestic and international audiences with the tacit assumption that they will be distributing their profits to shareholders.

The fourth defining characteristic of INGOs is that they are not formed for the expressed purpose of aiding one political candidate or cohesive set of political candidates. This is not to say that organizations cannot take political stands, recommending certain political actions and even political candidates. Human rights organizations, for example, often provide recommendations for political action, even going as far as to take a stand on humanitarian interventions or economic sanctions (Murdie and Peksen 2013, 2014). The characteristic is, however, mentioned to separate NGOs from political parties that routinely operate by supporting a set of candidates for political office within a country or set of countries. As Willetts (2002) points out, this de facto separation is still in place in the UN; organizations made up from coalitions of political parties can be classified as INGOs under the auspices of the UN ECOSOC structure, but political parties themselves cannot get UN ECOSOC consultative status for NGOs.

INGOs can include lobbying groups. This reflects the very difficult and gray area between general advocacy and private lobbying, where "one person's view of the public interest may be seen by another person as the assertion of unacceptable values, ideological extremism, or special pleading" (Willetts 2002, 6). In general, although the lobbying literature in political science is often distinct from the INGO literature, with the lobbying literature being far more critical of organizational practices and achievements, international lobbying groups are in fact INGOs. They are simply a type of organization that is utilizing one specific strategy set.

There has been much discussion about whether INGOs must be nonviolent or whether organizations that are primarily violent, non-governmental, and international should still be classified as INGOs (Martens 2002; Willetts 2002; Asal et al. 2007). In other words, are "terrorists, natural guerrilla or liberation organizations, and organized crime—such as the Irish Republican Army, the Palestinian Liberation Organization, or the mafia" considered INGOs? Some take a hard stance, defining INGOs explicitly as organizations that "cannot advocate the use of violence" (Ahmed and Potter 2006). Many are silent on the issue (Boli and Thomas 1999; Bob 2005). The UN ECOSOC, according to

Willetts (2002), will "question the suspension of an NGO's consultative status" if it is using "aggressive behavior" (10). Here, I take a somewhat more moderate definition and say that INGOs are organizations that cannot operate primarily by violent means outside of typical nonviolent or political channels. I do not contend that the IRA or al Qaeda are INGOs; on a scale of violence as opposed to the utilization of nonviolent or political channels, both of these organizations are more readily in the category of using violence as their primary mode of operation. However, to note, I will agree with Asal and colleagues (2007) and Frieden, Lake, and Schultz (2013) and say that there is some utility in examining the similarities and differences in the processes through which both transnational advocacy INGOs and primarily violent organizations affect political and behavioral change.

Nonetheless, I do not go as far as Ahmed and Potter (2006) and others and state that INGOs have to be completely nonviolent for a number of different reasons. First, advocacy organizations, like human rights INGOs, often work to increase domestic nonviolent protest within a state against a repressive regime. As part of their work, many organizations provide domestic actors, including domestic NGOs and individuals, with tools to aid in their nonviolent mobilization. For example, organizations in Cambodia and Ukraine have provided meeting spaces and cell phones for domestic groups to use in coordinating their mobilization against the state (Wallander 2005; Bunce and Wolchik 2006). There is a rich and diverse literature on the diffusion of protest tools; it is quite likely that tools given by advocacy INGOs to aid in nonviolent protest could be utilized by violent actors or in violent actions in larger nonviolent movements (Haines 1984; Andrews and Biggs 2006). In fact, my coauthored work with Tavishi Bhasin (2011) finds that human rights INGOs often do lead to increased domestic violent protest, in addition to their more expected effects on nonviolent protest mobilization against the state. In short, INGOs may not be advocating directly for the use of violence, but, through their work, violence may be heightened. It does not make sense to exclude INGOs definitionally for this process, through which their resources can diffuse to mobilized networks of domestic violent political actors.

Second, I do not exclude INGOs that for limited times or in particular instances would utilize violence. This is distinct, of course, from excluding organizations that primarily use violent means to meet their organizational objectives. There are many examples of organizations that have, at times, used violence against a state or nonstate actor; many environmental INGOs have held campaigns that have used violence (Wapner 1995; Chartier and Deléage 1998; Lyon 2010). These organizations do not, however, utilize violent actions exclusively or predominately (Lyon 2010). If they did, they would more readily be categorized as environmental terrorist organizations, like some groups are in the Global Terrorism Database or in other foreign policy lists of terrorist organizations. However, it must be acknowledged that many advocacy organizations, by their very nature, are confrontational and conflictual, at least verbally, with the regime in power. Workers of INGOs are often in danger of both nonstate and state violence. Certain isolated spillover violence can occur, and this should not negate the organization's inclusion in our definition of INGOs. More research is needed on (a) cases when violence is used as a strategy of otherwise nonviolent organizations and (b) whether this strategy is helpful or harmful to the organization's goals and to other organizations in the same sector (Lyon 2010).

Finally, organizations must be international to be classified as an *international* non-governmental organization. This was, at the very beginning, a part of the UN's definition of an NGO. However, even at the onset, there was little discussion of what made an organization "international." In general, I take a very inclusive stance here, similar to the one the UN ECOSOC took in 1950 and 1968 and has used in recent years when dealing with applications for consultative status from organizations. I refer to "international" as meaning that the organization has international interests, goals, or objectives, even if the organization is active in only a very defined and limited geographical area. This is somewhat more encompassing than the working definition used by the Union of International Associations in their definition in the *Yearbook of International Organizations*; they contend that an organization is international if it is "oriented to three or more countries" (UIA 2012). In practice, however, the *Yearbook* has since 1977 included organizations that are involved only in two countries as "transnational" organizations. The *Yearbook* still excludes organizations that are strictly bilateral. Many bilateral organizations could be said to not be "international" in scope, also limiting them from this book's definition of an INGO.

Although the UN system refers to international NGOs as just "NGOs," the academic literature has made a distinction between organizations that are completely domestic and organizations that are international (Boli and Thomas 1999; Ahmed and Potter 2006). I follow that distinction here. Organizations only involved within a particular country and only interested in working with their mission within that country can still be very important for international politics; as discussed below, these domestic NGOs are theoretically crucial players in the transnational advocacy networks where INGOs often work (Keck and Sikkink 1998; Risse, Ropp, and Sikkink 1999). However, domestic NGOs, often referred to as "nonprofits" in the American politics literature, are, in many ways, separate from our discussion and focus here on INGOs. These organizations may not be routinely working within both international and domestic arenas; they are more likely to just be working with domestic actors, both state and nonstate. Much of their decision calculus would be different from INGOs or, at the very least, may be on a very limited scale. For example, instead of trying to decide which countries to work in for a year, the organization may be deciding which neighborhoods to be working in for a year. Organizational members may not have aspirations of ever leaving the state. Instead of taking successful strategies from Argentina, for example, and using them in Peru, the organization may be taking strategies from, say, one area of Bolivia and using them in another area of Bolivia (Keck and Sikkink 1998; Boulding 2010). This is not to say that there are many similarities between domestic and international NGOs; in fact, many INGOs, like the March of Dimes, started out as specifically domestic NGOs and then expanded both their mission and their activities. Instead, for this book, I simply acknowledge that there are differences between international and domestic NGOs, both on-the-ground differences and differences in the academic literature, and restrict my focus to only organizations that can be classified as international. I do acknowledge, however, that many of the same dynamics I present in this chapter and then use to motivate my theoretical argument in Chapter 3 concerning organizational motivations and signaling apply readily to domestic nonprofits and have already been acknowledged within that literature (Rose-Ackerman 1996; Gugerty and Prakash 2010).

Many components of conventional INGO definitions are not included here. Most importantly, I do not require that the organization be classified as "legal" or registered in any country where it is working (Salamon and Anheier 1992). I do this for a number of reasons. First, country laws for INGOs vary; cross-nationally, it would be difficult to determine what to do with an organization that is legally operating in one country but illegally operating in another country at the same time. When laws within a country change, what would that mean to the organizations that no longer are legal? Would they lose their inclusion into the INGO classification? By not requiring the definition of INGOs to rest on legality requirements, these particularly vexing empirical dilemmas are avoided.

Moreover, there is some debate about the reasons for legal requirements concerning INGO registration in the first place. Some laws are designed to separate out taxation rates for INGOs from organizations that are for-profit, like the United States Internal Revenue Service 501(c) classification for nonprofits or charitable status with the Canadian Revenue Service. Other registration and donation laws have been passed under the formal goal of controlling funds going to terrorist groups (Bloodgood and Tremblay-Boire 2011). Unfortunately, in recent years, many of these regulations have been heavily critiqued as ways to control NGOs:

> A number of the laws considered or enacted [since 2007] have raised serious questions as to their compliance with international norms governing the right to free association as well as the practical obstacles that they raise to NGO operations. Among other issues, some of these laws impose restrictions on the ability of NGOs to form and become legal entities and carry out activities without undue government interference. Others provide governments with broad discretion to shut down NGOs. (ICNL 2009)

For example, a 2002 law in Egypt severely restricted the ability of organizations to take external funding; it was critiqued as a way for the regime "to exclude organizations it disfavors" (Elbayar 2012). After the Arab Spring uprisings in the Middle East and North Africa in 2011, moves by the interim government in Egypt expanded the use of the earlier legislation, leading many organizations to leave the country for fear of legal actions and violence. Laws concerning restrictions on associations were expanded in the fall of 2013. The UN High Commissioner for Human Rights at the time, Navi Pillay, spoke out against the proposed expansions of restrictions, saying, "It gives the government too much power to regulate, monitor, and restrict the work of civil society organizations" (OHCHR 2012).

A similar, widely reported, law restricted the work of INGOs operating in Russia. Under the law, organizations that work primarily in the political realm and that are receiving international funds must register as "foreign agents," a term that "carries a Soviet-era negative taint," and provide a listing of their activities to the government (BBC News, July 13, 2012). These requirements, according to many INGOs, could both undermine the abilities of organizations to work with local populations and make them easy targets for actions by regime supporters. These cases are not outliers; similar restrictions exist in Ethiopia, Jordan, Uganda, and Tajikistan, among others (ICNL 2009).

Because of the ways in which legal requirements can be used to control the behavior of INGOs and restrict citizens' freedom of association, many organizations try to work "under the radar" within a country; this is especially true for organizations that are advocating for policies that go against government practices, especially practices concerning governmental use of repression (Bosman 2012). Therefore, in defining an INGO, I do not restrict my focus to only organizations that have legal status. Doing so may, in fact, make it more likely that we are including groups that are effectively GONGOs, as discussed above, especially when looking at democracy or human rights–promoting organizations that are active in countries with these restrictive laws.

Tens of thousands of organizations fit the basic definition of an INGO used in this book, which characterizes INGOs by their formal organizational, nongovernmental, nonprofit, nonpolitical party, and international characteristics. Of course, there is still much variation within organizations that can be defined as INGOs. Many different typologies of INGOs exist across the social sciences, albeit with little attention within these typologies as to how differences among INGOs matter for their motivations or for the overall sector's effects on the outcomes of interest in this book (Gordenker and Weiss 1995, 1997; Vakil 1997; Alger 2002). Organizations may carry with them certain behaviors based on their Global South or North position, as well as their nation-of-origin peculiarities (Stroup 2011; Murdie 2014). For the most part, these distinctions and taxonomies are tangential to the primary focus here: understanding when and where organizations matter for a variety of human security outcomes.[2]

Further, most INGOs are not well known and may be of little interest to international relations scholars and human security promoters. For example, although World Association of Seaweed Processors or Starfleet—the International Star Trek Association may have a very diverse and vibrant membership base, it is difficult to see any direct linkage between these organizations and lessening repression or improving development conditions within a state.[3] As Boli and Thomas (1999) point out, most INGOs are in fact nonpolitical; they believe most are "highly specialized, drawing members worldwide from a particular occupation, technical field, branch of knowledge, industry, hobby, or sport, to promote and regulate their respective areas of concern" (20).

For this book, I do not focus on these specialized types of INGOs. Instead, the focus is on only organizations that have direct missions in line with the promotion of human security. By *human security*, as mentioned in Chapter 1,

I'm referring to outcomes that relate to freedom from "want" and "fear" within a population (UNDP 1994; Paris 2001).

HUMAN SECURITY FOCUS AND THE ADVOCACY/ SERVICE DISTINCTION

Human security is a term that has received a lot of attention since its first use in the 1994 United Nations Development Programme. Unlike conventional notions of security that focus on the state, human security, as a concept, rests on the individuals living within a state and their personal security. This security is recognized as coming both from freedoms that protect citizens from state repression and political violence and from the overall material well-being of the country. Many of these outcomes can be couched in language concerning the promotion of economic, social, and cultural rights (freedom from want) outlined in the Universal Declaration of Human Rights (UDHR) and in outcomes listed as political and civil rights (freedom from fear), also outlined in the UDHR (Howard-Hassman 2012).

Two specific groups of outcomes of human security are my focus here. First, I am interested in the effects of INGOs on basic service provision related to development; these are outcomes in line with human security ideas about freedom from want. By this, I'm referring to basic sanitation and access to potable water, as well as basic health services, like vaccinations, birth control, and tuberculosis treatment. Second, I am interested in the effects of INGOs on certain human rights—namely, physical integrity rights and empowerment rights, including these rights for women. These human rights could be classified as rights that fit in with the human security idea of freedom from fear.

Now, to be clear, all of these outcomes of human security fit in the general framework of rights outlined in the UDHR; all are, at their core, human rights. In general, however, there has been quite a bit of division between human rights that relate to development (like the right to health or an adequate standard of living) and human rights that relate to physical integrity (like the right to freedom from torture). These divisions are, in many regards, the result of Cold War politics, where the Soviet Union became the champion of economic, social, and cultural rights, like the right to development, while the United States and other Western powers became the champions of political and civil rights. This division led to the bifurcation of the first two binding UN human rights treaties: the International Covenant on Economic, Social, and Cultural Rights and the International Covenant on Civil and Political Rights (Donnelly 2003). The

United States, for example, has still not ratified the International Covenant on Economic, Social, and Cultural Rights, the treaty that would include the right to development. One of the major benefits of phrasing all of these outcomes within the recent human security rhetoric of freedom from want and fear is that this human security framework does not have this history of bifurcation. I do, however, acknowledge that all of these outcomes fall well within the human rights framework outlined in the UDHR.

Given that the focus, then, is on the influence of INGOs on human security outcomes, I restrict my theoretical and empirical focus to only organizations that have mission statements that refer to these outcomes. Doing this, however, introduces a very concrete division into the work of INGOs: organizations that focus on development and basic service provision often work in ways far different from organizations that focus on human rights advocacy and promotion. Development INGOs, like Oxfam, work predominantly through handing out basic services and setting up larger development projects. Although they may advocate for changes in hand-washing techniques, for the use of condoms, or for more government funding toward education or health, advocacy may be a small portion of their work. This is somewhat the opposite, of course, from the typical human rights organization. Although human rights organizations, like the very well-known Amnesty International or Human Rights Watch, may provide counseling or health services for repression victims, their main mode of operation is advocacy. Some organizations, of course, blur these lines—typically referred to as "hybrids" (Murdie and Davis 2012b). However, within the INGO world, this distinction in the modus operandi of various INGOs has been widely established, both by scholars and practitioners (Edwards and Hulme 1995; Gordenker and Weiss 1995, 1997; Vakil 1997; Baur and Schmitz 2012; World Bank 2012).

For example, the World Bank categorizes INGOs as either "operational" or "advocacy," with operational organizations being those whose "primary purpose is to fund, design, or implement" programs, while advocacy organizations are those whose "primary purpose is to defend or promote" policies and actions of state and nonstate actors (World Bank 2012). These distinctions are also in place outside of the World Bank; many organizations classify their work as either predominantly related to the operations of service delivery or advocacy efforts. Here, I refer to operational organizations as service provision organizations, reflecting the idea that organizations that are involved in "operations," in the World Bank sense of the term, are those that are providing social services to a population. This reflects some other academic labeling of this dichotomy of INGOs in the literature and the on-the-ground labels used by many organizations and volunteers (Edwards and Hulme 1995; Gordenker and Weiss 1995, 1997; Vakil 1997; Baur and Schmitz 2012; World Bank 2012).

This distinction becomes very important in developing a comprehensive theory of how INGOs influence human security. The processes by which service delivery organizations and advocacy organizations reach their organizational goals are sometimes very different. Likewise, the motivational pressures and interactions with outside audiences are different for these two types of organizations. Below, I begin with a discussion of the dominant theoretical framework of INGOs in international relations, which focuses primarily on advocacy organizations, and then focus on the different mechanisms through which advocacy and service INGOs are supposed to influence human security.

WHAT ARE THEY GOOD FOR? INGOS IN INTERNATIONAL RELATIONS

The dominant theoretical framework of INGOs within international relations, the transnational advocacy network (TAN) framework, centers on the role *TAN* that INGOs play in strengthening advocacy attempts (Keck and Sikkink 1998; Risse and Ropp 1999; Ahmed and Potter 2006; Reitan 2007). Within the TAN framework, INGOs are typically viewed as potential allies for domestic groups already interested in advocacy. If state actors are not sensitive to a domestic group's position, the domestic group seeks out INGOs to petition the state from abroad (Keck and Sikkink 1998). In TAN terminology, this is referred to as sending out a "boomerang" for help from the domestic state that is repressed to the international groups that are motivated to help (Keck and Sikkink 1998; DeMars 2005).

An example of this boomerang process can be seen after the overthrow of Salvador Allende in 1973. Many domestic groups in Chile wanted both the military junta and the successor, Augusto Pinochet, to answer for the widespread human rights atrocities occurring in their country. Many who attempted to stop government repression were themselves tortured, imprisoned, or killed by the regime, and many more just disappeared. As the authors of the TAN framework, Margaret Keck and Kathryn Sikkink (1998), point out, leaders of these domestic groups were able to leave the country and plead their case to many INGOs, including Amnesty International and various religious INGOs, which then joined the movement (91).

According to the TAN framework, INGOs supply the domestic group with connections, funds, and information to help them in their attempt to pressure the state. They also can provide meeting places, copy machines, nonviolence training, walkie-talkies, and, as has occurred more recently, cell phones. Domestic groups can then use these resources, often referred to as coordination goods, to heighten their domestic efforts to pressure the regime to change its practices (Bueno de Mesquita and Downs 2005).

At the same time, INGOs issue public statements about the plight of the domestic group and meet with various foreign policy actors to supply information about what problems the group is facing. Many of these statements, often termed "shaming" or "naming," include calls for the regime to stop its repressive practices and adopt the behaviors that the domestic group was advocating for in the first place. Through these activities, INGOs are encouraging the international community writ large, including foundations, the media, churches, intellectuals, intergovernmental organizations, and governments of third-party states, to pressure the state as well.

This concentrated pressure from various international and domestic actors creates a transnational advocacy network, which consists of all the organizations and individuals from different segments of society who are working toward the same goal. As Keck and Sikkink make clear, although these actors are all different, they form a network that includes "shared values" and "[frequent] exchange [of] information and services" (9). When international actors join in the INGO-headed campaign, the targeted state finds itself pressured by both heightened domestic activists and international activists, and this completes the "boomerang" pattern. According to this framework, if enough pressure is put on the state, the network is typically successful in reaching the goals of the advocacy movement (Keck and Sikkink 1998, 29).

In the case of Chile, INGOs were able to get the issue of political disappearances and killings in the country on the international radar. Representatives from INGOs spoke at international conferences, met with foreign policy leaders of states and donor foundations, and appeared in the popular media (Hawkins 2002). Because of this international campaign, largely spearheaded by human rights INGOs, many international actors joined the transnational network and issued their own demands for Pinochet's regime to stop its repression. Eventually, this combination of international and domestic pressure worked to improve the human rights situation in Chile, including a transition to democratic rule (Hawkins 2002; Ropp and Sikkink 2002). The process was so successful, in fact, that groups associated with the Chilean case became "models for human rights groups throughout Latin American and sources of information and inspiration for human rights activists in the United States and Europe" (Keck and Sikkink 1998, 90).

ASSUMPTIONS IN THE DOMINANT FRAMEWORK

This TAN framework and the later "spiral" model of transnational advocacy (discussed below) are rich with insights into the workings and potential effectiveness of INGOs. Before turning to the mechanisms through which these organizations are thought to influence human security and the extant empirical tests of the framework, a brief discussion on the theoretical assumptions of the TAN literature is certainly necessary.

First, as Price (2003) contends, most of the TAN literature "downplays the alleged constructivist-rationalist theoretical divide" within international relations (583). Katzenstein, Keohane, and Krasner (1998) argue that this divide "provide[s] the major points of contestation for international relations scholarship" currently (646). Other authors, including Fearon and Wendt (2002), argue that the debate between constructivism and rationalism in the general international relations literature has been overblown: "pragmatically," they are both "lenses for looking at social reality" (68). Even in these terms, however, the traditional focus of rationalism is still different from constructivism in many regards. As Katzenstein, Keohane, and Krasner (1998) point out:

> The core of the constructivist project is to explain variations in preferences, available strategies, and the nature of the players, across space and time. The core of the rationalist project is to explain strategies, given preferences, information, and common knowledge. Neither project can be complete without the other. (682)

As such, constructivism is typically concerned with "identities, norms, knowledge, and interests," while rationalists assume that actors are acting in an instrumental way and use this assumption "to provide the crucial link between features of the environment—power, interests, and institutional rules—and actor behavior" (Katzenstein, Keohane, and Krasner 1998, 678–679). Of the theoretical schools discussed in Chapter 1, realism would be typically classified as falling into the rationalist paradigm, as would liberal theory. Rationalism and constructivism, in the sense of this debate, are more far reaching than just theoretical schools or meta-theories. The debate between the two can be couched in terms of an "ontological" debate or, as Fearon and Wendt (2002) describe it, "a disagreement about substantive issues in the world, like how often actors follow a logic of consequences or logic of appropriateness, or whether preferences really are exogenous or endogenous to a given social interaction" (53).

However big this disagreement might be, as rationalist James Fearon and constructivist Alexander Wendt contend in *Handbook of International Relations*, "the most interesting research is likely to be work that ignores zero-sum interpretations of [rationalism and constructivism] and instead directly engages questions that cut across the rationalist/constructivist boundary as it is commonly understood" (52).

In his review of the common works that make up the core of the TAN framework, including Keck and Sikkink (1998), in *World Politics*, Price (2003) reiterates this idea that bridging the rationalist-constructivist divide is "for good reason" and exactly what the dominant framework has done "in that most of the case studies demonstrate an eclectic mix of persuasive and instrumentalist tactics" (583).

However, much of the dominant TAN literature, because of its overwhelming focus on ideas and social factors, has been categorized by later work as predominantly constructivist in orientation, perhaps with less emphasis on rationalism than prescribed by Fearon and Wendt (Kelly 2005; Prakash and Gugerty 2010; Risse 2010). These later pieces, in reviewing the TAN approach, characterize the traditional literature as constructivist typically because of the focus on norms transmission, preference formation, and the use of soft or discursive power. According to Hopf (1998), these are key characteristics of the constructivist paradigm within international relations (177).

Additionally, as mentioned, underpinning the traditional TAN literature is the assumption that INGOs are fundamentally different from for-profit organizations in their motivations (Keck and Sikkink 1998; Risse 2002). Unlike for-profit actors and states, advocacy network actors, as a whole, are argued to be motivated by "principles" and "values rather than material concerns" (Keck and Sikkink 1998, 2). In other words, while for-profit firms are assumed to be motivated by material goals, INGOs and other advocacy network actors are assumed to be motivated predominately by specific advocacy policy or behavior outcomes (Kelly 2005; Ahmed and Potter 2006). This is not to say, of course, that this literature assumes that INGOs and other advocacy actors do not behave strategically or with no consideration for staying financially afloat, but it does stress a fundamental difference between organizations with for-profit motivations and INGOs with motivations for shared values.

As Risse (2010) contends, "Advocacy network [actors] usually share a concern for universally accepted values or the global common good and, thus, pursue what they perceive as the public interest" (285). Within this literature, examples of shared values have included human security, in the broadest sense, environmental concerns, solidarity movements, minority rights, and democratization.

Worth noting, Risse (2010) does not go as far as Bob (2005) in categorizing the traditional advocacy literature as framing motivations as "cosmopolitan altruism" that focuses only on others (137). Instead, Risse categorizes shared values in the traditional advocacy network literature as allowing advocacy to occur both for other's interests as well as the interests of the advocates themselves. For example, the INGO World Committee on Human Rights for India includes individuals from India who, quite directly, could benefit from improvements in human rights conditions in India. Likewise, the organization Latin American Central of Workers is made up predominantly of workers from Latin American countries, the direct beneficiaries of the advocacy the organization is working for. More indirectly, however, the work of organizations is often motivated by the idea that advocacy for others will holistically benefit the advocates themselves. In 2001, for example, William Schultz, then director of the United States division of Amnesty International, stressed this blending of advocates' goals and the benefits to the population they are working to help when he said, "Caring about the fate of our 'neighbors' is far more than a matter of conscience. It is in truth a matter of survival—our own survival. Because our welfare is bound up in theirs, and when their dreams die, our health and security die with them" (xviii).

Additionally, unlike literature on lobbyist organizations, it is often implicitly assumed in the traditional TAN literature that all INGOs addressing a particular issue have the same shared principles; discussions that advocate for principles or norms that are conflicting or divergent are rare (Austen-Smith 1997; Bearce 2003; Bloodgood 2008, 2011; Hojnacki et al. 2012). For example, much of the TAN literature would assume that women's rights INGOs in Nigeria are all advocating for the same policies or behaviors. Little theoretical or empirical attention from within the TAN framework would explain why some women's rights INGOs in Africa advocate for abortion rights, while others believe that women's rights come only from natural family planning (UIA

2008/2009). Clifford Bob's (2012) recent literature on the workings of conservative organizations echoes this point.

Moreover, there is not much work from within the advocacy network framework concerning how even "shared values" among organizations may not automatically equate to shared desires for policy and behavioral outcomes. It is typically assumed that since organizations are advocating for norms that are "universally accepted" (Risse 2010), their goals with respect to these values are similar. This is not always the case on the ground, however, as groups advocating for transitional justice after civil war may radically disagree, for example, about the pathways through which this justice should be carried out. Although the shared value of transitional justice is present among these actors, solidifying their categorization as an advocacy network in the traditional sense, some organizations may work for international actions for justice, while others want the process of transitional justice to be completely domestic, such as the case in Nepal since the mid-2000s (Pasipanodya 2008). In the canonical literature, however, it appears that shared values are often assumed to equate to similar goals for advocacy outcomes.

Further, implicit within Keck and Sikkink (1998) and the larger TAN literature, is often the assumption that TAN actors are advocating for policies and behaviors that are largely consistent with the preferences of at least a small portion of the domestic citizenry within the state that the advocacy actor is targeting (Clark 2001; DeMars 2005).[4] As mentioned, within the TAN framework, the INGO is responding to domestic calls for help (Keck and Sikkink 1998; Risse et al. 1999). Therefore, it is often assumed that the ideas or norms that INGOs advocate have some resonance with the domestic citizenry, even if the norms do not resonate widely with state actors (Risse and Ropp 1999; Risse et al. 1999; Cortell and Davis 2000). In fact, as Price (2003) points out, the power of TAN actors "hinges on their legitimacy as agents addressing . . . democratic deficits" and, as such, INGOs are assumed to represent the interests of a repressed domestic citizenry (590).

Risse (1999) also points out that the "moral authority" of INGOs and other advocacy actors is based on their predominantly representing "public interests" or the "common good" rather than private interests (186). *Moral authority* is defined as power derived from the belief that activists are "not only (objectively) right in the sense of providing accurate information but also morally right in the purposes for which such knowledge is harnessed" (Price 2003, 539). This focus on power as moral authority would separate TAN actors, specifically

INGOs, from earlier studies of epistemic communities. In that literature, an epistemic community is a community of actors defined by their common knowledge base and ideas (Adler and Haas 1992; Evangelista 1999). Common epistemic communities would include the network of scholars, activists, lobbyists, and politicians attached to think tanks and university research centers. Unlike this literature, the TAN literature commonly assumes that the moral authority of advocacy actors comes from more than just a knowledge base. As Boli and Thomas (1999) contend, the power of INGOs comes also from their claim to represent "humanity," broadly defined (14).

By assuming that TAN actors are advocating for issues that have resonance with the domestic population, situations where international norms and the norms of a domestic population differ have received scant attention within the traditional TAN framework, despite the focus on these issues in the much broader constructivist literature (Checkel 1997; Cortell and Davis 2000; Risse 2002). In other words, unlike other literature that sees "resonance" as a variable, the assumption in much of the traditional advocacy network framework is that resonance is a given, at least during the boomerang process. In short, as Risse (2002) contends, within the traditional study of transnational advocacy, arguments about "ideational (in)compatibility [are] still underspecified" (267). I will return to these topics in the discussion of the revisionist literature later in this chapter.

MECHANISMS THROUGH WHICH ADVOCACY
INGOS AFFECT HUMAN SECURITY

Given this understanding of the TAN framework's basic workings and underlying assumptions, I now turn to the mechanisms through which this framework is connected to human security outcomes. Because the predominant focus in this framework is on advocacy organizations, I begin with the causal process connecting human rights advocacy INGOs to changes in human rights practices (freedom from fear). I then address the causal process through which development service provision INGOs are thought to influence development outcomes (freedom from want). Finally, I outline the existing empirical tests of this framework on both human security outcomes.

To begin, the TAN framework is reflected in the large cross-disciplinary literature that outlines the mechanisms through which advocacy INGOs impact policy and behavior outcomes. As Hahn and Holzscheiter (2005) point out, advocacy INGOs' efforts center on their collective "power of knowledge" (9).

Advocacy INGOs use "all forms of modern persuasion" and "multiple political tactics" to influence policy and behavioral outcomes (Yaziji 2004, 110; Schepers 2006, 283). Importantly, INGOs themselves, however, have "no direct ability to change policy" or behavior (Schepers 2006, 283). Instead, INGOs have to work with other actors, such as the international community and domestic citizens to cause actors to change behavior (Teegen et al. 2004; Yaziji 2004; Schepers 2006). This idea, again, forms the core of Keck and Sikkink's (1998) boomerang pattern of transnational advocacy.

Within this pattern are numerous tactics that INGOs use with the goal of influencing human rights practices on the ground. Many of these tactics are similar to those used by organizations in other issue areas, like advocacy related to the environment (Keck and Sikkink 1998).[5] Some organizations work to educate schoolchildren about human rights and hand out printed copies of the *Universal Declaration of Human Rights* (Welch 1995, 2001). Others, as mentioned, train domestic groups in nonviolent protest techniques or provide meeting spaces for individuals to plan domestic campaigns (Schock 2005). Many interview domestic victims of repression about the abuses they suffered and then work to get accounts of these abuses into the minds of the global public (Welch 1995). Some advocacy organizations perform multiple tactics simultaneously, while others specialize in advocating through one specific set of actions—for example, organizations that specialize in forensic anthropology to be used in transitional justice measures after civil wars (UIA 2008/2009).

In a piece with Dursun Peksen (2012), we organize these diverse tactics into two categories: "local population empowerment" and "information production." These categories meld well with the traditional transnational advocacy network framework in that they delineate a set of actions—"local population empowerment"—that organizations often perform from within a state, and a set of actions—"information production"—that organizations perform both internationally and domestically to complete the boomerang pattern of advocacy. By local population empowerment, I am referring to the set of actions that organizations can take with the goal of increasing pressure on the targeted government "from below" (Brysk 1993). These actions, like educating a population on their internationally guaranteed human rights or helping with nonviolent tactics, work to mobilize a population to bolster their domestic demands for human rights improvements. Often, these actions are also attempts to encourage more domestic actors to join in the movement (Davis, Murdie, and Steinmetz 2012).

At the same time, however, similar organizations within the advocacy network—perhaps some of the very same organizations—are collecting information to be dispersed to a wider domestic and international audience. Some organizations—like Amnesty International, for example—will send professionals and volunteers into the field to document human rights abuses and build reports and background documents about the alleged abuses. Other INGOs will use reports and information that domestic organizations and activists have provided. With this information in hand, INGOs then try to publicize the abuses in an attempt to add mainly international actors to the overall advocacy movement. This information can be utilized at many stages in the advocacy process; some information may be utilized first as a way to get an idea about a violation on the international agenda in the first place (Risse and Sikkink 1999). For example, recently, some human rights organizations have been releasing vivid information about the practice of "waterboarding" as a way to embed the practice into collective ideas about what constitutes torture in the international arena (AI 2008c).

Information production is often termed "shaming and blaming" or "naming and shaming" and refers to the conflictual or negative statements that an organization releases to the international media (Schmitz 2002; Ron, Ramos, and Rodgers 2005). For example, on March 5, 1990, in a Reuters Global News Service article, Human Rights Watch reported that a British journalist was hanged and some political prisoners were detained in Iraq; the headline read, "Iraq: Rights Group Condemns Iraq's Hanging of British Journalist." The purpose of the article was both to draw attention to the human rights practices of Saddam Hussein's regime and to call others to pressure the regime to stop its abusive practices. Similarly, later that same month, Human Rights Watch reported on problems with political and civil rights in Burma (Myanmar) with an article entitled "Burma: Human Rights Group Calls Burma's Coming Elections a Sham." The organization hoped that publishing the report before the Burmese election would generate international pressure to make immediate changes. Shaming, although mainly for international audiences, can also be designed to increase domestic mobilization about the human rights abuses; in fact, empirical research with David Davis and Coty Steinmetz indicates that shaming does lead to changes in domestic opinions about human rights abuses within a state, which could aid in fostering the grievances necessary for domestic mobilization (Gurr 1970).

After these shaming reports are released, however, improvements in human rights are (not) assured. At the very least, INGOs are hoping that other international actors join in the shaming of the state "from above" (Brysk 1993). This would be consistent with the out-of-country portion of the boomerang pattern; organizations do not have to be the only actors pressuring the state from above. Through their information production, they are trying to get other actors to join in and pressure the state as well. Actually, this happens quite often. For instance, after much shaming by many INGO actors, on June 14, 2007, the United States "sent [a] firmer signal to Pakistan on democracy," calling on President Musharraf to ensure that basic political and civil rights, including the rights to "freedom of press, freedom of assembly, an independent judiciary, and free and fair elections," were protected (Mohammed 2007). In the Reuters Global News Service report on the call for action from the United States, Human Rights Watch was cited as "welcom[ing] the firmer tone from Washington [DC]" (Mohammed 2007). Again, according to the mechanisms through which advocacy networks are supposed to work, INGO shaming and reporting led to Pakistani rights violations reaching the radar of the US government, leading to their own eventual "naming and shaming" of the human rights conditions under Musharraf.

The mechanisms through which INGO shaming leads to shaming by third-party states and other international actors are not very developed theoretically in the existing literature. As such, it is unclear when and how INGOs' information production leads to other international actors joining in the "from above" pressure on the targeted state. In general, it is clear that more shaming by INGOs should lead to these actors joining in the advocacy campaign (Keck and Sikkink 1998). Likewise, when INGO shaming reaches the attention of individuals within democratized third-party states, they can demand that their own governments pressure the state as well. These ideas are not fully outlined in the extant literature, but some of the very recent empirical literature on shaming determinants, as discussed below, illustrates which types of states INGOs shame the most, in particular INGO Amnesty International. Some of this work focuses on how shaming decisions are made not only with targeted state characteristics in mind but with characteristics of potential INGO advocacy partners (third-party states, intergovernmental organizations) (Ron, Ramos, and Rodgers 2005; Hendrix and Wong 2012). Extending this literature to examine the conditions when INGO shaming does in fact lead to shaming by other international actors would be a likely next step in this research agenda.

Very broadly, there are two mechanisms or general theoretical approaches that appear in the interdisciplinary literature concerning how international pressure, by both INGOs and third-party states, invokes policy or behavior outcomes in the targeted state: the spread of economic resources and the spread of norms (Feldman 1997; Poe et al. 1999; Van Tuijl 1999; Richards et al. 2001; Welch 2001). Although the mechanisms are often separated in the theoretical literature, in practice, advocacy INGOs frequently use these mechanisms simultaneously (Shigetomi 2002; Okafor 2006). The economic resources approach focuses on how advocacy INGO activities, especially shaming and blaming, can be linked to monetary assistance, investment and aid for a state; the "carrot and stick" incentives of these economic resources can induce targeted-state actors to change their behaviors or policies (Hahn and Holzscheiter 2005; Schepers 2006; Hafner-Burton 2008). Under this approach, advocacy organizations try to gain media attention on a specific human rights issue and get intergovernmental and powerful governmental actors to support the issue. Through these tactics, called "leverage politics," advocacy INGOs help pressure a target-state from above (Keck and Sikkink 1998; Hestres 2007). When their message reaches these international actors, INGO shaming could impact aid distribution and foreign direct investment, which in turn can cause a target government to adopt a policy or behavior line with the INGO's goal (Risse et al. 1999; Welch 2001). Under this mechanism, behavior change is based on the rational self-interest of target-state governmental officials, usually with no discussion of internalization (Johnston 2001; Checkel 2003).[6]

On the other hand, under the normative approach, advocacy INGO activities center on persuading targeted actors to internalize the goals of the advocacy network (Keck and Sikkink 1998; Tarrow 2005). By concentrating on normative change, this approach not only focuses on how INGOs work to obtain behavioral or policy outcomes but on how INGOs work to make a specific issue a domestic norm in the targeted regime, often defined as a "collective expectation . . . of proper behavior" (Katzenstein 1996). At the center of these activities is a process of international and domestic socialization (Finnemore and Sikkink 1998; Keck and Sikkink 1998; Johnston 2008).

By *international socialization*, I am referring to the process by which advocates work to convince a critical mass of states to adopt a norm (Finnemore and Sikkink 1998; Keck and Sikkink 1998; Johnston 2008). The process begins with norm "entrepreneurs" persuading states to adopt their idea, such as what happened with human rights at the end of World War II (Finnemore and Sikkink 1998, 895). Later, as more states begin to at least tacitly accept the norm, a critical mass of states begins to be embedded in a system where this norm is accepted. Finally, a "tipping point" occurs when latecomers support the idea that has become the "prevailing standard of appropriateness" (Finnemore and Sikkink 1998, 895).

Under this approach, a state adopts the norm to retain its identity or to be legitimized (Checkel 2005; Johnston 2005). The larger socialization process usually involves education, habituation, and repetition, all activities that many advocacy INGOs try to work through (Welch 2001; Checkel 2005; Johnston 2005; Ahmed and Potter 2006). Frequent interactions between the international persuader and the persuadee can help expand the identity of the self, which can also encourage conformity (Checkel 2005; Johnston 2005). Socialization of norms also can be understood as being achieved through peer pressure— blaming and shaming behavior that goes against the norm, while praising the behavior associated with the norm (Finnemore and Sikkink 1998; Keck and Sikkink 1998). Under this approach, the point is that the advocacy INGO impacts policy and behavior outcomes by changing the identity and expectations of the targeted state; this actor does not just adopt a policy or behavior because of material concerns. Because the focus is on how numerous states adopt a norm, international socialization has been useful in addressing how norms of behavior are introduced into the public discourse or how they become codified in international treaties (Finnemore and Sikkink 1998).

Soon after Keck and Sikkink's (1998) award-winning book was published, *The Power of Human Rights: International Norms and Domestic Change*, edited by Thomas Risse, Stephen C. Ropp, and Kathryn Sikkink (1999), was released. This book extends both Keck and Sikkink's boomerang pattern and the concepts of norm socialization to the enactment of changes in domestic human rights practices. According to their framework, there is a five-part "spiral" pattern of socialization related to human rights, with the work of human rights INGOs at the center. To begin, both information production and domestic empowerment work to bring a targeted state on the international stage for its repressive practices. This process of shaming and domestic mobilization is heightened in the second stage. At these early stages, although the discourse of human rights may be heightened, few changes in the actual human rights practices occur.

Later, however, if domestic and international pressure continues, the tar-geted state begins to make "tactical concessions" or "cosmetic changes" in order to counter criticism from the international community (Risse and Sikkink 1999, 25). Given the lack of "teeth" in human rights international treaties, these tactical concessions may be the "window dressing" of treaty ratification (Hafner-Burton and Tsutsui 2005). Human rights treaties, like the Convention against Torture or the International Covenant on Civil and Political Rights, have long been criti-cized for their ineffective enforcement mechanisms and little power to actually require compliance (Hathaway 2002; Vreeland 2008). By signing and ratifying these treaties, however, governments in targeted states are signaling that they are responding to the human rights shaming and plan to make changes in on-the-ground practices (Risse and Sikkink 1999). However, given recent research on the ineffectiveness of human rights treaties, states may be ratifying these agreements only as a way to "camouflage" themselves against further criticism (Simmons 2009). In other words, at this stage of tactical concessions, the regime elite do not actually believe in the norms that the advocacy network is touting; they are simply trying to appease activists into leaving the state alone.

After these concessions, however, if information production and domestic mobilization remain high, a fourth stage in the spiral process can occur where discussions among activists and regime leaders expand and the regime begins to adopt some behaviors that are consistent with the norm being advocated (Risse and Sikkink 1999). For example, at this stage, the regime may release prisoners or begin offering training to police officers about interrogations; the regime may allow dissent in the popular press. These changes in behavior may be part of a process of "controlled liberalization" where the regime extends tac-tical concessions to allow some opening of the political process and improve-ments in human rights practices (Risse and Sikkink 1999, 28). At the last stage, if domestic and international pressure continues, the regime begins to internalize the norm associated with these "rule-consistent" human rights behaviors (Risse and Sikkink 1999, 259). At these latter stages of the spiral process, domestic mobilization is thought to be incredibly important for the socialization process necessary for internalization to occur within the regime.

Worth mentioning, the mechanisms through which advocacy INGOs im-pact policy and behavior outcomes, as discussed above, are also similar to the mechanisms linking international governmental organizations (Ios or IGOs) to domestic political outcomes in the "second image reversed" literature

(Reiter 2001; Pevehouse 2005; Gleditsch and Ward 2006). Though this literature has focused almost exclusively on IGOs, as Pevehouse (2005) points out, the international community can encourage domestic political outcomes through direct pressure, socialization and preference change, and "bribery" (170).

Additionally, although this literature clearly outlines the mechanisms and process through which advocacy actors influence human rights outcomes, the focus is almost predominantly on governmental human rights practices. In other words, the state is seen as central in human rights violations and human rights protection. However, recent human rights advocacy has expanded beyond the traditional focus on the state as the only violator of human rights and has acknowledged that nonstate actors, including transnational terrorist organizations and multinational corporations, can still violate human rights and can be shamed by advocacy networks themselves (Spar and LaMure 2003). The mechanisms through which INGO activities lead these nonstate actors to "rule-consistent" behavior, however, have not been as clearly delineated in the extant literature.

MECHANISMS THROUGH WHICH SERVICE INGOS AFFECT HUMAN SECURITY

Given the above discussion of the mechanisms through which human rights advocacy INGOs influence human security outcomes related to freedom from fear, what are the mechanisms connecting service INGOs to human rights outcomes related to freedom from want? As mentioned, the TAN framework does not focus on the work and influence of organizations that typically focus on service provision. In general, however, the literature on service INGOs in international relations does draw on the TAN framework and often associates similar behaviors across subcategories of organizations (Cooley and Ron 2002; Busby 2010).

Although largely missing from the TAN framework, the extant cross-disciplinary literature provides a largely straightforward account of how service INGOs impact an individual's ability to receive services that make them free from want (Masud and Yontcheva 2005; Mohanty 2006; Sparr and Moser 2007). In general, three mechanisms are worthy of mention here: organizations can provide social services directly themselves or train individuals in service provision, organizations can provide funds for individuals to later receive services, and organizations can set up partnerships with governments or advocate for changes in government policies that lead to better government provision of services. I address each in detail below.

First, although it may be commonsensical, these organizations affect human security outcomes because they often provide the outcome themselves within the state where they are working.[7] Service provision INGOs provide relief aid, health care and sanitation services, vocational education, and access to business-development training to local populations (Streeten 1997; Clarke 1998; Makoba 2002; Ahmed and Potter 2006). For example, the conglomerate organization Oxfam International has been involved in Ghana since 1986. It has dug wells and administered vaccines within the country. Currently, Oxfam work in Ghana also focuses on sustainable agriculture education; by educating local citizens on how to increase the food production on their land without negatively impacting land quality, Oxfam is working for the goal of food security for all Ghanaians in the state. Oxfam, like many INGOs, also works with domestic organizations and tries to aid in coordination between various international and domestic organizations within a set locale.

Direct service provision within a country is not without critics. Alexander Cooley and James Ron's (2002) important piece, "The NGO Scramble: Organizational Insecurity and the Political Economy of Transnational Action," discusses how NGOs involved in relief in the immediate aftermath of the fighting in Goma, Democratic Republic of Congo may have inadvertently aided "Hutu war criminals" through their handing out of relief items to those linked to the fighting (28). Early critics of direct service provision also highlighted the dependence that might be a result of INGO aid (Edwards and Hulme 1996).

Because of these criticisms, many organizations now use tactics that both provide basic services when necessary and work to increase long-term sustainability through education and health services. In other words, by first improving health and education, many organizations hope that a host state's population will then have the tools necessary to provide services related to the "freedom from want" themselves. Jakub Kakietek and I (2012) address this in our article "Do NGOs Really Work?" In the article, we show empirically that development INGOs improve both female life expectancy and secondary enrollment. These indicators have then been linked to improvements in economic development, through which a population may be better able to provide necessary basic necessities themselves.

Worth noting, tactics used in direct service provision are constantly changing as service provision organizations reevaluate what is working and what is not. Sometimes, an organization's large "output" does not actually translate to a sustainable outcome in service provision. For example, the organization

Engineers Without Borders reported that when it provided Zambia with con-
struction equipment, its "output" (the equipment) did not equate to any real
service provision outcome in the state because the organization did not also
supply the parts and repairs necessary to keep the equipment in good working
order.[8] Perhaps more troubling, septic work by organizations early in the 1970s
in Bangladesh and East Asia has been linked to increases in arsenic poisoning.
Certainly, then, this output did not sustainably improve human security provision in those countries. One Cambodian NGO official spoke of the failure:

> In the 1990s, a lot of poorly planned NGOs built wells for villages and did not
> fully understand the long-term situation after they left. . . . Many were short-
> term volunteer programmes that didn't teach people about the dangers of arse-
> nic from their wells. (IRIN 2008a)

Service INGOs typically provide services through funds collected from the
international community, including aid from developed countries, individual
and private donations, and aid from intergovernmental organizations (Hulme
and Edwards 1997; Ahmed and Potter 2006). As such, development INGOs are
often seen as part of the overall aid sector; some are simply delivery channels
through which both state and IGO aid are funneled. As Simone Dietrich (2013)
points out, some aid is often funneled into the INGO sector when states lack
the governance structures through which intended outcomes are likely. For example, when corruption is widespread within a country, aid typically bypasses
the government, going to INGOs or IGOs instead, which are seen as more reliable and efficient actors on the whole (12).

Sometimes overlooked, another mechanism through which service INGOs
influence service outcomes is through direct transfers of money. Some service
INGOs provide funds for domestic citizens to get a specific good or service
themselves (Edwards and Hulme 1996; Hulme and Edwards 1997; Masud and
Yontcheva 2005). Many service INGOs, especially faith-based INGOs, transfer
funds directly to local households (Sparr and Moser 2007). These "social transfers" can be limited to lodging or food monies, but they can also include larger
amounts of funds to support local business initiatives. Social transfers usually
do not require reciprocity or accountability of the recipient: the funds trans-
ferred are noncontingent on results and do not need to be repaid.

Recently, one particular form of direct transfer has received a lot of attention: microfinance by INGOs. Unlike the traditional transfers discussed above,
these transfers involve the agreement that all of the funds provided by the

INGO, or a large percentage of the funds provided, will be paid back; basically, they are loans. In general, the idea here, for which the Grameen Bank, a for-profit company out of Bangladesh, received the Nobel Prize in 2006, is that small loans, mainly to impoverished peoples without access to credit, fuel entrepreneurial endeavors that in turn enable these individuals to both pay back the loan and provide services that help them get out of poverty. Many microfinance institutions, both for-profit and INGOs, specialize in providing funds to women, who are argued to be more likely to use the funds to help provide health and educational services for their children. Sometimes the loans are attached to promises that the loan recipient must enroll her children in school or get water only from certain wells. The growth in microfinance projects is staggering: an estimated US$70 billion industry that has reached 200 million individuals worldwide (Sinclair and Korten 2012). Well-known INGO endeavors in microfinance include organizations like Kiva, which partners donors with loan recipients over the Internet.

Despite this growth in the tactic of microlending by INGOs, complaints about such microfinance do exist, including stories that equate microfinance institutions, even those that operate as nonprofits, with being nothing less than pawn shops or payday loan brokers, where people are encouraged to take out another loan to pay for their existing loan, which could have a total interest rate of over 100 percent (Karnani 2007; Sinclair and Korten 2012). Empirical literature, as discussed below, is in its infancy, but evidence shows that microfinance helps the poor, even those who did not take out the loan (Khandker 2005). In general, though, microfinance represents a mechanism that some INGOs use that connects direct transfers of money to both investment and consumption, leading theoretically to increased provision of services. In short, either through providing services themselves or providing funds that are utilized in ways that allow personal purchases of services, service INGOs are connected to the freedom from want aspects of human security. As Makoba (2002) points out, in many developing countries, these organizations "are considered good substitutes for weak states and markets in . . . the provision of basic services to most people" (62).

The third mechanism connecting the work of service provision INGOs to human security is through government partnerships and work that increases a state's own provision of these services. This mechanism is somewhat counterintuitive; many critics of the work of INGOs have highlighted that organizations are "being used to slowly remove all the flesh of the state" (Ell 2008) and that the organizations, in providing services themselves, will eliminate any desire or need for the host state to provide their own services. Despite these criticisms, many INGOs recognize that their provision of goods could lead to some sort of dependence and work through government partnerships and agreements where the government is providing some assistance and complementing the work of the INGO. In our article "Can International Nongovernmental Services Boost Government Services? The Case of Health," Alex Hicks and I (2013) address how current INGO practices can lead to an increase in government service provision, focusing on the issue of health services. Interviews with decision makers at service INGOs indicated that their goals reflected government provision of services instead of INGO provision. An official at one INGO reported that their goal was to "[try] to leave or increase government programs" instead of "proving services in lieu of the government providing them."

There are at least three mechanisms through which service provision INGOs work to increase government provision of the services themselves: indirectly working to change the policy making climate, aiding in domestic organized mobilization for health services, and directly pressuring the state to change its practices. Empirically, in my earlier work, I find much evidence for the first two mechanisms, indicating that organizations often change both government and citizen expectations about what services should be provided. Unlike conventional wisdom, service INGOs aid in service provision *through* the state in addition to their work to provide services *around* the state.

Further, INGOs also could influence a host state's service provision by changing the state's governance structures internally in ways that increase service provision. For example, Zinnes and Bell (2002) argue that service INGOs, through increasing civil society within a state, can lead to increases in respect for the rule of law. Respect for the rule of law may make existing government efforts for service provision more efficient.

In short, although service INGOs are largely missing from the TAN framework, the microprocesses connecting them to human security outcomes are very straightforward: service INGOs impact policy and behavior through their own service provision, direct transfers, and influences on government service provision.

EMPIRICAL TESTS OF INGO EFFECTS
ON HUMAN SECURITY

So far, I have outlined the general transnational advocacy network literature and its assumptions about INGOs. I then addressed the theoretical mechanisms through which advocacy and service organizations have been connected to human security outcomes. In these sections, however, I did not directly address the existing empirical evidence of these mechanisms or the evidence of any overall INGO effects on human security. Below, I address this literature, focusing first on advocacy INGOs and their empirical effects, and then turn back to service INGOs and the empirical literature concerning them.

Advocacy INGOs To begin, it is worth noting that the TAN framework does offer some predictions concerning the conditions when advocacy movements are more likely to affect policy and behavior outcomes. The framework predicts that advocacy attempts are more likely to be successful (a) if the advocacy network is dense, (b) if the targeted state is vulnerable or embedded in the international system, and (c) if the issue "involves bodily harm" or "legal equality" (Keck and Sikkink 1998, 26–29).

Existing case studies have provided some support to the conditional effectiveness predictions from the TAN framework. Human rights INGOs were successful in changing policies in the Philippines in the 1980s and 1990s because of their density (Jetschke 2000). Similarly, the success of the South African apartheid movement has been linked to the density of the advocacy network (Black 1999). Risse (2002) points out, however, that some advocacy network movements have involved a small number of advocacy actors, perhaps in contrast to the density hypothesis.

Case studies have also indicated that the vulnerability of the state does influence the conditional effectiveness of advocacy movements. Increases in state vulnerability explained why TAN actors were able to affect human rights conditions in Mexico in the 1990s but not earlier (Sikkink 1993; Donnelly 1998; Keck and Sikkink 1998). Evangelista (1999) found that state vulnerability increases also explained the conditional efficacy of epistemic communities in Russia at the end of the Cold War. Also, Princen (1995) found that the advocacy movement to end the ivory trade was more successful in Kenya than in Zimbabwe because of state vulnerability to internal and external pressure. However, many have noticed that state vulnerability offers little in explaining why advocacy networks can have divergent outcomes on two issues in the same state (Keck and Sikkink 1998; Risse 2002; Ahmed and Potter 2006).

Finally, the "bodily harm" or "legal equality" contention has received very little attention in case studies; it is typically only mentioned in passing (Keck and Sikkink 1998), or the study is limited at the onset to focusing only on a specific subsegment of rights that reflect these issues (Risse, Ropp, and Sikkink 1999).

Worth noting, however, with respect to some case study empirical research within the TAN framework, as Risse (2002) points out:

> Many studies do suffer from methodological problems such as case selection on the dependent variable. There are many single case studies of successful transnational campaigns, while we know much less about failed campaigns. (264)

Risse's statement could explain the limited attention given to the bodily harm/legal equality contention with the TAN framework; other issues would be less likely to have a successful outcome on the dependent variable.

Perhaps more important than the problem Risse outlines with respect to the extant empirical literature, these predictions from the TAN framework center not on INGOs themselves but on the total advocacy network, including INGO ties to the domestic and international communities. As such, the TAN framework offers little in the form of predictions concerning when and how INGOs are able to get and maintain these ties or concerning the impact of INGOs themselves. This is reflected in much of the case study empirical research that focuses not on the effect of INGOs but on the effect of the whole advocacy network. In other words, the INGO's ability to get and maintain other potential advocacy actors has been somewhat black-boxed in the conventional TAN approach and has not been the focus on the existing theoretical or empirical literature.

More recently, however, there is a growing cross-national literature on the impact of INGO activities on human rights outcomes and, to a lesser extent, on the impact of INGO activities on various steps in the spiral process. To begin, Landman (2005) and Hafner-Burton and Tsutsui (2005) both make the case and find that general civil society, measured as all types of INGOs in a country, is associated with higher respect for basic physical integrity rights, including the rights to freedom from torture, political imprisonment, political disappearances, and political killings. Neumeyer (2005) also finds that many types of INGOs in a country act as a conditioning variable for the relationship between human rights treaty ratification and actual human rights practices. When more INGOs are present, human rights treaties can have a positive effect on human rights performance. In all these works, however, the focus is not on human rights organizations per se but on the impacts of all organizations, many of which, as mentioned above, have no link to advocacy for human rights or service provision.

Very recently, many pieces have moved to examining the influence of the activities of specifically human rights INGOs. Cardenas (2007) used a static measure of human rights INGOs in a country and found that organizations had no statistically significant impact on human rights outcomes. My 2009 article "The Impact of Human Rights INGOs on Human Rights Practices" reported on human rights INGOs' effects on empowerment rights at three static points in time (1978, 1988, and 1998): the rights to freedom of movement, freedom of speech, political participation, and religion and workers' rights. In all these works, the mechanisms the authors addressed focused on a combination of domestic empowerment and international information production.

Focusing specifically on INGO shaming activities in a small sample of Latin American countries, Franklin (2008) found that shaming can lessen government repression only in states that are vulnerable to outside pressure, which he defines as the combination of high levels of foreign aid dependence and foreign direct investment in the targeted country. Franklin codes human rights domestic and international NGO shaming as criticism mentioned in "Facts on File or Keesing's Record of World Events" (193). Expanding beyond Latin America, however, Hafner-Burton (2008) examined the influence of the INGO Amnesty International's press releases and background reports on repression. Hafner-Burton (2008), however, did not find that more reports equated to a higher level of human rights protection in the following year. In other words, by itself, the total number of reports that are intended to be used for shaming are not associated with higher levels of human rights performance.

My cross-national global empirical work with David Davis (2012a), "Shaming and Blaming," examined the interaction between human rights INGO shaming and the domestic presence of particularly human rights INGOs. We found that when human rights INGO shaming to states in Reuters Global News Service is coupled with a larger domestic presence of human rights INGOs, improvements in human rights were more likely. Additionally, we found that the combination of human rights INGO shaming and shaming by third-party actors that cite a human rights INGO also led to a more likely improvement in human rights.

Even more recent work has also found a positive effect of shaming on a variety of human rights outcomes and in a variety of conditional scenarios.

For example, Krain (2012) found that more Amnesty International background reports reduced the severity of ongoing genocides and politicides. DeMeritt (2012) found something similar with respect to overall human rights INGO shaming. Hendrix and Wong (2013) found that human rights INGO shaming, as measured by Amnesty International reports, was associated with human rights improvements only in autocratic regimes. Hendrix and Wong believe this effect is due to the larger impact on "public perceptions" that naming and shaming can bring in the absence of opposition parties and free media (1–2). In other words, democracies and hybrid regimes are likely to have more information when they decide to repress in the first place and thus feel less of an impact of shaming on their decision-calculus to repress.

In a piece with Sam Bell and K. Chad Clay (2012) entitled "Neighborhood Watch," we examined the role of human rights INGOs in the state "next door" to the targeted state and found that higher numbers of human rights INGOs with members or volunteers in neighboring states can have a spillover effect on the human rights in the targeted state. We believe this is true because coordination goods can cross borders with human rights INGO officials and help in mobilization "from below" (Brysk 1993). This effect, however, is conditioned by more respect for foreign movement in the neighborhood; when individuals are free to leave their country, they are more willing to aid in mobilization "next door."

In addition to these empirical pieces on the influence of INGOs on human rights or improvements in human rights, various empirical pieces have also examined the influence of human rights INGOs on some of the intermediary steps necessary for the boomerang pattern/spiral model of human rights change (Keck and Sikkink 1998; Risse, Ropp, and Sikkink 1999). First, at least two pieces looked at the influence of general INGOs (Olzak and Tsutsui 1998) and human rights INGOs (Murdie and Bhasin 2011) on domestic protest and found that INGOs that are present domestically help protest mobilization. Murdie and Bhasin (2011) even argue that human rights INGOs can help domestic violent protest through providing collective action resources that diffuse to "radical flanks" of larger domestic movements (Haines 1984). Further, and somewhat implicit within the TAN framework, my work with David Davis and Coty Steinmetz (2012) showed how shaming can influence public opinion in a country. When human rights INGOs shame a country, the citizens of that country feel their human rights are not being respected.

Shaming also influences foreign policy decisions and behaviors in ways consistent with the boomerang pattern. Dursun Peksen and I (2012) showed that shaming can increase a targeted country's likelihood of economic sanctions, even when we accounted for the human rights conditions in a country. Likewise, Barry, Clay, and Flynn (2013) showed that foreign direct investment actually diminishes for the state targeted by INGO shaming.

Service INGOs   Moving toward service INGOs' influence on human security service outcomes, the empirical literature is much scarcer than advocacy INGOs. However, the literature that does exist supports the idea that these organizations do often deliver services in developing countries. First, much of the case study research, including an influential book edited by Edwards and Hulme (1996), indicates that development INGOs can provide services in developing countries. Their use of credit programs in Bangladesh aids in diminishing child mortality rates (Amin and Li 1997). Other research in Bangladesh indicates that development INGO partnerships with governments help in fighting tuberculosis (Ullah et al. 2006). Focusing on the country of Timor, Alonso and Brugha (2006) concluded that health INGOs can help government health systems. Campos and colleagues (2004) found that INGOs fill gaps in government service provision and aid in political organizations among rural low-income people in Pakistan. In Africa, Rose (2009) found that NGOs can be good providers of basic educational services, although only second best when compared to state provision. With Eastern Europe, as mentioned, Zinnes and Bell (2002) found that NGOs can improve the rule of law.

Few global studies on the effects of service INGOs are available. Shandra and colleagues (2010) found that health INGOs reduce infant mortality, but this is true only in democracies. A similar finding holds with respect to HIV prevalence (Shircliff and Shandra 2011). My work with Jakub Kakietek (2012) showed development INGOs' direct effects on female life expectancy and education, as well as both direct and indirect effects on economic growth rates in developing countries.

In short, consistent with the dominant framework on INGOs, existing empirical work does indicate likely positive influences of the organizations on some human security outcomes. This work, however, did not take into account the empirical implications of many of the theoretical critiques of the dominant framework and, thus, failed to provide many concrete answers into the conditions in which INGOs are most likely to succeed. It is on this topic of theoretical critiques that the chapter now turns.

CRITIQUES OF THE DOMINANT FRAMEWORK

Despite its indisputable importance, existing TAN framework has been criticized on many fronts (Brown and Moore 2001; Cooley and Ron 2002; Bob 2005; Kelly 2005; Carpenter 2007). First, as mentioned, the TAN framework, often cited as the INGO theory of international relations, focuses solely on advocacy INGOs, especially human rights INGOs advocating for the realization of political or civil rights (Keck and Sikkink 1998; DeMars 2005; Kelly 2005). No existing theoretical framework focuses on both service and advocacy INGOs or offers predictions concerning the differences between the two.

Additionally, as Kelly (2005) points out, within international relations, "too many scholars in the field overidentify with the NGOs" (62). This "overidentification" could be causing a "wishful academic conjecture" about the behavior and impact of the organizations (62–63). In critiquing the TAN framework, Kelly goes as far as arguing that "international relations research on [I]NGOs needs less ideological excitement for them and more theoretical and empirical research" (60). Worth noting, some of these critiques of INGO motivations even predate the TAN framework (Brett 1993).

Perhaps this "ideological excitement" is to blame for the TAN framework's somewhat overly positive view of INGO motivations and the lack of attention that very personalistic rent-seeking behaviors by INGOs have received in the dominant framework. As many revisionist works and journalistic accounts of INGOs point out, however, some INGOs' motivations appear counter to the principled or "shared values" assumption that has dominated the TAN literature (Petras 1997; Cooley and Ron 2002; Bob 2005; Khidr 2006; Omara-Otunnu 2007). Below, I highlight these critiques, paying special attention to how non-principled motivations differ for service as opposed to advocacy INGOs.

ADVOCACY INGOS: INTERNATIONALLY BIASED ADVOCACY

INGOs at work within a state may not be responding to domestic needs or desires (Cooley and Ron 2002; Bob 2005; Goonatilake 2006; Sundstrom 2006). Instead, INGOs can have their own operational and normative agenda, which can run counter to the goals and objectives of the domestic population. Many times, this agenda can take a very non-"shared values" patronizing or paternalistic tone that reflects a particular international bias; as Manji and O'Coill (2002) put it so vividly, some INGOs have taken the "missionary position."

This problem appears to be especially prevalent in advocacy INGOs, such as environmental or human rights INGOs. Unlike that described by the TAN framework, advocacy INGOs are often involved in a state or on an issue not because they have been called there by domestic groups but because that state or issue fits the INGO's existing goals (Cooley and Ron 2002; Bob 2005; Goonatilake 2006; Sundstrom 2006). As such, much of the revisionist literature contends that instead of the boomerang process, organizations go where they want to for personalistic reasons, even if they have not been called by a repressed domestic population. Lisa Sundstrom's 2006 book *Funding Civil Society: Foreign Assistance and NGO Development in Russia* provides a fascinating account of this process. Instead of responding to domestic calls for assistance, at the end of the Cold War, Western democracy promoting agencies actually sent advocates to Russia to create a domestic NGO sector that would be supportive of democracy. As such, foreign donors wanted INGOs to focus on expanding domestic NGO sectors in soldiers' rights and women's rights, even if there had been very few domestic calls for assistance in these areas. A similar account of INGOs responding to international funding in their decision to get involved on an issue and not on domestic calls for assistance is found in Susantha Goonatilake's 2006 book *Recolonisation: Foreign Funded NGOs in Sri Lanka*.

Also counter to the TAN framework, Clifford Bob (2005) points out that INGOs may not be interested in all calls for help by domestic populations. Instead, INGOs may only respond to domestic groups if the group's issue fits the strategic needs of the organization. Bob refers to this process as one of "organizational matching," explaining that organizations want issues that "will not harm and may in fact help them" (37). As such, just like Goonatilake (2006) and Sundstrom (2006) point out, organizations will highly value the desires of their donors when deciding what to focus on. Prakash and Gugerty (2010) showed that this behavior by INGOs is more like for-profit "firms" than the dichotomy of nonprofit and for-profit organizations suggested in Keck and Sikkink (1998).

Practitioner and journalistic accounts of advocacy INGOs are also critical of many organizational motivations. These critiques highlight an often "imperial" or "Western" bias in the workings of some advocacy INGOs, often calling these INGOs a modern-day missionary or colonizing force (Roelofs 2006). As one aid worker in Afghanistan contended:

> The "work" of NGOs sometimes seems to have more to do with the ideas of donor agencies than of actual local needs. Timetables are likely to be set to please donors rather than to pursue the best-quality outcomes. Projects are often determined based on what donors want to fund rather than starting with what local people are asking for. (Wenzel 2006)

An op-ed piece in the *Yemen Times* reiterated this contention:

> Every NGO has its own agenda that is not necessarily identical to all domestic interests of the peoples and states that are the target of the organizations' activities. Those organizations are not the angels who we have seen on television. (Khidr 2006)

Roelofs (2006) equates INGOs to the "heirs of missionaries," who "did many good deeds" but "also served as scouts for corporations and colonizers."

As these reports highlight, critiques of advocacy INGO motivations are often couched as concerns with international "donor dominance" within the INGO community (Clark et al. 2006). In other words, because INGOs get most of their funding and support from international actors, particularly from the Western community, some INGOs might have little or no incentive to do what domestic groups would like them to and more incentive to advocate for what their international donors desire (Gourevitch and Lake 2012). To be clear, this criticism is not unaware of the idea that INGOs can be advocating for changes in personal opinions within a domestic population; even within the traditional framework, INGOs do work to raise awareness of the issue. However, within the traditional framework, INGO involvement would still be predicated by some domestic awareness and agreement with the organization as to the importance of the changes being advocated.

Let me briefly illustrate these dynamics with a discussion of the antifemale genital cutting (FGC) movement in North Africa. During the late 1970s and early 1980s, most advocacy INGOs in North Africa framed FGC issues in medical terms (Boulware-Miller 1985). As such, most advocacy groups, such as Doctors Without Borders, were only pressing for policy changes requiring the practice to be performed in hospitals or doctors' offices by trained medical staff and age-specific restrictions on the practice (Boulware-Miller 1985). By many accounts, these early efforts for medicalization and age restrictions of the practice were successful and in line with the preferences of the domestic population (Parker 1995; Gruenbaum 2001).

At the end of the Cold War, however, preferences of the international community changed; now the international community wanted all-out FGC eradication. In 1995, four major donor foundations issued a joint statement that the previous advocacy attempts for medicalization policies concerning FGC were "mistake[s]" (Boyle 2002). Many INGOs thus joined larger IGO groups or policy statements concerning their goals for total FGC eradication (Boyle 2002).

In the 1990s, both the number of INGOs active on anti-FGC projects and funds directed at these INGOs increased. In fact, as Clark and colleagues (2006) point out, all other funding to human rights or women's INGOs already active within the region dried up; INGOs with long-standing commitments to the region could join the bandwagon of anti-FGC and gain international community funds, or they were forced to look elsewhere for funds and support.

Given the vast amount of funding and attention to FGC eradication advocacy, the extant TAN framework would predict the advocacy attempt by INGOs to be wildly successful (Keck and Sikkink 1998; Risse et al. 1999). In addition, the issue concerned states that were vulnerable to international pressure and involved bodily harm—all factors that, according to the TAN framework, would increase the likelihood of the advocacy effort influencing policy and behavior outcomes in line with the INGO's preferences. In reality, however, although INGO efforts led to some policy changes and treaty adoption by targeted governments, the project was largely considered unsuccessful in eradicating FGC practices (Boyle et al. 2001; Grande 2004). Many scholars writing on the subject conclude that human rights INGO efforts might have actually increased FGC prevalence, especially among middle- and upper-class highly educated women in North Africa (Gruenbaum 2001; Boyle 2002).

As the case of FGC eradication advocacy highlights, INGOs are often not motivated to help a domestic population reach its own goals. Instead, INGOs can have self-interested motivations to be involved on an issue or in a state. Many of these motivations reflect an international bias on the part of the advocacy INGO. These motivations can be in stark contrast to the goals and desires of the domestic population that the INGO, by its very mission statement and the canonical literature, is supposedly trying to help. The FGC case would imply that this type of behavior by INGOs could condition when and where INGOs have an impact in world politics.

One explanation for the lack of FGC advocacy success has to do with issue resonance and universal norms. In general, as both the traditional and the revisionist literatures point out, some issues are simply likely to resonate with the general public more. As mentioned, Keck and Sikkink (1998) contend that issues to do with "bodily harm" and "legal equality of opportunity" can be "framed more easily" so as to resonate. Sundstrom (2005, 2006) contends that INGOs had more success with domestic NGO mobilization on issues that reflected well-established universal norms where the local community is more in tune with the international community's ideas of appropriate behavior. Within this literature, however, little focus is paid to how specific policy and behavior recommendations by varying INGOs, even within a strictly defined issue area, can still differ in their resonance. For example, early FGC advocacy may have found a common ground with medicalization and age restrictions; these recommendations, however, were avoided by many latter advocates who favored policies and advocacy efforts that had less resonance with the domestic community but were more in line with what their international donors wanted.

In sum, all of these accounts, both practitioner and academic, definitively highlight a potential problem with one of the assumptions underlying the working of the dominant TAN framework and the boomerang process of advocacy: INGOs can work for issues where they have not been called by a domestic population and advocate for policies that have little or no resonance with the local domestic community they are trying to help.

What is interesting, however, is that much of this revisionist work equates some organizations' behaviors and motivations with those of all INGOs on an issue. As such, if some organizations are internationally biased in line with what their donors want, all organizations must share those same nonprincipled motivations. If some organizations behave like firms, all must be equal in their firmlike behavior. However, this doesn't appear to be the case. Organizations differ in the extent to which they exhibit behavior in line with the canonical Keck and Sikkink (1998) idea of principles and shared values or behavior in line with this personalistic, internationally biased motivation. In the FGC case, for example, many organizations in the region were involved with issues of women's rights that actually had goals in line with what domestic groups and individuals actually wanted at the time. Some of these groups were outraged at their internationally biased counterparts; as quoted in Clark and colleagues (2006), one women's rights INGO official reported:

> Look at FGM [female genital mutilation]. We can get funding for awareness raising that has nothing to do with women's empowerment. But we can't find support for something beyond counting the number of clitorises that have been cut. (83)

There are very few existing theoretical insights on the impact of varying motivational types of INGOs within a single locale. The presence of INGOs that advocate for issues that run counter to the desires of local communities could make domestic populations leery of supporting any INGO, even an INGO that has preferences for policy and behavior outcomes similar to the domestic community. Both the TAN framework and the revisionist literature offer few predictions into how this phenomenon could impact overall advocacy INGO effectiveness in world politics. No theoretical framework examines how the presence of advocacy INGOs that are internationally biased could impact the behavior of other advocacy INGOs without this bias, how other international and domestic actors regard advocacy INGOs, or, perhaps most importantly, how this phenomenon influences the effectiveness of overall advocacy INGO efforts on improving human security outcomes.

SERVICE INGOS: NONPRINCIPLES AS RENT-SEEKING

There are very few channels of accountability for INGOs (Gordenker and Weiss 1997; Hillhorst 2002; Cooley and Ron 2002; Grant and Keohane 2005; Gourevitch and Lake 2012). Unlike governments or private companies, there are very rarely boards or constituents who oversee their decisions. Many donation channels have little formal reporting requirements; often INGOs do not even have to prove their projects were successful—only that donations were actually spent (Petras 1997). Issues of INGO accountability are not addressed within the TAN framework and bring up many debatable issues for both international relations scholars and practitioners (Cooley and Ron 2002; Hillhorst 2002; Grant and Keohane 2005; Gourevitch and Lake 2012). For example, are INGOs accountable to their host government or to the government where they were founded? How accountable should INGOs be to donors? Or, as the above section on advocacy INGOs might suggest, could accountability to international donors limit accountability to local populations? Additionally, will accountability from above (i.e., accountability to governments and international organizations) limit the creativity and low overhead that are supposed to be the strengths of the INGO sector? These issues have been similarly raised in recent American politics and public policy research on nonprofits (Najam 1996; Frumkin 2002; Darnall and Carmin 2005; Gugerty 2008; Gugerty and Prakash 2010).

Regardless of where INGO accountability should lie, a lack of overall accountability, coupled with a growing amount of funds directed at INGOs, has been argued to have led to an increase in the number of INGOs that are motivated not to help a domestic population but to fill their own private coffers (Cooley and Ron 2002; Ben Attia 2004; Petras 1997). As such, these INGOs are rent-seekers; they are using donor funds for a private benefit that is not in line with the expected use of the funds. Like before, this type of nonprincipled motivation is contrary to the TAN's assumption that INGOs are motivated by "values rather than material concerns" (Keck and Sikkink 1998, 2).

The issue of rent-seeking by INGOs seems especially prevalent in service INGOs. This could also explain the lack of attention to rent-seeking INGOs from within the TAN framework, which, as mentioned, focuses almost solely on advocacy INGOs. Service INGOs, which typically take large donations for development or health projects, often have much larger operating budgets than advocacy INGOs (Ahmed and Potter 2006; UIA 2008/2009). These organizations also characteristically have far more overhead than advocacy INGOs, perhaps making the siphoning of funds from large donations easier.

Within the academic literature, Cooley and Ron (2002) best lay out the problems with service INGO projects and rent-seeking. They maintain that the problem of rent-seeking really stems from the "marketization" of INGO activities, seen in the "use of competitive tenders and renewable contracting" by the donor sector (6). According to this work, the market-based structures of the aid industry create opportunism and insecurity, which causes "self-interested action, inter-INGO competition, and poor project implementation" (14). In line with the rent-seeking behavior I'm discussing, Cooley and Ron point out how the process of aid contracting gives INGOs very little oversight:

> Recipients may genuinely welcome all project support and use aid resources for the purposes for which they were intended. On the other hand, without adequate monitoring, recipients may appropriate the contractor's resources for opportunistic gain. . . . When faced with pressure to renew existing contracts, aid contractors will be reluctant to report recipients' opportunistic behavior unless donors can credibly guarantee that they will not terminate or reduce funding for the project. (15–16)

Cooley and Ron do not go as far as to discuss how INGOs can differ in this behavior, with some organizations behaving in ways that appear far more consistent with nonprincipled motivations than others. In fact, they conclude with the idea that, in the face of these market-based structures, INGOs can be a "homogenous" lot:

> There is no doubt that many of today's INGOs are motivated by normative agenda. Insecurity and competition, however, often push them to behave in rational and rent-seeking ways. As scholars of institutional isomorphism have long suspected, organizational environments have powerfully homogenizing effects on their constituent units. (36)

Unlike this view of rent-seeking as a main motivation for all INGOs, however, it seems likely that organizations differ in their rent-seeking motivations. As Arundhati Roy reported in *Le Monde diplomatique* in 2004:

> It will be easy to twist what I say into an indictment of all NGOs, but that would be false. There are NGOs doing valuable work; there are also fake NGOs set up either to siphon off grant money or as tax dodges.

Roy is not alone in this contention; most of the practitioner and journalist accounts of INGO rent-seeking highlight how INGOs differ in their rent-seeking behaviors. Various reporters and practitioners, however, seem to see the distribution of rent-seeking and non-rent-seeking organizations differently. For example, writing about Somalia in 2002, Sereke Berhan contends:

> In what seems to be an open secret, NGOs these days are mostly instituted for reasons that have nothing to do with humanitarian and social causes. The large majority of NGOs, according to the way they operate, seem to have been created with hidden objectives. In many cases they have come to serve as lucrative means of amassing personal wealth.

Berhan goes on to say that in "most cases" INGOs are being created by "selfish and greedy individuals" for the gathering of private rents.

Similar sentiment comes out of Ghana, where Fadda Dickson said the following in a 2004 BBC article:

> NGOs are doing well, but the majority of them are in it to make money. There are instances where some will just go to the villages, take photographs, and present them to the donors.

The same was said about HIV/AIDS service organizations in Tanzania, where in a 2003 report, organizations reported the common problem of "briefcase" NGOs, which were defined as those without offices and "a well-defined administrative machinery and organizational structure" but that "are normally established to target donor funds" (UNAIDS 2003, 6).

Articles about Nepal in 2000, however, indicate that there may be a lower proportion of rent-seeking organizations there: "Most NGOs are result oriented, effective, and efficient. But there are some NGOs which do not function well" (ACCU 2000, 8).

These quotes all point out a very nonprincipled motivation of many service INGOs: the use of funds for private purposes. These funds can be fully embezzled, or some of the money can be used to buy "$40,000 four-wheel-drive sports vehicles" and "maids" for private purposes (Petras 1999). This self-interested use of funds donated to help a domestic population is in stark contrast to the principled or "virtuous" assumption dominant in the TAN framework (Keck and Sikkink 1998; Gourevitch and Lake 2012).

To conclude this section, however, let me be clear that, based on these practitioner criticisms, I am not contending that all INGOs share this rent-seeking motivation. Some organizations are behaving in ways that appear completely in tune with the shared values or principled ideals of the dominant theoretical framework. Some, however, are not. Unfortunately, the underlying motivations of INGOs are not public knowledge. No one besides the INGO really knows whether the organization is motivated mainly to help a domestic population achieve its goals or whether it is self-interested (Berhan 2002; Roy 2004; Vaknin 2005). Berhan (2002) points out that the true motivations of INGOs are often "hidden . . . and vehemently denied." INGOs have incentives to disclose and disguise their true type. In other words, they may want to appear as legitimate and altruistic as possible, even if they are not. This was also the case historically with many religious-based advocacy INGOs; they wanted to disguise their proselytizing and not appear internationally biased (Paine and Gratzer 2001).

In short, discussions of heterogeneity in INGOs' motivations are almost completely missing in the dominant TAN framework. As such, INGOs' behaviors and impacts discussed in the TAN literature fail to reflect reality. Not only does this TAN framework, then, fail to account for INGOs with nonprincipled motivations, but it fails to address how these heterogeneous motivations could complicate the interactions all INGOs have with other actors in the world system and condition, by extension, any impact INGOs have on human security.

THE SIGNALS INGOS SEND

The previous discussion served to make one point: even though we know a lot about the possible human security "goods" that some INGOs can bring to a situation, INGOs do not all share the same principled motivations. Instead, organizations can be principled or nonprincipled, and it can be difficult to tell the two apart (Hundley and Taggart 2013). Many INGOs are concerned that an increase in nonprincipled INGOs could undermine their ability to gain international and domestic support (Steinberg 2001; Ben Attia 2004; Mojumdar 2006). As Lee (2007) put it, could a few "bad apples" cause the international and domestic community to throw out the whole barrel? Given that INGOs do differ in their underlying motivations, what can those with principled motivations do to separate themselves from the pack? In this section, I address how INGOs themselves have sought to deal with issues concerning their underlying motivations and outline the cross-disciplinary literature concerning the actions and procedures INGOs have tried to use as an indication of their motivations. In short, these actions can be seen as *signals* and can, when credible, help the INGO indicate its underlying motivations to both the international and domestic communities. I situate these actions within the larger signaling literature in international relations.

To begin, the TAN framework makes clear that INGOs do not operate alone. INGOs need and desire the support of both international and domestic actors. By *international actors*, I am referring to the third-party states, donor agencies, and parts of intergovernmental organizations that are often critical to INGO work. By *domestic actors*, I am referring to domestic NGOs, civil society activists, and host country populations that work with the organization within a state. Unfortunately, these actors are ignorant of the INGOs' true motivations. In the domain of advocacy, INGOs could be motivated by shared values with the domestic community, working to help domestic communities reach their own goals when otherwise repressed, or they could be internationally biased, working for the policy or behavior outcomes that their international donors or stakeholders want that are not consistent with the domestic population they are supposedly trying to help. Conversely, in the service realm, INGOs could be either principled, working to provide goods and services to a domestic population, or rent-seeking, taking money from international donors to fill their own private coffers. When they are uncertain about the INGO's motives, it is hard for international and domestic actors to support any organization they are dealing with (Bekkers 2007).

For both service and advocacy organizations, issues of heterogeneous motivations have been an important topic at INGO conferences and networking meetings. As these conferences have concluded, it is often up to the INGOs themselves to try to indicate their underlying motivations to the domestic and international actors that are crucial to their work (Ben Attia 2004). Providing their motivations can be done with no expense, such as creating a website or writing a mission statement, or it can be expensive, such as releasing financial documents or signing larger issue and policy statements on an advocacy issue. As Hundley and Taggart (2013) said of US nonprofits, these signals could come from well-functioning staff who are expected to raise money instead of a for-profit fund-raising firm.

In many cases, these actions differ for advocacy as opposed to service INGOs. Below, I discuss the different ways in which advocacy and service INGOs have sought to indicate their underlying motivations to the domestic and international actors that can offer them support. First, however, I want to stress that such actions fit squarely within the larger signaling literature in international relations. As such, I believe these actions are signals that are meant to reduce the uncertainty that domestic and international actors have concerning the INGO's underlying preferences and motivations.

In the fields of both international relations and economics, a large literature has formed concerning signals (Jervis 1970; Kreps 1990; Morrow 1994; Sartori 2003; McCarty and Meirowitz 2007; Chapman 2009). Much of this literature is formal, using game-theoretic models to examine signaling dynamics (Kreps 1990; Morrow 1994; McCarty and Meirowitz 2007). This signaling literature all reflects one basic dynamic: some private information, typically concerning an actor's underlying motivations, exists, and other actors want access to it. The uninformed actors may think they know what the information consists of, but they can't be sure. The fully informed actors can send a signal to the uninformed actors about its private information in an attempt to throw them off and get them to do what they want (Kreps 1990; Morrow 1994; McCarty and Meirowitz 2007). Game-theoretic discussions of these dynamics also refer to signaling as an adverse selection principal-agent situation. The fully informed player is the agent, and the uninformed player is the principal. The principal must rely upon signals sent by the agent when selecting which type of agent to support (Kreps 1990; Morrow 1994; McCarty and Meirowitz 2007).

This is clearly the case with respect to INGOs: the domestic and international communities want to know the underlying motivations of the INGO they could support. These communities could receive some benefit from the INGOs' work. However, if the service INGO is a rent-seeker, for example, the INGO might provide no benefit for the international and domestic communities and just use the support it receives privately. If the advocacy INGO is internationally biased, likewise, the domestic community may also receive no benefit from the policy and behavior outcome the INGO is advocating for. The INGOs would like to indicate their underlying motivations to these communities, either signaling that they are non-rent-seekers, in the case of service INGOs, or signaling whether they are predominantly motivated to help the domestic population or are internationally biased, as is the case with advocacy INGOs.

This signaling literature in relation to INGOs lets us make a connection to signaling in international relations, which has not typically extended its focus to actions by nonstate actors (Chapman 2007, 2009; Fang 2008; Weeks 2008). It also provides a theoretically satisfying framework to examine these actions by INGOs that connects to other literatures on nonprofit organizations. Previous research on similar actions by domestic nonprofits and international actors has not extended the framework to focus on how these signals could affect policy or behavior outcomes by the overall INGO/nonprofit community (Reinhardt 2006, 2009; Gugerty 2008; Gugerty and Prakash 2010).

Likewise, a publication edited by Gourevitch, Lake, and Stein (2012) discusses how INGOs have to address issues of credibility "beyond virtue" (1). Gourevitch and Lake (2012) contend that "signals" can be one way for organizations to show their credibility. I argue, however, that all of the actions they discuss fit nicely within the signaling framework. Moreover, Gourevitch and Lake's work, which complements the approach taken here, does not systematically address the fundamental dynamic for which I argue signaling is necessary: differences in INGOs' underlying motivations and a lack of information about these motivations to both the domestic and international communities. Instead of focusing on INGOs as a very heterogeneous lot with differing motivations, Gourevitch and Lake see organizations as "virtuous" but argue that "virtue is not enough" (xi). As shown above, however, virtue in the INGO community is not a given. Signals are ways for organizations to show they are "virtuous" in a world where underlying motivations differ. My argument also builds off Gourevitch and Lake in addressing how actions to signal "credibility" can influence the behavior of domestic and international audiences and, ultimately, can matter for human security outcomes.

By considering INGOs' attempts to distinguish themselves from nonprincipled actors as signals to uninformed communities, many theoretical and empirical factors can be examined. First, by drawing on the signaling literature, the costs of these actions are highlighted (Jervis 1970; Sartori 2003). In other words, for a signal to inform the uninformed actor, the signal has to be discriminating and can't be copied or mimicked by the undesired type (Kreps 1990; Morrow 1994; McCarty and Meirowitz 2007). To ensure that the signal isn't copied, it must be costly—too costly for the undesired type to copy. However, the signal typically can't be *too* expensive, or the desired type won't be willing to send the

signal (McCarty and Meirowitz 2007). This concept from the signaling literature helps us understand how INGOs focus on their costs and how their costs
are borne by both principled and nonprincipled types of INGOs.

Second, the signaling literature addresses when and where signals are more
likely to be observed. In certain situations, such as when the uninformed player
faces predominantly one type of actor or when the uninformed player's benefits from the two types are similar, we are less likely to see signals at all (Kreps
1990; Morrow 1994; McCarty and Meirowitz 2007). Attention to these signaling
dynamics is important for understanding when heterogeneous types of INGOs
will try to indicate their underlying motivations in the first place. Worth noting, however, as Sartori (2003) points out, some signals, even if inexpensive
"cheap talk," can reveal repeated interactions, so uninformed actors know the
history of the actor that sent the signal, and there is the possibility of pun-
ishment. I would contend that a cheap talk approach to signaling would not
as aptly apply to INGOs because the international and domestic communities
rarely know the full history of the INGO they are interacting with.

Third, the signaling literature in international relations has separated costly
signals into categories based on when the costs are paid in relation to when the
uninformed player updates its beliefs (Fearon 1997). If costs are paid ex post,
these signals are typically thought of as "tying hands" signals (Fearon 1997).
These signals inform the uninformed player by showing resolve and involve an
audience that can punish the signal sender for not following through (Fearon
1997; Weeks 2008). Public statements of resolve by a state's leadership, for example, have been thought of as tying hands signals.

Conversely, if costs are paid ex ante, these signals are typically referred to as
"sunk costs" signals (Fearon 1997). In other words, these signals inform because
of the financial costs that are taken up front, showing the uninformed player
the commitment, for example, of the signal sender. I contend that the INGOs'
signals are typically sunk costs signals. Because of issues of overall accountability of INGOs, as discussed above, there rarely exists an audience that can
coordinate and punish the INGO ex post. As Weeks (2008) points out, this
coordination is necessary for tying hands signals to inform and be credible.

Finally, the previous signaling literature in international relations has focused on how signals sent by actors condition the behavior of others and, thus,
impact many different political outcomes, including war, foreign direct investment, and diplomacy (Jervis 1970; Mansfield et al. 2003; Sartori 2003; Chapman
2009). Similarly, through examining how these signals impact the behavior of

other actors, a more theoretically satisfying account of the conditional impact of INGOs can be constructed. In short, there are many theoretical reasons for drawing on the signaling literature to understand the actions of INGOs. I return to these ideas further in the next chapter when I draw upon the signaling literature to construct a game-theoretic model of INGO behavior and derive expectations about where INGOs will be most likely to influence human security.

SIGNALS BY ADVOCACY INGOS

For both advocacy and service INGOs, signals of underlying motivations can be sent to both the domestic and international communities. For advocacy INGOs, the signal is a way to inform these communities if the organization is internationally biased or if it has preferences for advocacy outcomes consistent with the desires of the domestic community. For service INGOs, the signal is a way to inform the domestic and international community whether or not it is a rent-seeking organization. This type of signaling to multiple uninformed actors has been referred to as a common agency situation within the larger literature (Stole 1991; Martimort 1996; Dixit et al. 1997).

Briefly, to indicate their underlying motivations, advocacy INGOs typically have relied upon signing on to larger policy position statements on an advocacy issue or joining intergovernmental policy positions and organizations (WRC 2001; CSD 2005; CAN 2007; NGO Statement on US IDP Policy 2008). Much of the time, these policy statements are used to signal that an INGO is internationally biased (WRC 2001; CSD 2005; CAN 2007). This was definitely the case with the above example of female genital cutting advocacy by INGOs; many internationally biased INGOs signed on to large Western statements concerning the need for the full eradication of FGC, indicating that there would be no efforts for the medicalization or age restriction of the practice (Boyle et al. 2001; Boyle 2002). These policy statements, as Boyle (2002) points out, indicated to the domestic populations in North Africa and the Middle East that their preferences were not paramount for the advocacy INGO.

However, as mentioned, signals by advocacy INGOs can also indicate their interest in supporting the preferences of domestic communities. As an example, in December 2008, 21 human rights and refugee INGOs signed a policy statement entitled "NGO Statement on US IDP Policy." This statement laid out a policy position that was contrary to the United States' position on internally displaced people (IDP). In addition to advocating for a change in this policy, this statement can be viewed as a signal that these groups are not internationally biased but, instead, have advocacy preferences that are more in line with the domestic communities they are trying to help.

Signals through policy statements occur in many different advocacy situations. For example, in 2007, many INGOs joined the European Union in a joint policy statement on climate and energy (CAN 2007). This policy statement was very internationally biased, offering little discussion of the desires of domestic groups, specifically domestic groups in developing countries, with respect to environmental concerns (Steinberg 2002, 2005). Therefore, by signing this statement, these advocacy INGOs were indicating that their underlying motivations were in line with the international community and not in line with the domestic communities of many developing states.

A similar signal of underlying motivations for advocacy INGOs has occurred through their involvement with large intergovernmental organizations (Otto 1996; Clark et al. 1998; Willetts 2000; Alger 2002). Many intergovernmental organizations, such as the United Nations and the World Bank, have consultative status or working relationship status that INGOs can apply for (Willetts 2002; Kelly 2005). These consultative status arrangements provide the INGO with some additional access to the workings of the intergovernmental organization but can, especially with the case of advocacy INGOs, be seen as a signal of the INGO's international bias (Otto 1996; Clark et al. 1998; Willetts 2000; Alger 2002). In fact, to gain status with the UN or the World Bank, an INGO has to state how its motivations and policy positions reflect the overall goals of the intergovernmental organization (Willetts 2002; Kelly 2005; UN 2011). As such, the vast majority of INGOs with consultative status are based in the Western world. Recent reports from the UN show that 66 percent of organizations with consultative status are based in either Europe or North America (UN 2011). Organizations with preferences for advocacy issues that are not in line with international preferences are typically not given consultative status (Willetts 2002; UN 2011). In short, consultative status, although perhaps desired for a variety of networking reasons, also serves as a signal of motivational preferences for advocacy INGOs.

THE SIGNALS SERVICE INGOS SEND

For service INGOs with principled motivations, the goal of the signal is to differentiate itself from its rent-seeking counterpart. As a first effort, the organization may make its funding sources and activities transparent; it could release its financial statements or post them on its website. It might set out to design its staff and organizational structure in such a way as to ensure oversight. These actions, however, may not be enough to completely differentiate themselves from nonprincipled INGOs. In an uncertain environment following a natural disaster, for example, donors may not see these signals as enough to verify motivations. Donors and domestic populations may seek more clear-cut signals of motivations, especially if costs are very high. Perhaps because of these dynamics, INGOs and domestic nonprofits have sought ways to create voluntary accountability mechanisms or programs to signal that their underlying motivations are not for rent-seeking activities and that they will, instead, use donated funds to help domestic populations (Gugerty 2008; Gugerty and Prakash 2010; Tschirhart 2010). Like the US Better Business Bureau that deals with for-profit firms, these voluntary accountability groups are very prevalent for service INGOs, where concerns of rent-seeking behaviors are paramount.

As Gugerty and Prakash (2010) contend, voluntary accountability mechanisms, often termed voluntary accountability "groups" or "clubs," are a way for NGOs to signal their motivations to donors and other actors concerned about the organization's underlying motivations. As a recent practitioner article concluded, "It has come full circle, with NGOs forming their own NGO government in order to establish some kind of order" (SP 2008). In effect, this is exactly what service INGOs have tried to do through these mechanisms: they have tried to form a voluntary "government" or program though which their underlying motivations can become clear to both the international and domestic communities.

Many voluntary accountability programs exist; in fact, Bowman (2010) found over 200 such programs in the United States for domestic nonprofits. For service INGOs, which are often involved in multiple states and regions in a single year, the UN ECOSOC consultative status program represents a similar type of accountability mechanism.[9] To gain consultative status, organizations must fill out a lengthy application and participate in a review process (UN 2011). INGOs are asked about their governing structures and their relationships to any governments, and they must list all monies received in the last five years, with detailed explanations of how the funds were used. These applications are then reviewed by both governmental and non-governmental representatives to ECOSOC, and if the documentation is sufficient, the INGO is granted consultative status (UN 2011). This process, which is very arduous and time-consuming, thus can serve as a signal to both the international and domestic communities of a service INGO's underlying motivations not to rent-seek. Once accredited, many INGOs proudly list their UN Consultative Status on their organization's stationery and website. Organizations with consultative status are subjected to quadrennial reporting requirements (UN 2008). In short, the ECOSOC consultative status program perhaps could be argued to be the longest and most well-known of any voluntary accountability program and one that would be observable to both the domestic and international communities (Dieng 2001).

The impact of these accountability programs on service INGOs' behavior and the responses to these programs by the international and domestic communities have not been theoretically or empirically established. More importantly, issues of heterogeneous motivations of INGOs on the conditional effectiveness of the sector on human security have been undertheorized and never empirically examined.

CONCLUSION

This chapter makes three interrelated points. First, INGOs interact with actors from both the international and domestic communities in trying to impact policy or behavior outcomes. Second, unlike the dominant TAN framework, INGOs differ in their underlying motivations; some are principled in the traditional sense and some display behavior that would be consistent with very nonprincipled or self-interested motivations. For service INGOs, nonprincipled motivations are typically observed as rent-seeking behaviors. For advocacy INGO, nonprincipled motivations are typically seen as an international bias as opposed to advocating for policies or behavior outcomes that are desired by the domestic population of the state that the INGO is targeting. Third, INGOs can act in ways that signal to the domestic and international communities concerning their underlying motivations. This chapter is not designed to be an overarching typology for all of the variations in the INGO world; instead, the focus centers on one key variation among INGOs—their motivations— and the extant literature that addresses how INGOs try to signal their motivations to others.

In the next chapter, I use these basic points to develop a theoretical framework of the behavior and conditional impact of INGOs in world politics. This framework, by relaxing the assumption that all INGOs are principled, provides excess empirical implications over the dominant TAN theory and offers rich empirical implications for when and where we can expect INGOs to impact human security.

3 SIGNALING PRINCIPLES
INGOs, Domestic and International Communities,
the State, and Human Security Effectiveness

WHEN SHOULD WE EXPECT INGOS to actually matter in human security? Across issues and states, what makes it more likely that INGOs will influence human security outcomes? What, if anything, could be done to aid INGO efforts? In Chapter 2, I laid out my critique of both the dominant theoretical literature and the existing revisionist work. Both strains of literature tend to see INGOs as a homogeneous lot. The traditional theoretical framework, the transnational advocacy network (TAN) framework, views all INGOs as motivated primarily by principles or "shared values" that differentiate the organizations from all other actors in world politics (Keck and Sikkink 1998; Risse 2010). The revisionist literature, by both practitioners and academics, takes the opposite stance and sees INGOs as nonprincipled, self-interested actors resembling for-profit firms, with INGOs operating in corrupt ways that only further their own personalistic agenda. As such, the traditional literature sees INGOs as extremely capable at providing human security, while the revisionist literature questions whether INGOs will actually have any noticeable impact on the ground.

I contend that neither existing theoretical approach truly captures the complexity of the INGO sector. Instead of an either/or situation, the INGO world consists of *both* principled and nonprincipled actors. Unfortunately, the domestic and international communities—those actors that work with INGOs—do not know what type of organization they are facing and have to rely on cues or *signals* from INGOs themselves as to their underlying motivations.

This chapter takes this basic contention—that not all INGOs share the same underlying motivations—and uses it to develop an alternative theory for when and where we should see INGOs be effective actors for human security outcomes. Understanding that (a) uncertainty about the motivational composition of the INGO sector, (b) the peculiarities of the domestic political structures and conditions where the work is taking place, (c) the signals that the organizations send, and (d) the responses of the domestic and international communities are all critical for determining when and where INGOs will actually matter for human security.

Unlike the traditional avoidance of service provision INGOs in the theoretical literature, the theoretical framework developed here specifically applies to both INGOs that focus predominantly on service provision and those that focus predominantly on advocacy. The framework, however, does not equate the same basic tensions and problems to both INGO sectors: service INGOs and advocacy INGOs differ in what a "nonprincipled" organization looks like, and the communities, both domestic and international, that work with the organizations often differ in their fundamental goal alignment with these INGOs. Because of these differences, the theory developed here is based on two very basic game-theoretic models, one that focuses only on service INGOs and one that focuses only on advocacy organizations. Although there are differences in the driving tensions of these theoretical models, the model structures are similar and discussed in tandem whenever possible.

Why game-theoretic models? Most INGO studies do not take a formal game theory approach in their theory building. In fact, across disciplines, only a very small handful of formal theoretic models concerning INGOs exist (Reinhardt 2009; Aldashev and Verdier 2010). Most theory building within the literature has taken a nonformal approach, even if the underlying logic could have been easily formalized (Cooley and Ron 2002; Bob 2005). Here, I use game theory as a way to ensure that my logic is sound and that my empirical implications flow directly from my understanding of actor motivations and interactions. In no regard, however, do I contend that game theory is the *only* way to make sure my logic is sound; it just is the way I choose. Worth noting, the use of a game-theoretic approach requires only instrumental rationality, defined as "whether people act in accordance with their motivations, regardless of what those motivations may be" (Quackenbush 2004, 94). As such, using game theory to develop my theory and hypotheses does not in any way negate the importance of norms or ideas. It does not, in any sense, require that organizations only form their preferences without any regard to the populations they are trying to help. In other words, game theory allows that organizations can form preferences based solely or primarily on helping others; an organization can have motivations that are "other interested" and still rational in the game-theoretic sense. I stress this point to situate, at the onset, the use of game theory squarely into the existing ideas of INGOs. The simple use of game theory does not make the theory developed here fundamentally different from either the traditional or the revisionist literature on INGOs. It is only my actors' preferences and my model's structure—the "stuff" that goes into the game-theoretic model—that separate my approach from the existing literature. Whether or not that "stuff" was discussed in a game-theoretic way, I want the empirical implications that come from my alternative framework to be logically consistent, and the use of game theory is just a tool through which I can better ensure that these implications are logical. In fact, many of the hypotheses that come from my game-theoretic approach are consistent with existing hypotheses and practitioner ideas that were derived in a nonformal way. This should serve as an important "reality check" on the use of formal models here.

At the end of the day, the approach developed here provides a rich array of empirical implications concerning when service and advocacy INGOs will be powerful conduits of human security—and when they will not. In general, when INGOs are working on issues that are of value to both the domestic and international communities they are interacting with—and send sufficient signals to these communities concerning their underlying preferences—we should see that INGOs actually matter for human security outcomes. All of these implications are subjected to rigorous empirical tests in the following two chapters.

RELAXING THE PRINCIPLED ASSUMPTION

As discussed in Chapter 2, many of the critiques of the transnational advocacy network approach are not based on issues with the actors and structure of the boomerang model or Keck and Sikkink's (1998) discussions about what makes a state vulnerable to external and internal pressure. Instead, at their core, many of the critiques concern the model's baseline assumption about the motivations of INGOs. While Keck and Sikkink (1998) and other work in this vein see INGOs as motivated by "principles" and "shared values," the critiques see INGOs as motivated in various ways inconsistent with this assumption.

For example, even Bob (2005), whose critique of Keck and Sikkink (1998) centers on the ways that organizations respond to calls for help from domestic communities, does not throw out the basic structure of the boomerang model, just the idea that organizations are completely principled in their responses to domestic calls for help. Cooley and Ron (2002) also focus on how material incentives, here brought on by the aid industry, color both advocacy and service work; their critique, however, does not call into question the basic structure of INGO interactions with the domestic and international actors first outlined in Keck and Sikkink (1998). Similarly, Prakash and Gugerty's (2010) edited volume, in categorizing INGO motivations as comparable to firms, also revises assumptions about the motivations of organizations and not the structure of interactions central to the canonical literature. In other words, all of these pieces question the "principled" assumption underlying Keck and Sikkink's (1998) canonical work. In all these revisionist pieces, however, the end result of questioning the canonical literature's principled assumption is to largely abandon the idea that INGOs are motivated mainly by principles. Instead of all INGOs motivated by principles, all INGOs in this revisionist literature are predominantly nonprincipled in their motivations.

Like these revisionist pieces, my theory begins by relaxing the principled assumption that all INGOs are distinct from other actors in world politics in that they are motivated by principles or "shared values" to help a domestic population with what that population wants but is not able to achieve on its own. Unlike other existing revisionist work, however, when I relax the principled assumption, I allow for two fundamentally distinct types of organizations: those motivated predominantly by principles consistent with the traditional transnational advocacy network framework and those motivated in some sort of nonprincipled way. By relaxing the principled assumption, I am acknowledging the critiques of the dominant framework from both the revisionist scholarly work and the practitioner world, as discussed at length in Chapter 2. More importantly, however, by still allowing for organizations with principled motivations like those assumed in Keck and Sikkink (1998), I am not "throwing out the baby with the bathwater" and making some INGOs' "bad behavior" equate to an assumption of nonprincipled motivations for all INGOs (Poskitt 2012).

This division of INGO motivations into two types—principled and nonprincipled—provides much theoretical leverage over both completely homogeneous alternatives. Unlike the traditional theoretical literature, I can account for how the presence of organizations with nonprincipled motivations may limit support from outside actors. I can also account for how these nonprincipled organizations may use funds in ways that are not in line with what the domestic community wants, perhaps limiting the final human security outcome. Unlike other revisionist pieces that assume homogeneous nonprincipled motivations, my theory still allows for organizations that are motivated predominately like those in the TAN framework are assumed to be and, as such, are theoretically supposed to matter for human security in ways already outlined.

In other words, relaxing, but not abandoning, the principled assumption allows me to incorporate insights from each existing strain of literature. Moreover, allowing for both principled and nonprincipled organizations makes it possible for me to acknowledge that the possibility of the presence of both of these types of organizations within a locale can color how other actors respond to all INGOs and the various actions that organizations can take to separate themselves from their counterparts.

Now, to be clear, my distinction of INGOs into principle and nonprincipled types is not the only possible way to categorize INGOs; as mentioned in Chapter 2, many typologies exist for organizations, with divisions among INGOs including where the organizations receive their funding (Gordenker and Weiss 1995), their religious ideology (Boli and Brewington 2007), and their nation of origin (Stroup 2012; Stroup and Murdie 2012). Some of these typologies do not stress differences in motivations; likewise, they do not extend the typological differences to differences in outputs or outcomes. I contend, however, that for the question of the conditional effectiveness of organizations on human security outcomes, understanding the dynamics associated with the principled/nonprincipled distinction outlined here is key: it is what creates uncertainty in the minds of the domestic and international communities, ultimately influencing human security outcomes. To the extent that other divisions among INGOs could be important, I would contend that it is because these divisions reflect (a) the principled/nonprincipled distinction or (b) the signaling dynamics I lay out in this chapter. In fact, to the extent that an existing typology outlines a group or division of INGOs that would be nonprincipled in their motivations, divisions could then be empirically examined through the same theoretical lens developed here. Whenever possible, I point out how these typological divisions could fit within the framework I develop in the discussion below.

One more thing deserves restating: I am not the first person to think about the INGO sector as composed of both principled and nonprincipled groups. Some of these dynamics have been discussed in work that predates Keck and Sikkink (1998), like Brett (1993) or Vakil (1997); it is simply that the bulk of the theoretical literature within IR sees organizations as one homogeneous unit: principled or not. What is novel here, I hope, is the way I extend these differences in preferences to the actions of INGOs themselves and the communities they interact with, all of which stands to influence when and where INGOs can provide much-needed improvements in human security.

NONPRINCIPLED ORGANIZATIONS: SERVICE AND ADVOCACY

For both service and advocacy INGOs, what does an organization with non-principled motivations look like? I contend that relaxing the principled assumption leads to conceptually different behaviors for service as opposed to advocacy INGOs. As discussed in Chapter 2, existing critiques of service INGOs center on how many organizations appear to be motivated to fill their own coffers, taking money designed to go to service provision and using the money instead to buy flashy SUVs and condos or to embezzle the funds in other ways for their private use. These nonprincipled service-provision INGOs can be largely categorized as rent-seekers in the traditional sense; they are using their position for private gain by manipulating the environment in which they are embedded.

For advocacy INGOs, however, nonprincipled organizations look much different. Consistent with the overwhelming practitioner and journalistic critiques of advocacy INGOs discussed in Chapter 2, nonprincipled advocacy organizations can be thought of as those that are motivated by what their donors want instead of what the domestic community they are supposedly trying to help actually desires. In other words, and given that INGOs predominantly have monetary donations from international instead of domestic donors, these organizations have motivations that are internationally biased instead of being motivated by "shared values" with the domestic population they are supposed to be working on behalf of. Principled advocacy organizations, in line with the existing framework, have preferences for human security advocacy outcomes essentially in line with the domestic community they are trying to help; they are domestically consistent, at least with the portion of the domestic population that called them into the state for advocacy help in the first place. Nonprincipled advocacy INGOs, however, have preferences that are more in line with the international donor community they are trying to court for largely personalistic, materialistic reasons. Some of the "donor-organized" and "quasi-non-governmental" organizations outlined in Gordenker and Weiss's (1995) typology may be nonprincipled—if, of course, their motivations are internationally biased for personalistic or materialistic reasons instead of in line with what the domestic population wants.

Although these organizations still may "share values" with the international community, they have motivations different from the organizations assumed to be at work in the TAN approach: these groups are not advocating in line with the domestic population that is supposed to start the boomerang process and instead, like other actors in world politics, are motivated predominantly by material gain. Instead of responding to domestic calls for help with assistance, these organizations are active in states and on issues because of their personal, private, and—this is key—materialistic motivations to gain donations from the international community. These private motivations are inconsistent with our conventional understandings of "principles" or "shared values" from Keck and Sikkink (1998) and other works in the canonical TAN framework.

I stress these differences in what a nonprincipled organization looks like for service as opposed to advocacy INGOs not to belabor the point but because it matters for the underlying tensions at play in these two realms of human security work. For service provision work, all actors want to avoid supporting a nonprincipled service INGO; no one—domestic or international—wants to support an organization that is primarily motivated to fill its own coffers. All would rather support the principled type of organization that is actually providing services on the ground.

For the advocacy realm, however, an underlying tension exists in the fact that not all actors that work with INGOs have to share the same order of preferences with regards to possible advocacy outcomes. As such, communities may actually have preferences for supporting very different types of advocacy INGOs. In line with Keck and Sikkink and the canonical literature, principled advocacy INGOs have preferences for advocacy outcomes that are consistent with what the domestic community wants but has not been able to achieve on its own. For example, this was the case for advocacy related to the end of physical integrity rights violations in Chile in the 1970s; the domestic community called on international actors to help them in ending domestic repression, and the INGOs that responded mainly had preferences to help the domestic community reach these same policy objectives (Keck and Sikkink 1998).

However, nonprincipled advocacy INGOs, as mentioned, have preferences mainly to get international donor community support, even if this is not consistent with the domestic community with which they are traditionally thought to be sharing values. Think, for example, about the issue of female genital cutting. Some early advocacy INGOs active on the issue wanted age restrictions or medicalization of cutting practices. This advocacy objective would have been more in line with what domestic groups and individuals in the region wanted; these preferences could be thought of as being "shared" with the community the organizations were trying to help. Other organizations, however, were advocating only for the full eradication of the practice; many took up this issue as a way to get international donor funds (Clark et al. 2006). Their work would be not consistent with what the domestic community wanted and could be categorized as nonprincipled in the sense that the work was motivated by private organizational desires—mainly motivated by a desire for materialistic gain. However, this "nonprincipled" work still reflected the desires of the international community. This is the basic difference between service and advocacy INGOs: the tension in the advocacy INGO realm is that not all actors have to share the same order of preferences. The international community may have preferences that are drastically more in line with the "nonprincipled" organization, even if this is for human security outcomes that are not at all consistent with what the domestic community the organizations are supposedly working on behalf of actually want. In the general sense, these advocated outcomes are typically more extreme than what the domestic community desires.

One way to think about how these differences in what nonprincipled organizations look like in the advocacy and service realms—and how these differences create different underlying tensions for the actors that are traditionally thought to work with INGOs—is to organize principled INGOs, nonprincipled INGOs, the domestic community, and the international community on a theoretical preference line. As shown in Figure 3.1, if we do this for the service realm, we see that both the domestic community for which the INGO is supposed to be providing human security goods and services and the international

Principled service INGO	Nonprincipled service INGO
Domestic community	
International community	

Figure 3.1a Preferences of service INGOs and the actors with which they work

Principled advocacy INGO	Nonprincipled advocacy INGO
Domestic community	International community

Figure 3.1b Preferences of advocacy INGOs and the actors with which they work

community that supports INGOs both have preferences that are in line with the principled service INGO: they all want the provision of goods and services. On the other end of the theoretical preference line, however, is the nonprincipled service INGO; its preferences are for personalistic rent-seeking and are not in line with the other actors in the human security service provision realm.

Contrast this with the theoretical preference line for advocacy INGOs, also shown in Figure 3.1. Here, the organization that is thought of as principled in the traditional sense is the one that has preferences consistent with the domestic community it is advocating on behalf of; it is sharing values with at least some of the individuals who called the organization to the locale it is advocating for. The nonprincipled organization, however, is after whatever the international community wants and has these preferences largely, although perhaps not completely, for materialistic gain. As such, its preferences would line up with the international community's preferences, even if these preferences are distinct and separate from what the domestic community desires. This idea has been discussed with reference to "resonance," "domestic legitimacy," or "input legitimacy" in previous works, and the argument presented here is that nonprincipled advocacy INGOs lack this resonance with the domestic community because their motivations are for international donations instead of advocating on behalf of the domestic community with which they were assumed to be sharing values (Scharpf 1999; Risse 2002; Sundstrom 2006).

Of course, the distance between what the international and domestic communities want on the preference line can vary by issue and locale and with creative (re)framing. When this distance varies, this information will be important to include in our theory of the conditional impact of advocacy INGOs on human security outcomes. For some issues, the distance between what international donors desire from advocacy and what the domestic community prefers may be slight. For other issues, the distance may be greater. Regardless of where all actors are situated on any particular preference line for a particular issue, nonprincipled advocacy INGOs have material motivations and personalistic interests that make them chose the preferences of their potential international donors over the domestic community they are supposed to be working on behalf of. This creates a key underlying tension in that not all actors in the advocacy realm that work with advocacy INGOs necessarily want the same advocacy outcome.

This discussion is not to imply any normative agenda about what advocacy INGOs or service INGOs *should* be motivated by; it is just to highlight differences in their motivations on the ground. Using the idea that there are both principled and nonprincipled organizations, together with the understanding of what both types look like for advocacy and service, I can incorporate these dynamics and tensions into game-theoretic models of the conditional effectiveness of INGOs on human security outcomes.

Because of the differences between the service and advocacy realms, I build two separate game-theoretic models: one for service INGOs, where the underlying tension again is that all actors would like to avoid supporting a rent-seeking nonprincipled organization, and an advocacy INGO model, where the underlying tension is that not all the actors that work with INGOs share the same order of preferences about advocacy outcomes. These models are bifurcated due to the differences in what a nonprincipled organization looks like on the ground and the ways these differences translate into distinct underlying tensions for each realm (advocacy and service) of human security work. Despite these differences, the two models are very similar in the actors specified and the structure of the interactions, as discussed below.

THE INGO-EFFECTIVENESS WORLD: ACTORS CRITICAL TO INGOS

INGOs do not act in a vacuum. While anecdotal evidence suggests that INGOs can be critical in improving human security for many local populations, they do not have many formal powers or unlimited funds. Instead, the mechanisms through which INGOs work to improve human security, as outlined in Chapter 2, depend on the cooperation of additional actors. This is consistent with both the extant TAN framework and the cross-disciplinary literature on INGOs (Keck and Sikkink 1998; Risse, Ropp, and Sikkink 1999; Cooley and Ron 2002).

As touched on above, two groups of actors work with human security INGOs: the domestic population of the state that the INGO is supposedly working for and the international community that can offer support and funds to the organization. By the domestic or substate population, I am referring to domestic NGOs and domestic citizens in the state where the organization is working. In the TAN framework, these actors are supposed to work with the INGO from the onset, calling the organization into the state and then working with the INGO to build increased pressure "from below" in the name of advocacy against a recalcitrant state (Brysk 1993). In the cross-disciplinary and practitioner literature on how service INGOs connect to service outcomes, the domestic population is also essential to the workings of the organization; the domestic population is supposed to attend the service INGO's seminars and workings, pick up and use any goods provided, and attend any medical clinics or food drives that the INGO holds. The support of the domestic population is essential for service INGO activities to have any lasting impact on political or developmental outcomes (Hulme and Edwards 1997; Petras 1997, 1999).

By the international community, I mean intergovernmental organizations, like the World Bank or the United Nations; donor foundations; and third-party states that often interact with human security organizations. The support of these actors aids in the funding and operations of service INGOs; the organizations must have funds in order to hand out goods and services. These actors can also provide security and coordination goods to aid in service INGO work (Cooley and Ron 2002). For advocacy INGOs, this set of actors is also clearly defined as necessary for the ways in which advocacy INGO work is connected to human security outcomes (Keck and Sikkink 1998; Risse, Ropp, and Sikkink 1999). INGOs call on these actors to join them in pressuring a state "from above" (Brysk 1993).

INFORMATION AND UNCERTAINTY:
THE MODELS' STRUCTURE

In the game-theoretic models built here, a key function of INGOs is to facilitate domestic and international community support in the name of human security. In other words, the INGO wants the support of these two communities, and its influence on human security is determined, at least in part, by the support it receives from these communities. Domestic and international support for an INGO is not automatic; each actor has a choice of whether or not to support the INGO it is interacting with. This assumption, although very straightforward, is largely distinct from the TAN framework, which often assumes that the domestic community calls out to and would welcome any INGO with open arms.[1] Instead, the framework developed here acknowledges that organizations may not receive the support of the domestic community it is working with.

Within both the service and the advocacy models, the model structures are very similar and reflect a slightly altered format of a traditional continuous choice costly signaling game (McCarty and Meirowitz 2007). The sequence of the game-theoretic models is outlined in Figure 3.2. As the figure shows, within both the service and advocacy models, the game starts with a random draw, which determines whether or not the INGO in the game can be categorized as principled. With a set and known probability (P), this random draw

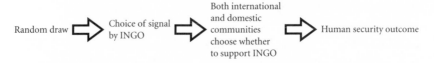

Figure 3.2 Sequences of the games

determines that the organization is principled. Likewise, with a set and known probability $(1 - P)$, the random draw determines that the organization is not principled. Only the INGO that is in the game knows at this point whether or not it is principled; in other words, it is the only actor that truly knows its core motivations. The international and domestic communities from which the INGO is trying to get support do not know the result of this random draw; they just know the underlying probability that an organization it is facing in this game could be principled.

For example, the domestic and international communities that have the opportunity to work with an INGO in post-earthquake Haiti may know there is a problem with service INGOs' rent-seeking in their state; they know the underlying base probability that any organization they are facing is likely to be a non-principled rent-seeker. The communities would not know, however, whether or not the particular organization they are interacting with at that moment is a rent-seeker. These communities may be suspicious of the organization because of the high baseline probability of facing a rent-seeking nonprincipled INGO in Haiti, but they are not informed of the actual motivations of the specific organization they are interacting with.

The next move in both the advocacy and service models, as shown in Figure 3.2, involves the costly signal that the INGO can send to the international and domestic communities in an effort to reveal (or conceal) its underlying motivational type. After observing the costly signal the INGO sends, the international and domestic communities make simultaneous moves; these actors can choose to invest or support the INGO—or not—as seen in Figure 3.2. These are the last moves in the game. Supporting the INGO is costly for the international and domestic communities. For the international community, this cost would entail funds directed at the service INGO or diplomacy costs entailed from supporting an advocacy INGO's stance against a targeted state. For the domestic community, these costs include time, effort, and energy spent working on the INGO's programs and projects. For example, domestic support of a service INGO that provides training on sustainable agriculture practices, like the Asian Farmers' Association for Sustainable Rural Development, entails real opportunity costs to the individuals sitting in on the training programs instead of partaking in their normal income-generating activities. For the domestic community in the advocacy INGO game, these costs would include a loss of time and energy from supporting the organization's advocacy mobilization efforts. After these moves, in both game-theoretic models, the INGO's effect on human security outcomes is determined, in part, as a function of the support it received from the international and domestic communities.

I outline the payoffs of both games for all actors below. Before doing so, a few points on the use of a signaling game are worth highlighting. First, like all signaling games, these games are useful in addressing principal-agent dynamics. Principal-agent game-theoretic models all involve information asymmetries (Miller 2005). One fully informed player, typically called an agent, interacts with a set number of principals, who have less information than the agent. In a signaling game, the principals typically have less information than the agent about the agent's underlying "type." Here, the principals (domestic and international communities) are ignorant of the agent's (the INGO's) underlying motivations (i.e., whether or not the INGO is principled). The agent can send a signal to the uninformed principals as a way to signify their underlying type. Like all signals, there are times when the uninformed players will be able to see this signal and know, for certain, what type of organization they are facing; this would be referred to as a "separating" signal because the signal separates one type of actor (the principled organization, for example) from the other type (nonprincipled). The information from the signal would then help the principals update their beliefs about the type of agent they are dealing with, and they could make decisions based on this updated belief. There are other times, however, when this signal may not inform the principals. It could be, for example, that both types of principles choose to send the same signal or send no signal at all; this is known as a "pooling" signal, and it would not help the principals update their beliefs about the type of organization they are facing. One type of signal that could be "pooling" that has been observed among US nonprofits is the adoption of organizational names that sound like well-established organizations or make reference to a specific outcome. For example, as Hundley and Taggart (2013) report, one rent-seeking nonprofit organization in the United States adopted the name Kids Wish Network to mimic organizations that were established (like Make-A-Wish) and, by all accounts, were acting in ways consistent with principled motivations.

To illustrate, take again our example of rent-seeking service INGOs in Haiti. Suppose all non-rent-seeking organizations have volunteers that wear gold stars on their lapels and all rent-seeking organizations have volunteers that do not wear gold stars. The gold star, then, would be a separating signal. Perhaps organizations only get the gold star if they have publicly released their accounting statements to other organizations, and only non-rent-seeking INGOs are willing to release their accounting statements. In this world, if a domestic citizen or an international donor saw a representative with a gold star, she could then update her belief about the type of organization she is dealing with: she would know she was dealing with a non-rent-seeking INGO and might be more willing to support it. If, however, she was interacting with a representative from an INGO that was not wearing a gold star, she might decide not to support this organization, knowing it is a rent-seeker.

Although gold stars on lapels may not actually be used as a signal by INGOs in Haiti, as discussed in Chapter 2, INGOs perform many actions that indicate their underlying motivations. In the service realm, signals sent to indicate that an INGO is not a rent-seeker could involve setting up costly structural controls against rent-seeking, registering with voluntary accountability programs, and joining accountability clubs. This would be consistent with Vakil's (1997) discussion of actions that organizations have taken to show their accountability and transparency. In the advocacy realm, signals that INGOs send typically involve joining intergovernmental policy positions and larger umbrella organizations or policy positions. In other words, consistent with Gordenker and Weiss (1995), these signals could include actions by "quasi-non-governmental" advocacy organizations to assert that "their own priorities rather than those of donor governments dominate" (361).

Although it might be self-evident, it is worth noting that both types of INGOs, principled and nonprincipled, can signal. In the case of rent-seeking service INGOs, for example, rent-seekers can also try to signal their transparency or register with voluntary accountability programs just like non-rent-seekers (Ben Attia 2004). In the case of internationally biased advocacy INGOs, they may be signing on to policy statements just like domestically consistent advocacy organizations.

Relatedly, these signals are assumed to be costly. An INGO has a continuous choice of the amount of the signal it wants to send. If it chooses to send more of the signal, the INGO faces more costs. This is consistent with the nonprofit literature and many of the practitioner descriptions of these signals (Akhtar

2006; Gugerty 2009; SP 2008; Gugerty and Prakash 2010; UN 2011).[2] Many signals add an additional burden on the part of the INGOs, forcing them to hire additional staff for "endless meetings, paperwork, and accounting" (Dolhinow 2005, 165). As Akhtar (2006) pointed out with reference to voluntary accountability programs, the requirements of many of these programs make "report writing . . . a mandatory skill" of INGOs, often taking time and resources away from other more mission-oriented activities (94). Additionally, the signaling choice is assumed here to be continuous because INGOs could, in theory, register with unlimited numbers of voluntary accountability programs or participate in many umbrella groups and sign endless group policy positions. In other words, the signal is costly because it involves a loss of resources and time to the organization at the onset. In the game-theoretic model, these costs are paid ex ante, or prior to the offering of support by the international and domestic communities.

To illustrate the costliness of one possible signal that can be informative both in the advocacy and service realms, let me outline the process of gaining consultative status with the United Nations Economic and Social Council (ECOSOC). ECOSOC is not the only IGO that offers a consultative status arrangement for NGOs; however, it is the "only main UN body with a formal framework for NGO participation" (UN 2011, 6). It allows organizations to enter the premises of the UN and participate as observers in the UN Human Rights Council and work with the UN Commission on Sustainable Development, among other UN bodies.

The first step in gaining consultative status involves a formal letter of intent, copies of financial statements, annual reports, and the bylaws of the organization (Willetts 2000; Wieczorek-Zeul 2005; UN 2011). The organization also has to fill out a questionnaire about how it "contributed to any areas with substantive UN concern," their structure, and the executive board of the organization (UN 2011). More importantly, the organization must supply information about all donations and expenses (UN 2011). Many complain that these reports take a large portion of time for even the most professional INGOs (Dhunpath 2003; Dolhinow 2005; Akhtar 2006).

After this information is submitted, it is then screened by the NGO Committee of ECOSOC. In 2009, 64 of the 153 applications were recommended for consultative status by the Committee (UNECOSOC 2009). Typically, the [I]NGO is also questioned by members of the Committee. If the Committee recommends the organization, the organization's status is then decided by

ECOSOC, typically within the same year (UN 2011). Once consultative status is granted, the organization must provide quadrennial reports and can be suspended for not adhering to ECOSOC's goals, for failing to submit required reports, or at the request of UN members.

One final thing worth mentioning about INGOs' signals: unlike the classic signaling game involving one principal and one agent, the game utilized here involves two principals: the domestic community and the international community. As such, the INGO, as the agent in these games, is sending one signal to multiple audiences who may have preferences that differ. If the preferences of the principals differ with respect to which type of organization they want to support, this could lead the two principals to react to the signal the organization sends differently. Existing research in American politics has shown that the presence of multiple principals can sometimes be advantageous for the agent, which can use the information asymmetry to its advantage. It can also result in agents that take very centralist positions, neither type signaling a position that is in favor of either agent when principal preferences differ greatly (Moe 1985, 1987; Miller 2005). These issues are often referred to as the "multiple principals problem" or as an issue of "common agency" and reflect the idea that the agent will have to calculate its decision of how and whether to signal with the diverging preferences of these multiple principals in mind (Miller 2005). Multiple principal models have not been widely used in international relations.

Remember again that the central tension in the advocacy INGO model is that the domestic and international communities may have preferences for advocacy outcomes that reflect differences in the underlying motivations and preferences of the domestically oriented and internationally biased advocacy INGO. Because of this, the signals that advocacy INGOs send will likely be driven, at least in part, by this multiple principals problem. This problem may be less important in the service INGO model, where both principals have the same preference for a non-rent-seeking service INGO.

UTILITIES AND OUTCOMES:
THE SERVICE AND ADVOCACY REALMS

Although both models share the same basic structure, the different underlying tensions and dynamics of the interactions in the service INGO realm as opposed to the advocacy INGO realm are reflected in different payoffs in these two games for all actors in the models. In the following discussion, I start by outlining the components of the utilities for all players in all possible outcomes of the service INGO model and then focus on the advocacy INGO model.

Service INGO Model Like most of the stories of rent-seeking INGOs in the practitioner literature, in the model, I assume that a nonprincipled service INGO fails to produce any outcome of value to the international or domestic communities. Therefore, the international and domestic communities receive no benefit for supporting this rent-seeking organization; both communities just entail the costs of their support. These costs are summarized as C_I, in the case of the international community, and C_D, in the case of the domestic community. Additionally, the nonprincipled organization does not produce any outcome of value for itself besides the rent it receives if it gets the international community to support and invest in it; this rent is summarized as K. All service INGOs, whether principled or not, have to pay for any costly signals they send; this is summarized as C_{INGO} in the model. Consistent with the formal signaling literature, this cost is endogenously determined (Kreps 1990).

When the service INGO is a non-rent-seeking INGO, consistent with the extant literature, it is critical that the domestic community supports the service INGO; without the support of the domestic community, I assume that any effect of the principled organization's activities and services are not sustainable (Edwards and Hulme 1996; Petras 1997, 1999). Also, I assume that the international community's support can be critical to getting greater service provision.

Therefore, in the service INGO game, if the principled service organization gets both the domestic and the international communities to support the project or service provision, all actors (international community, domestic community, and principled INGO) receive a payoff that reflects this high-service outcome. I call this value H and subscript it for each relevant actor. If the principled service INGO is only supported by the domestic community, however each actor receives a value for a lower-service outcome, L, which is also subscripted for each actor. And, as mentioned, if the actor is only supported by the international community, any impact of the service INGO is not sustainable, and, thus, all actors receive no benefit from the project or activity. Like the case with a nonprincipled service INGO, if the principled organization sends a signal, the cost of this signal, C_{INGO}, is subtracted from the overall payoff to the principled service INGO. Further, both the international and domestic communities incur costs for supporting the principled organization. Again, these costs are summarized as C_I for the international community and C_D for the domestic community.

Advocacy INGO Model   Many components of the payoffs for the actors in the advocacy INGO model are similar to the service INGO model. As in the service INGO model, the international and domestic communities face costs, C, for any support they give the advocacy INGO they are facing. These costs are subscripted for each actor and subtracted from any benefit they receive from the advocacy outcome. Additionally, advocacy INGOs face costs in time, effort, and energy for signaling. These costs, C_{INGO}, are again endogenously determined in the model and are subtracted from the utility the INGO receives from any advocated policy or behavior outcome.

However, other components of the advocacy INGO model are fundamentally different from the service INGO model and reflect both differences in advocacy work and the nature of the interactions in the advocacy realm, as discussed above. First, remember again that the underlying tension in the advocacy INGO model is that not all actors have to share the same order of preferences with regard to possible outcomes of the advocacy efforts. As discussed in Chapter 2, the international community and the internationally biased advocacy INGO would prefer one outcome. Conversely, the domestic community and the domestically oriented advocacy INGO would prefer a different outcome. Typically, the internationally biased actors' advocacy desires can be thought of as more extreme than the domestic community's desires.

To illustrate, these dynamics were apparent in the case of FGC advocacy, as outlined in Chapter 2. The international community and internationally biased INGOs wanted the full eradication of FGC. However, the general domestic community and domestically aligned INGOs would have preferred only age-specific restrictions or the medicalization of the practice. The full eradication of FGC was definitely the more extreme possible outcome concerning FGC, while the age-specific restrictions and medicalization outcomes were more moderate advocacy outcomes (Boulware-Miller 1985; Boyle 2002).

To extend these dynamics to the game-theoretic model, therefore, I assume that there are two possible advocacy outcomes that INGOs can be working for on all issues: E, the extreme outcome, and M, the more moderate outcome. The international community and the internationally biased INGO, as the INGO that is wanting mainly to get the private benefits that come from the international community, prefer (or are indifferent between) the extreme outcome, which provides them a payoff of E_I for the international community and E_{IB} for the internationally biased INGO, to the moderate outcome, M, which is also subscripted for each actor. The domestic community prefers (or is indifferent between) the more moderate outcome, M_D to the extreme outcome, E_D. The domestically oriented INGO only works for the moderate outcome, for which it receives a payoff M_{ID}. In short, then, in this model, it is assumed that $M_D \geq E_D$ and that $E_I \geq M_I$ and $E_{IB} \geq M_{IB}$.

Although the preference order of the international community and internationally biased INGO, on the one hand, and the domestic community and the domestically oriented INGO, on the other hand, are assumed to be different, the model makes no assumption about the importance or value the actors place on these various outcomes. In other words, although it is assumed that the international community would always prefer or be indifferent between the extreme advocacy outcome and the more moderate outcome, I do not assume that the moderate outcome has no value at all to the international community. On some issues, the distance on some imaginary preference line between the moderate and extreme outcome could be negligible, with the moderate outcome being also greatly valued by the international community. This setup provides much leverage in the model because it allows me to make predictions about the likelihood of success on various issue areas, some where the values of the extreme and moderate outcomes are great to both the domestic and international communities and some where the distance between these two outcomes is substantial, with one community placing little value on what the other community wants as an advocacy outcome.

Additionally, unlike the service INGO model, outcomes in the advocacy INGO model are assumed to be probabilistic, depending on domestic regime characteristics such as the internal vulnerability of the state to political pressure and the state's embeddedness within the international system (Keck and Sikkink 1998). This is illustrated in the advocacy INGO model by the terms B and Q. These probabilities reflect the idea that the outcomes of advocacy attempts depend not only on the international and domestic communities' support but also on regime-specific characteristics, as outlined in the extant TAN literature.

Therefore, if both the international and the domestic communities support the internationally biased advocacy INGO, there is a set probability, B, that the outcome will be extreme, E, and a set probability, $1 - B$, that the outcome will be the more moderate outcome, M. If only one community (domestic or international) supports the INGO, the probability of advocated change drops to Q, where $B > Q$. To note, this probability Q remains the same regardless of which one of the relevant actors supports the INGO. In other words, I make no assumption about whether the support of the international or domestic community matters more for advocacy outcomes; it is just assumed that a lack of support of one of these communities will result in a less likely extreme advocacy outcome than if both of the communities were supporting the organization.

As mentioned, I set up the model such that a domestically oriented INGO is never working for the more extreme advocacy outcome. Therefore, there is no probability B of an extreme outcome when both relevant actors are supporting the INGO. Instead, if both the international and the domestic community supports the domestically oriented INGO, there is an assured moderate outcome. Thus, like discussed in the TAN framework, if both relevant actors support the INGO in its attempt at moderate policy or behavior outcomes in line with what the domestic community desires, the advocacy is typically successful (Keck and Sikkink 1998). However, like above, if only one of the relevant actors supports the domestically oriented INGO, there is still a probability Q of the moderate outcome, M, and a probability $1 - Q$ of no advocacy outcome. Finally, if no actor supports the INGO, regardless of INGO type, there is no lasting impact in advocated policy or behavior; thus, all actors receive no benefit from the advocacy INGO's activity.

SOLUTIONS TO THE FORMAL MODELS

Given these dynamics, what behaviors by INGOs are likely? What are the likely reactions of the international and domestic communities? Solving the formal models provides several insights into the likely behavior of each actor in the model. Attention to these solutions is the first step in deriving logically consistent empirical implications for when, where, and on what issues INGOs will have an impact on human security outcomes. Below, I outline the solutions to the service and the advocacy INGO game, first focusing on the service INGO game and then the advocacy model. In both discussions, I simply highlight the logic of the games in the text of the chapter; formal proof of this discussion can be found in the book's online appendix.

In both games, I use perfect Bayesian equilibria as the solution concept. This allows me to focus on only outcomes, or equilibria, that involve sequentially rational moves given certain consistent beliefs about the incomplete information critical to the game. In other words, using this solution concept allows me to focus only on likely outcomes where all actors would be allowed to update their beliefs about the type of organization they are facing once an organization sends a signal.

I restrict my focus to pure strategy equilibria in both the service and the advocacy INGO games. Like other signaling games, I am interested in the existence of both separating and pooling equilibria. In a separating equilibrium, again, one type of organization would be sending a signal that is not mimicked by the other type of organization, leading the domestic and international communities to know for certain what type of organization it is facing simply by the signal that it observes. However, in a pooling equilibrium, the signal the organizations send is the same; as such, the domestic and international communities are not able to update their beliefs about the type of organization they are facing. Since signaling is costly, in a pooling equilibrium, we typically think of the agents as not sending a signal at all in a pooling equilibrium.

Service INGO Model   The service INGO game has two separating equilibria and three pooling equilibria. Both separating equilibria that hold for the model involve a signal the principled service INGO sends that is too costly for the nonprincipled service INGO to follow. As such, the domestic and international communities are able to know for certain what type of organization they are facing based solely on the INGO's signal. If the signal is sufficiently costly, these communities know for certain they are facing a principled service INGO that will use their support for the provision of goods and services within the locale. I call this separating signal C^*_{INGO}. For example, this signal could entail registering with a sufficient number of voluntary accountability programs. If the signal the domestic and international communities receives is less than C^*_{INGO}, the communities know for certain they are facing a nonprincipled service INGO that will use any support it receives only for its personal rent.

What does this information do for the other actors in the model? In the first separating equilibrium, which I term the *Ideal Behavior Equilibrium*, both the international and domestic communities only support a service INGO if—and only if—they observe the separating signal C^*_{INGO} or greater. For the domestic community to decide to support service INGOs that send this signal, the domestic community's costs for supporting the INGO must be sufficiently low in comparison to the benefit it receives from the high service outcome that will result when both it and the international community support the INGO. This can be summarized as $C_D \leq H_D$. For the international community to support any INGO that sends the separating signal C^*_{INGO} or greater, its costs of support to the INGO must be also sufficiently small—smaller than the difference between its value of the high- and the low-service outcomes ($C_I \leq H_I - L_I$).

When the international community is facing costs that are larger than its value for the difference between the high- and low-service outcomes ($C_I \geq H_I - L_I$), we get the second separating equilibrium, which I term the *Domestic Desires Equilibrium*. In this scenario, the international community does not support any service INGO it is facing, regardless of the signal sent. Here the domestic community continues to support an INGO that is sending the separating signal C^*_{INGO} or greater. This requires that the domestic community's costs are sufficiently low in comparison to their value for the low-service outcome that only comes when they, and not the international community, support the principled service INGO. In other words, $C_D \leq L_D$.

For the international and domestic communities, the decision of whether or not to support the principled service organization that is signaling C^*_{INGO} or greater rests on the costs it faces in giving its support in relation to the benefit it will receive if it supports the signaling organization. If the costs to each actor are sufficiently small, below the value of the difference between the high and low outcomes for the international community and below the value of the high outcome for the domestic community, we have the *Ideal Behavior Equilibrium* with each actor, seeing C^*_{INGO} or greater, supporting the INGO. If the costs to the international community rise past the difference between the high outcome and the low outcome, we have the *Domestic Desires Equilibrium*. However, this equilibrium holds only if the costs to the domestic actor are smaller than or equal to its value of the low-service outcome, L_D.

When will the two types of service INGOs separate, allowing the communities to know for certain that they are facing a principled organization when they observe C^*_{INGO} or greater? For the principled INGO to want to signal knowing that this signal will garner the support of both communities in the *Ideal Behavior Equilibrium*, the costs of C^*_{INGO} must be less than or equal to the benefit it receives from the high outcome, H_{INGO}. In other words, $C^*_{INGO} \leq H_{INGO}$. In order to ensure that the signal will not be mimicked by the nonprincipled type, however, this cost is as least as great as the rent, K, that the nonprincipled INGO would receive if it was to get the international community's support. Because the principled service INGO does not want to send any more of the costly signal than she has to, the organization will then send a signal where $C^*_{INGO} = K$. Given this cost, the nonprincipled INGO will be indifferent between sending the signal to get its private rent and sending a signal less than C_{INGO}; in equilibrium, therefore, I can assume that it sends a signal less than C^*_{INGO}.

A very similar dynamic occurs in determining the cost of the signal in the *Domestic Desires Equilibrium.* Here, the principled organization will only signal C^*_{INGO} if the costs of signaling are less than the benefit it will receive from the lower-service outcome that comes just when the domestic community supports a principled service INGO, L_{INGO}. As such, $C^*_{INGO} \leq L_{INGO}$. In addition to this upper bound on C^*_{INGO}, like before, C^*_{INGO} must also be greater than or equal to the value of the rent, K, for the rent-seeking service INGO.

In both of these separating equilibriums, then, the principled INGO must be willing to incur as much cost in the signal as the nonprincipled INGO would get as benefits for its private rent. However, if the costs of the signal are more than the benefit the principled INGO will get by signaling, the signaling equilibrium breaks down. Though this might seem straightforward, it represents a powerful constraint for voluntary accountability programs and other signaling devices the service INGO uses: in order for these programs to work, they must be costly, as costly as the rent received by the nonprincipled type. However, if the value of the rent received to the nonprincipled service INGO is greater than the value of the likely outcome to the principled service INGO, we will never see separation.

If a separating signal is not sent, one of three different pooling equilibria are possible. In each of these pooling equilibria, the international and domestic actors must rely on the base probabilities that they are facing a non-rent-seeking, principled service INGO, P, or a nonprincipled, rent-seeking service INGO, $1 - P$, when determining whether to support the organization they are interacting with. During the game, since the INGOs do not send separating signals, the domestic and international communities are not able to update their beliefs about the underlying probability that they are facing a principled INGO. Because signaling is costly here and does not separate out types, in each of these equilibria, both types of INGOs send no signal. In the first equilibria, which I term the *Take Your Chances Equilibrium,* both the domestic and international communities decide to support all INGOs, regardless of the signal sent. For this decision to be rational for each of these communities, the baseline probability of facing a principled organization has to be sufficiently high. If this random draw or baseline probability of facing a principled service INGO is higher than or equal to (a) the ratio of the cost of support to the difference in value of the high outcome to low outcome for the international community

$(P \geq (C_I / (H_I - L_I)))$ and (b) the ratio of the cost of support to the high-outcome value for the domestic community $(P \geq (C_D / H_D))$, the domestic and international community will take a chance and support any service INGOs, regardless of any signal sent.

At the other extreme, if the probability of facing a principled service INGO is sufficiently low—lower than the ratio of the costs for the domestic community to the benefit of the lower-service outcome $(P \leq (C_D / L_D))$—neither the international nor the domestic community will want to support any INGO, regardless of the signal sent. Remember again that I assume that the principled service INGO will not produce any sustainable service outcome if not supported by the domestic community; as such, if the domestic community is facing this sufficiently low probability of interacting with a principled organization, the international community will also not support the organization. Both communities will "throw out the baby with the bathwater" and not support any INGO for fear of supporting a rent-seeker. Thus, this second pooling equilibrium, the *Throw Out the Baby Equilibrium*, entails no signal by either type of service INGO and no support from either community, regardless of the signal sent.

If the probability of dealing with a principled service INGO is in a midrange, however—too small for the international community to want to support it (determined by the ratio of the cost of support to the difference in value of the high outcome to low outcome for the international community again) and yet too large for the domestic community to want to *Throw Out the Baby* (determined by the ratio of the cost of support to the low-outcome value for the domestic community)—then the domestic community will still support all INGOs, regardless of the signal sent, but the international community will not support any organization. Because this probability implies that the cost of support for the domestic community must be smaller than the cost of support constraint in the *Take Your Chances Equilibrium* (smaller than L_D instead of H_D), I have called this equilibrium *Small Potatoes*. This equilibrium would only hold, therefore, if the costs of support for the domestic community are sufficiently low; the costs must be minimal for the domestic community, just colloquial "small potatoes."

Advocacy INGO Model   Like the service INGO model, the solution to the advocacy INGO model provides many insights into the behavior of advocacy INGOs and the actors that can support them. By focusing on these dynamics, logically consistent empirical implications concerning the conditional effects of advocacy INGOs can be derived. I first walk through the solutions to the game-theoretic advocacy INGO model and then focus on how the solutions to both the service and advocacy models provide many testable empirical implications.

The advocacy INGO model has both separating and pooling equilibria. Interestingly, some of the separating equilibria involve signals sent by the internationally biased INGO, and some involve signals sent by the domestically consistent advocacy INGO. This is different from the service INGO model, since that model only had equilibria behavior where the organization that is motivated in ways consistent with our canonical idea of "principled" was signaling. The different types of separating equilibria in the advocacy INGO model, however, are dependent on changes in many parameters, especially the values of the moderate and extreme outcomes for all various actors. In this way, the model results reflect the multiple principal dynamics discussed in the larger principal-agent literature (Miller 2005).

Somewhat surprisingly, the signaling equilibria that hold for the advocacy INGO model all involve a signal that only garners the support of either the domestic or international community; the signal makes no impact on the decision of support for the alternative audience, which is either never going to support an advocacy INGO, regardless of the signal sent, or is always going to support an advocacy INGO, regardless of the signal sent. This, in effect, could represent a *signaling dilemma* on behalf of advocacy INGOs, in which the signals that are sent are not effective at influencing the behavior of both potential audiences but can be effective at gaining the support of an audience that would not support it without the signal. Proof of all these equilibria can be found in the book's online appendix.

First, there are two separating equilibria where it is the internationally biased advocacy INGO that sends a costly signal that is not copied by the domestically consistent advocacy INGO. Much differently than suggested by Keck and Sikkink (1998), these separating equilibria never involve both the international and the domestic communities' support. In other words, by relaxing the principled assumption and focusing on how uncertainty over the preference order of advocacy INGOs impacts the interactions of advocacy INGOs with international and domestic communities, the model shows that internationally biased INGOs are only signaling as a way to gain the support of one potential community when it knows that the other community is not supporting any INGOs on that particular issue.

As could be expected, in the first separating equilibrium, which I term the *Missionary Force Equilibrium*, the internationally biased advocacy INGO is signaling its type to gain the international community's support, which is only supporting INGOs that send a sufficient signal. The domestically consistent INGO is not signaling at all. Likewise, in this equilibrium the domestic community is not supporting any organization, regardless of the signal sent.

The second separating equilibrium involving a signal the internationally biased INGO sends is interesting in that the signal garners the support only of the domestic community. The domestic community is supporting only INGOs that send a sufficient signal, which in equilibrium is not copied by the domestically consistent INGO. The international community in this scenario is not supporting any advocacy INGO, regardless of the signal sent. This is a somewhat surprising scenario in that it involves a signal the internationally biased organization sends that influences the domestic community's behavior, which does not share the same order of preferences. I term this equilibrium the *Foreign Helper Equilibrium* in that the domestic community is supporting only the internationally aligned INGO and using this internationally biased organization to help reach its own goals.

What explains the decision calculus behind these two separating equilibria? Though this may seem a little counterintuitive, the domestic community's behavior in these two situations can be understood to be largely a function of Q—that is, the underlying likelihood of getting what the advocacy INGO is requesting from the state with the support of either the domestic or the international community. If the domestic community is located in a state where an advocacy INGO is unlikely to get its preferred outcome if it is supported by only one actor, again, as captured in the model by Q, the domestic community will actually prefer to work with the more extreme internationally biased INGO because it knows that if Q is low enough, it is more likely to get its preferred moderate outcome, M_D. This occurs because the internationally biased INGO, though working for the more extreme outcome, can still get the moderate outcome with $1 - Q$ probability in the *Foreign Helper Equilibrium*. In effect, the domestic community, in a very repressive environment where the targeted actor is invulnerable to advocacy pressure, may actually want to work with the more extreme, internationally biased actor simply because it doubts the actor will be successful in getting the extreme advocacy change in the first place and will instead be able to get the domestically preferred moderate advocacy outcome with its support. In this scenario, the domestic community does not want to support its own domestically aligned INGO because it fears this same lack of vulnerability will prevent the INGO from getting its preferred moderate outcome if it doesn't ask for the extreme advocacy outcome in the first place.

This logic, however, makes it necessary for the international community not to support any INGO on this issue, regardless of the signal sent. It therefore must have high costs in relation to its value placed on the advocacy outcomes, both moderate and extreme. Therefore, as captured in this *Foreign Helper Equilibrium*, when costs for supporting advocacy INGOs are too high for the international community, the domestic community decides it can then use the internationally biased INGO for its purposes—namely moderate change under a very repressive or invulnerable regime.

For this equilibrium to hold, the INGOs themselves are also being influenced by the value of Q and their values of both the moderate and the extreme advocacy outcomes. For example, the internationally biased INGO is willing to endure a costlier signal as Q, the probability of its preferred outcome, increases. Likewise, it will endure a costlier signal both if its value for this extreme outcome increases and its value for the more moderate advocacy outcome increases. In short, if the value it places on any advocacy outcome—extreme or moderate—increases, the expense of it signing on to a joint policy statement or joining a larger group of INGOs as a signal of its underlying motivations can increase, since it knows that sending this signal will garner the support of the domestic community, with which it can at least get a moderate advocacy outcome. This separating signal, however, also requires that the domestically aligned INGO either places little value on the moderate outcome or, perhaps more likely, is in a repressive state where it doubts its ability to get this moderate outcome due to low Q probability and thus is not willing to exert much time or energy on the signal. The internationally biased INGO thus sends a signal exactly equal to the domestically aligned INGO's value of the moderate advocacy outcome times the likelihood it would receive this outcome given only the domestic community's support ($C^*_{INGO} = Q(M_{ID})$).

This behavior described in the *Foreign Helper Equilibrium* appears to have occurred early during the Cold War, when some human rights and other advocacy INGOs from Western Europe and the United States spoke out against Communist dictators (Korey 1998; Romankov 2000; Thomas 2001). These INGOs were often not supported by the international community, which feared instigating Cold War aggressions and violating norms of nonintervention but were supported by the domestic community, which did not have a very active domestically aligned civil society (Romankov 2000; Thomas 2001; Hopgood 2006). During and especially after the Helsinki Final Accords of 1975, the costs of supporting advocacy INGOs diminished for the international community (Korey 1998; Thomas 2001).

Although the *Foreign Helper Equilibrium*'s behavior is somewhat surprising and counterintuitive, the *Missionary Force Equilibrium*'s behavior is more in line with academic and practitioner stories of how internationally biased organizations signal for international-community support, isolating the domestic community that really does not value any advocacy outcomes on the particular issue (Clark et al. 2006; Sundstrom 2006; Wenzel 2006). Here, the international community wants to support only INGOs that share their order preferences. The domestic community, which really doesn't place much value on any advocated outcome on the particular issue, can be thought of as ignoring or not supporting advocacy INGOs altogether on the issue, regardless of the signal sent.

As a "reality check" to the formal equilibrium, *Missionary Force* behavior could be argued to have been what occurred in the case of female genital cutting (FGC) (Boyle 2002) or Western efforts at building women's rights and domestic groups at the fall of the Soviet Union (Sundstrom 2006). For FGC, the domestic population did not place much value on the extreme outcome—total FGC eradication—but also, perhaps, it didn't place much value on the moderate outcome—medicalization. This issue was divisive for the domestic community; thus, costs for supporting the advocacy movement could be argued to have been relatively high—higher than any expected benefit from a possible moderate outcome (Boyle 2002). For the international community, however, costs were low compared to the value placed on total FGC eradication, especially considering that this was an issue in vulnerable states, as captured in the model by Q. Therefore, this behavior is likely on issues where the domestic community does not strongly value even the moderate advocacy outcome, but the international community values extreme advocated outcomes and is dealing with a vulnerable state.

Environmental protection advocacy in developing countries during the 1980s and 1990s could also fall into this category (Soto 1991–1992; Jakobsen 1999, 2000). Though Western-based advocacy INGOs were very active on environmental policy making in developed countries and widely supported by the international community, domestic citizens in less-developed countries typically did not support their advocacy efforts (Soto 1991–1992; Brenton 1994;

Jakobsen 1999, 2000). In fact, many have argued that the domestic communities saw little value from the outcomes that environmental INGOs were advocating for (Soto 1991–1992; Brenton 1994; Jakobsen 1999, 2000). As Soto (1991–1992) commented:

> Air pollution, carbon dioxide emissions, and the loss of biological diversity have little meaning to people who see their children die of malnutrition and who lack even the most basic health care. (680)

As Soto's comment points out, INGO advocacy on environmental protection in less-developed countries during this time period may be thought of as missionary force behavior, with little support by the domestic citizenry. Worth noting, however, more recent advocacy INGO efforts on environmental protection that take a sustainable development approach alongside environmental protection have been supported by local populations within developing states (Brenton 1994; Jakobsen 1999).

This equilibrium also depends on the domestically aligned INGO not wanting to signal as much as the internationally biased INGO. This occurs when either Q or the value the internationally biased INGO places on the moderate advocacy outcome is low compared to the price of the signal. This implies that the domestically consistent INGO really doesn't gain much utility from the issue at all, even from its preferred moderate outcome. Like before, then, the internationally biased INGO sends a signal equal to the likelihood of the domestically consistent INGO getting its preferred moderate advocacy outcome times the value it places on this outcome ($C^*_{INGO} = Q(M_{DC})$).

In addition to these separating equilibria where it is the internationally biased advocacy INGO that is signaling, there are three separating equilibria where it is the domestically consistent advocacy INGOs that is sending a sufficient signal for domestic and/or international community support and the internationally biased INGO that is not signaling. Unlike the above equilibria, two of these equilibria involve support by both the domestic and the international communities.

In all of these three separating equilibria, the domestic community supports the advocacy INGO that shares its same preference order: the domestically consistent INGO. Interestingly, however, in the first of these equilibria, which I term the *Domestic Leader Equilibrium*, the domestic community supports all advocacy INGOs, regardless of the signal sent. This would occur if costs for the domestic community are sufficiently low for it to want to support both types of organizations and, very surprisingly, would also depend on the international community only supporting domestically consistent organizations. For this to occur, the international community must greatly value the ensured moderate outcome it will get when it joins the domestic community and supports the domestically consistent advocacy INGO. In other words, for this move to be sequentially rational for the international community, the international community must get a lot of utility not from the possibility of the extreme outcome that the internationally biased organization is working for but from the moderate outcome it is ensured when it joins the domestic community in supporting the domestically oriented INGO. Therefore, this behavior could be observed in situations where the international community is searching for domestically oriented INGOs to work in states that are not very vulnerable to outside intervention or requests for extreme advocated change.

What about reality: does this dynamic appear even anecdotally? A good example is the attempt to change environmental regulations in the United States in the early 1990s. The US government was not very vulnerable to outside pressures, but there was much to be gained from small advocated changes in policies and behavior (McCormick 1999; Schofer and Hironaka 2005). For example, even though the United States eventually did not ratify the Kyoto Protocol, Betsill (2008) notes that environmental INGOs played a substantial role in changing the United States' position to one not solely reflecting "domestic pressure from the fossil-fuel industry" (60). Specifically, Betsill (2008) points out the role environmental INGOs had in changing the position of then vice president Gore, later awarded the Nobel Peace Prize for his work on environmental issues. Since then, there has been a "growing impetus for a domestic US climate policy that can provide meaningful reductions in emissions of CO_2 and other greenhouse gases" (Stavins 2008). Additionally, many individual states within the US have either reduced carbon emissions through voluntary cutbacks or are projected to reduce carbon emissions voluntarily (DePalma 2005; Auffhammer and Steinhauser 2007).

In the next two separating equilibria involving a signal the domestically consistent advocacy INGO sends that the internationally biased INGO does not mimic, it is the domestically consistent organization that signals to the domestic audience; its signal does not influence the behavior of the international community at all. Instead, the international community is either supporting all INGOs, regardless of the signal, in the case of the equilibrium I term the *International Fad Equilibrium,* or not supporting any INGO, regardless of the signal sent, as in the *Domestic Signaling Equilibrium*. For the *International Fad* to occur, the international community's cost of supporting any INGO has to be very small: below $(1 - Q)M_r$. This could occur, for example, if the costs of support to the international community involve only office space at intergovernmental organizations or making references to the INGO's work when dealing with the state in question. For this equilibrium to hold, the domestic community has to greatly value the moderate outcome and be in a situation where its support could prove valuable to the domestically consistent INGO, as determined by a low Q probability of an INGO being effective if only gaining the support of the international community.

Conversely, in the last separating equilibrium in the advocacy INGO model, the *Domestic Signaling Equilibrium*, the domestic community, being the only actor to support an INGO, would require a moderately high Q probability and must not put much value on the extreme outcome that an internationally biased INGO could bring. Additionally, in this situation, the cost of support for the international community must be very high in relation to the benefits it could receive if any advocacy attempt was successful.

As mentioned, all of these equilibria in which the domestically consistent INGO is signaling depend on the internationally biased INGO not wanting to replicate the costly signal. In both the *International Fad* and the *Domestic Leader Equilibria*, this occurs if the probability of getting an extreme outcome with both actors is not that great compared to the probability of getting an extreme outcome with one actor, as determined by the values of B and Q. In the *Domestic Signaling Equilibrium*, the internationally biased INGO must not value either outcome very much, similar to the behavior of the international community discussed above. Perhaps this would be an advocacy issue that does not fit with the international community's agenda, as discussed by Bob (2005) and Carpenter (2007) but is something that the domestic community strongly supports.

In addition to these various separating equilibria, there are four different types of pooling equilibria to the advocacy INGO model: an *All Support Equilibrium*, where both the domestic and international communities support all INGOs; a *No Support Equilibrium*, where neither community supports any INGOs; an *International Support Only Equilibrium*; and a *Domestic Only Support Equilibrium*. In each, like the pooling equilibria of the service INGO model, advocacy INGOs do not signal, and the international and domestic communities rely on the baseline probabilities that they are facing a domestically consistent advocacy INGO, P, or an internationally biased INGO, $1 - P$, when deciding whether to support the organization it is interacting with. Since signals are costly and do not influence the behavior of the communities, both types of organizations rationally decide not to send any costly signal, given the behavior of the other actors in the model.

Perhaps the best way to understand the logic underlying these pooling equilibrium is with reference to P and each community's value on its most preferred and alternative advocacy outcome. Very basically, the international and domestic communities react differently to changes in the value of P. This is somewhat self-evident: since the domestic community prefers to deal with a domestically oriented INGO, it would prefer a world where P is very large and is more likely to support all organizations as this probability increases. However, the international community would prefer a world where P is small and is more likely to support organizations as this probability decreases.

In a world without signals, the behavior of the domestic community is also contingent on its value for the extreme advocacy outcome. If the international community is going to support all advocacy INGOs, as in the *All Support Equilibrium*, or if the international community is not going to support any INGOs, as in the *Domestic Only Support Equilibrium*, the domestic community is more likely to support all INGOs as it gains more utility from the extreme advocacy outcome. This makes intuitive sense: if extreme outcome is still valuable to the domestic community, although less valuable than their preferred moderate outcome, it will support all INGOs, even if P is relatively low. Similarly, without signals, the international community's decision to support an advocacy INGO is largely determined by the probability it is interacting with an INGO that shares its preference order and the distance between its preferred extreme outcome and the moderate advocacy outcome it could get by supporting the domestically consistent advocacy INGO.

In short, the *All Support Equilibrium* requires a likely mix of domestic and internationally oriented types of advocacy INGOs—P cannot be too large or too small. This is a strikingly different situation than what occurred in the *Take Your Chances Equilibrium* in the service INGO model, which also involved support by both the domestic and international communities to all service INGOs, regardless of the signal sent. This reflects differences in the underlying dynamics of the two games; in the advocacy INGO model, the differences in advocacy preferences for the domestic and international communities lead the actors to react differently to a rising proportion of principled, domestically consistent INGOs.

EMPIRICAL IMPLICATIONS OF THE THEORETICAL MODELS

Given the various separating and pooling equilibria for the service and advocacy INGO models, when, where, and on what issues can we expect INGOs to have an impact in human security? This question, of course, is the reason why I went to the pains of setting up and solving the game-theoretic models in the first place. And, in many regards, solutions to the game provide rich empirical implications. Below, I first outline some of the pertinent implications that come from the solutions to the service INGO model and then address the implication that flow from the advocacy INGO model. All implications rely on comparative statics over the various parameters of the models; in other words, I focus on how increasing or decreasing a value of a parameter makes certain behaviors more or less likely in the model (Carrubba, Yuen, and Zorn 2007). The appendix contains tables with comparative statics for all parameters in the models. Here, I focus only on a few of the most important ones for the question of when and where INGOs will matter for human security.

Service INGO Model   First off, remember that in the service INGO model, even in a world without signals, the domestic and international communities are more likely to support all service INGOs they face in the *Take Your Chances Equilibrium* as the probability of facing a non-rent-seeking principled organization increases. This makes intuitive sense: as the world of INGOs becomes one that is more "principled," it is easier for both the domestic and international communities to take a chance and support all INGOs, leading this group of organizations to have a more likely high level of service delivery related to human security. Conversely, in an environment where these communities feel less certain that they are going to be interacting with INGOs that have a preference for actual service delivery as opposed to rent-seeking, it becomes more difficult for these actors to support any INGOs. In other words, in an environment where "bad apples" in the service INGO community are likely to flourish, the international and domestic communities do exactly what Lee (2007) predicted: they throw out the whole barrel. In these situations, then, we should see little or no impact of the whole service INGO sector on human security goods and services; the baseline likelihood of facing a rent-seeker has limited the level of support the whole sector will receive from both the domestic and international communities, leading to little overall impact on human security.

So from the *Take Your Chances Equilibrium*, we can see that the underlying proportion of rent-seeking service INGOs impacts the likelihood of support from actors critical to INGO work, ultimately influencing the impact of the sector on service-delivery human security outcomes. What does this logic imply? Quite basically, where the proportion of rent-seekers is likely high, we should see little impact of service INGOs. Where this proportion is low, we should see more of an effect of service INGOs. In other words, based on the domestic conditions of the state, we should expect some variation in the proportion of rent-seekers, which will ultimately influence when and where we see service INGOs influence human security. What domestic conditions may make it less likely that this proportion of rent-seekers will be high? At the most basic level, existing practitioner and journalistic accounts of the INGO community imply that rent-seeking INGOs tend to flourish in states where they are less likely to get caught (Berhan 2002; Roy 2004; Lee 2007). Additionally, similar reports often highlight how some corrupt regimes will actually use rent-seeking service INGOs to gain international donations or take bribes from rent-seekers (Steinberg 2001; Ben Attia 2004). In other words, if the underlying corruption level within a country is high, it is likely that the level of corruption in the INGO sector is also high. Given this observation, together with the logic observed in the *Take Your Chances Equilibrium*, the following is implied.

Service INGO Hypothesis 1: Service INGOs' impact on service delivery human security outcomes will likely be conditional to the overall level of corruption in the state. When corruption is controlled, it is more likely that service INGOs will matter for service delivery related to human security.

In addition to the role of domestic control of corruption on conditioning the influence of service INGOs, we can expect certain government structures to either serve this purpose of lessening corruption (Lambsdorff 1999; Nur-Tegin and Czap 2012) or provide alternative ways in which rent-seeker INGOs could be controlled. For example, a democratic state may be less likely to have a large proportion of rent-seeking INGOs simply because citizens can reject rent-seeking behaviors and create their own organizations. I return to these dynamics in some of the robustness checks in Chapter 4.

The role of state corruption as a conditioning variable has not been theoretically linked to service INGOs' behavior or effectiveness. In fact, many assume that INGOs are a likely alternative to state service delivery and aid funding in corrupt countries (Edwards and Hulme 1996; Dietrich 2013). However, by relaxing the underlying assumption that all INGOs share the same underlying motivations and explicitly modeling how INGOs of various motivational types interact with the domestic and international communities, we see that this strategy may not actually improve service delivery. In corrupt countries, rent-seeking INGOs can flourish. When this occurs, if signals are not sent indicating that the rent-seeking organization should be distinguished from the principled organization, it is less likely that the communities necessary for the principled INGO's work will be willing to support the INGO sector, leading to little actual effect on the ground. Although this hypothesis is pretty straightforward, if supported empirically, it represents a powerful constraint on INGOs' ability to matter in insecure countries without adequate corruption controls.

What happens, however, if we move from this world of no signals to one of INGOs signaling their underlying preferences? In other words, what happens when we take the INGOs' signals of service into account? When and where will we see a human security effect by service INGOs? Remember again that the service INGO model had two separating equilibria that held: when the principled service INGO signaled to a level that the nonprincipled service INGO did not mimic, resulting in the principled organization being supported by either just the domestic community, as in the *Domestic Desires Equilibrium*, or both the domestic and the international communities, as in the *Ideal Behavior Equilibrium*. If we look at the constraint on the costliness of support for the domestic community in the *Ideal Behavior Equilibrium* compared to the constraint in support on the similar equilibrium where there were no signals—the *Take Your Chances Equilibrium*—it is easy to see that as long as the likelihood of only facing principled INGOs is less than 100 percent, the domestic community will accept higher costs of support if it is only supporting principled organizations instead of both principled and nonprincipled organizations. As long as the baseline probability of facing a principled type is less than 100 percent, an assured high-service outcome for the domestic community that comes from the *Ideal Behavior Equilibrium* is always greater than P times the value for the high outcome that occurs in the *Take Your Chances Equilibrium*. A similar dynamic occurs for the international community when we compare its cost restrictions in the *Ideal Behavior Equilibrium* and the *Take Your Chances* scenario. Because both communities know they are supporting only INGOs that will provide them with human security services instead of filling their own coffers, these communities are willing to invest more in supporting the service organizations.

This logic implies that service INGOs have a greater impact on human security outcomes when there are more service INGOs in an area that have signaled their principled motivations through voluntary accountability programs or other common signaling channels for service INGOs. In these scenarios, we should see a better human security service outcome because the international and domestic communities will very likely invest more in supporting the INGOs.

To get a testable hypothesis about this phenomenon, however, we need to extend the logic of the separating equilibrium a little further. When can we expect to see service INGOs willing to send these separating signals? Remember again that the separating equilibria for the service INGO model only held when the principled service INGO felt that the cost of the signal was greater than the benefit it could receive from providing goods and services in that locale. In other words, principled service INGOs are more likely to send a separating signal as their value of the high- and low-service delivery outcomes increases. This statement is based on the comparative statics of the parameters relating to the high and low outcomes for the principled service INGO in the two separating equilibria: *Ideal Behavior* and *Domestic Desires*. Although the exact value of the costly signal is set to make the nonprincipled service INGO not care whether it sends a signal or not, as mentioned above, as the values of the high and low outcomes increase, the more likely the principled organization is to send this signal. This logic implies that a principled service INGO is more likely to sign up for voluntary accountability programs or send other related signals in states they value or where they expect a positive gain for the organization and from the outcome. This would imply a potential selection dynamic on behalf of principled service INGOs: they should be more willing to send signals of their underlying motivations in countries where high outcomes are ensured. This potential selection dynamic has not been theoretically argued within the burgeoning cross-disciplinary literature on the common signals INGOs send through their joining of voluntary accountability programs (Reinhardt 2009; Gugerty and Prakash 2010).

So when service INGOs signal, the domestic and international communities are more likely to offer their support; thus, the impact of service INGOs will be greater. However, extending the logic underlying the separating equilibria a little further, issues of self-selection arise when service INGOs signal; these INGOs are more likely to pay the costly signal when they expect a higher outcome. This makes empirical attention to self-selection necessary when examining the impact of signals and signaling INGOs on human security outcomes. This has not been theoretically examined in the cross-disciplinary literature. The logic can be restated as the following empirical implication.

Service INGO Hypothesis 2: Service INGOs' impact on service delivery human security outcomes will likely be greater when more service INGOs have signaled their underlying motivations. When examining the influence of service INGOs that have signaled, however, special attention will have to be paid to self-selection.

In Chapter 4, I test this hypothesis using the signal of consultative status with UN ECOSOC. This signal, as discussed above, closely reflects the signaling behavior that motivated the model and could be classified loosely as a voluntary accountability program, as discussed in the larger nonprofit literature, mainly from American politics.

In general, what other implications can be derived from the service INGO model? In looking at the constraints on gaining support for service INGOs, in both a signaling and a nonsignaling environment, the international community is more likely to support service INGOs as the value it receives from the high-service outcome increases and as its costs of support decrease. This is very intuitive: when the international community highly values the human security outcome that the service INGO is providing, it is more likely to support the INGO. Likewise, if support is too costly, the international community will not extend any assistance to INGOs, even if it knows it is facing a principled organization.

By looking at the international community's behavior in the equilibria a little more, we also see that that it is less likely to support service INGOs as its value of the second best outcome, the L outcome, that can be received without its support increases. Although this may appear counterintuitive, the logic underlying this is also straightforward. As its value of the lower-service outcome the principled service INGO can achieve with just domestic support increases, it is more likely not to offer support to the INGO and simply reap the benefits of the lower–human security outcome. In other words, the international community will not support projects where its support does not greatly improve project outcome; if the potential outcome without its support is sufficiently large, the international community is more likely not to support service INGOs at all. Taken with the above logic on the international community, this implies that the international community should have a great impact on INGOs' observable policy and behavior outcomes. The amount of funds the international community invests in service INGOs should create greater policy and behavior outcomes. This implication, though straightforward, has not been readily articulated within the INGO literature and never been empirically tested.

Service INGO Hypothesis 3: Service INGOs' impact on service delivery human security outcomes will likely be greater when there is more support from the international community.

Because the international community will tolerate higher costs for greater benefits from the service INGO, the service INGOs' impact should be conditional to the support this community provides to the service INGO. This argument, if empirically supported, could have important policy implications. As mentioned in the introduction, much of the support service INGOs receive from the international community is often questioned; not much is currently known about the impact this support has on service INGOs' human security outcomes (Masud and Yontcheva 2005). Please note, however that this hypothesis, as it stands, does not differentiate among potential donors. Based on the decisions taken in the game-theoretic model, mostly for parsimony, the model only accounts for one international community and its collective decision whether or not to fund an INGO. Theoretical extensions to this work could definitely include multiple possible international donors with different preferences. Empirically, extensions of this work could also examine whether certain types of aid donors condition the influence of INGO outcomes more than others. Looking at variation in the conditional influence of specific donors may be a way to combine the logic of Hypothesis 3 with Hypothesis 1: certain donors (countries, foundations, etc.) may place more value on the high outcome and be willing to face higher costs, even if it is just taking a chance.

Does this hypothesis hold up to a "reality check"? Anecdotally, however, many practitioners would contend that rent-seeking INGOs are more prevalent where there is a history of more funds directed at service INGOs; this is part of the critique concerning INGOs in Haiti (Valbrun 2012). This idea is shared by Cooley and Ron (2002). By all accounts, however, such support is necessary for organizations to survive: if an organization receives little support and attention internationally, the human security plight is often "forgotten," making it more difficult for INGOs to provide goods and services (Oxfam 2011). The logic underlying this hypothesis, then, together with the logic underlying Hypothesis 1, implies that funds directed at INGOs are something of a double-edged sword for human security service outcomes. Although donor funds can drastically increase results, they also can make it less likely for communities to broadly fund service INGOs. In these situations, we should see voluntary accountability programs being utilized.

What can the logic underlying the domestic community's behavior in the equilibria imply empirically? Like with the international community, the domestic community is more likely to support service INGOs as the costliness of their support diminishes. This appears consistent with any sort of nonformal "reality check": individuals are more likely to support things when their opportunity costs are lower. When the domestic community faces fewer costs for associating with and supporting service INGOs, the domestic community is more likely to support INGOs. This intuitive statement implies that service INGOs might not be able to impact human security outcomes in areas where the domestic community's costs of travel to work with service INGOs are high, such as in rural communities. If INGOs typically reside in urbanized areas where they can travel in and out of a state, urbanized states may have lower costs of interaction for the domestic community simply because of lower travel costs for the domestic population to work with service INGOs. This logic could be restated as the following formal hypothesis.

Service INGO Hypothesis 4: Service INGOs' impact on service delivery human security outcomes will likely be conditional on urbanization in the state where the service INGO is working.

This empirical implication is interesting because it runs counter to the conventional wisdom on when and where development INGOs are necessary. Most often, service INGOs are thought to be necessary in rural, underdeveloped areas. However, when we consider that the costs for the domestic community to work with the service INGO are probably greater in these areas, it is implied that service INGOs may not get the support necessary for a human security outcome in rural countries.

Further, like the international community, in looking at the logic underlying when the domestic community is likely to support service INGOs in the equilibria, it is easy to see that the domestic community's support of service INGOs is more likely as its value of the high service outcome that comes from both international and domestic community support of INGOs increases. Unlike the international community, however, which can still receive a benefit of the low-service outcomes when it does not support the INGO while the other community is supporting it, we must remember that the domestic community must support the INGO for there to be a sustainable outcome. As such, as the value for the low-service outcome that comes just from domestic community support increases, the domestic community is more likely to want to support the service INGO it is interacting with.

What does this logic imply? Very basically, but often overlooked, it implies that not all of the issues service INGOs tackle will result in human security service provision outcomes. Issues or projects that are of little value to the domestic community will not get its support and will thus not be sustainably influenced, despite service INGOs' attention. For a nonformal "reality check," these ideas mold well with earlier ideas of issue resonance, which have previously been discussed mainly in reference to advocacy INGOs and outcomes (Risse 2002; Sundstrom 2006). As the value of a service INGO program diminishes for the domestic community, domestic actors will be less likely to invest their time and energy into the service INGO. For example, some issues, such as those dealing with basic health and development provision, could be argued to be of more value to domestic communities than controversial birth control goods provision or women-in-development programs in areas without a well-established domestic community that wants these services provided. When these issues are sufficiently valued by some segment of the domestic community, however, we should see service INGOs have a positive influence on even controversial human security outcomes. In other words, this would imply the following.

Service INGO Hypothesis 5: Service INGOs' impact on service delivery human security outcomes will likely be conditional on the preexisting value the domestic community places on the particular human security issue.

This hypothesis, if supported, highlights the tremendous attention service INGOs need to devote into making their agendas and programming relevant to the domestic communities in which they work. To note, this does not say anything about the potential for long-term changes in the value placed on certain human security issues within a locale; the model results simply imply that human security service delivery outcomes are more likely in locations where the domestic community places more value on that issue at the time it is interacting with the INGO. In this regard, this result is consistent with Sundstrom (2006) and others who talk about issue resonance in the advocacy realm. Because the domestic community is more likely to support service INGOs when it places greater values on the services the INGO is providing, there should be some issue-specific factors that condition the effectiveness of service INGOs

Advocacy INGO Model   Unlike the service INGO model, remember again that the underlying tension of the advocacy model is that not all actors shared the same order of preferences. The international community prefers the extreme outcome that the internationally biased organization is advocating for, while the domestic community prefers the more moderate outcome that the domestically consistent advocacy INGO is working for. With this is mind, one of the most fundamental, and yet interesting, facts that come out of the equilibria conditions is that the value of each community's least-preferred outcome matters for the likelihood of support. First, as the domestic community's value of the extreme advocacy outcome, E, increases, it is more likely to support signals from INGOs that do not share its preference order and to support all INGOs when INGOs are not sending separating signals. In other words, as the domestic community gets more utility out of the extreme advocacy outcome that the internationally biased organization is peddling, it is more likely to support it when it can discern that the organization is internationally biased from the signals it is sending. It is also more likely to support any organizations it encounters on that issue in a world without signals. Similarly, like the domestic community, the international community is more likely to support the domestically oriented organizations it encounters, knowing they are domestically oriented from the signals it observes, as the international community's value of the more moderate advocacy outcome increases. In the case of a world without signals, the international community will still be more likely to support all INGOs as its value for the more moderate advocacy outcome increases. In this pooling scenario, however, this result holds only in situations where the extreme outcome is not valued too much, as outlined in the book's appendix.

What does this imply? At the most basic level, it means that issue-focus matters when it comes to advocacy success. Nondivisive issues, where the international and domestic communities, though still different in their exact preference orders place sufficiently high values on their least-preferred outcomes, are more likely to get the support of both communities than divisive issues. Given that the model assumes that support by both communities relates to a better chance of the advocated policy and behavior outcome, these results imply that advocacy INGOs will have a greater effect on nondivisive issues than on divisive issues.

Advocacy INGO Hypothesis 1: Advocacy INGOs' impact on advocacy human security outcomes will be greater on issues that the domestic and international communities consider nondivisive.

This hypothesis counters the focus on "hot button" issues that have dominated some advocacy attempts. Just because an issue is one that is highly controversial and receives a lot of attention from the international community, it does not imply that the issue will automatically get results. By acknowledging that not all advocacy INGOs are motivated for what the domestic community wants, we can see that issues where the advocated change is one that is not valued by the domestic community, which would rather have a more moderate issue outcome, measurable human security outcomes are less likely. When the international and domestic communities have similar views about what successful advocacy should look like, it is more likely that human security advocacy organizations will gain their support and have a more likely positive outcome, even if still facing a recalcitrant state. If supported, this hypothesis would imply that advocacy INGOs must find ways to make their advocacy reflect some middle ground between the international community and the domestic community in order to get results. Whenever internationally biased organizations can still frame advocacy outcomes in ways that get sufficient "buy-in" from the domestic community, they are more likely to see results on the ground. Although straightforward, this logic implies an importance on domestic issue resonance that is often assumed to be present in the INGO advocacy (Risse 2002). In other words, this logic is consistent with existing theoretical expectations derived nonformally.

On an issue that is valued sufficiently by the domestic community, perhaps like an end to torture or political imprisonment or some other physical integrity right, when are we likely to see an effect on the ground? First, based on comparative statics on equilibria where both the international and domestic communities are supporting the advocacy INGO they are interacting with, it is easy to see that results depend on B, the vulnerability of the state. When the state is more vulnerable to international and domestic pressure, advocacy INGOs will have a greater impact on nondivisive advocacy outcomes. In other words, this leads us to the following.

Advocacy INGO Hypothesis 2: Advocacy INGOs' impact on nondivisive advocacy human security outcomes will be greater as both international and domestic vulnerability increase.

Although this hypothesis is completely consistent with earlier nonformal ideas (Keck and Sikkink 1998; Risse, Ropp, and Sikkink 1999), it has received very limited empirical support in some extant studies (Franklin 2008; Hafner-Burton 2008; Murdie and Davis 2012a). However, existing cross-national studies have not simultaneously examined both international and domestic pressure, even though this dual pressure is implied by even the canonical dominant theoretical framework.

What about signals by advocacy INGOs? Unlike the case with service INGOs, remember again that signals in the advocacy INGO model only hold in equilibria where organizations are sending the signal to garner the support of either the domestic or international community. Regardless of whether it is the domestically oriented or internationally biased organization that is signaling, the signal only works to influence the behavior of one community. The other community is either always going to support any advocacy INGOs it comes across, as is the case in the *International Fad* or the *Domestic Leader Equilibria*, or is not supporting any advocacy INGOs, regardless of the signal sent, as what occurs in the *Domestic Signaling, Foreign Helper*, and *Missionary Force Equilibria*. In the signaling equilibria titled *Missionary Force* and *Foreign Helper*, remember again that the internationally biased organization is only signaling to get the support of one community, knowing that the other community will not support any organization, regardless of the signal sent. As such, this organization in a scenario where it is more likely to get a moderated advocacy outcome, not the more extreme advocacy outcome it would prefer.

Conversely, the domestically oriented organization sends a signal when it is assured of the domestic community's support, regardless of the signal sent, as is the case in the *Domestic Leader Equilibrium*, or sending a signal to the domestic community when it already has the international community's support, as what occurs in the *International Fad Equilibrium*, or for just the support of the domestic community when the international community is not supporting any organization in the *Domestic Signaling Equilibrium*. As such, their signals should also increase the support necessary for either an assured or a more likely moderate advocacy outcome. This would imply that—regardless of which type of organization is signaling—we should see signals aid in garnering the support necessary for moderate advocacy outcomes.

Advocacy INGO Hypothesis 3: Advocacy INGOs that signal should be associated with a more likely moderate advocacy outcome.

Similar to Service INGO Hypothesis 2, Advocacy INGO Hypothesis 3 requires that attention be paid to self-selection by the INGOs themselves when they signal.

As in the service INGO model, the model equilibria here also indicate that the domestic community will be more likely to support advocacy INGOs, of any type, when the costs the domestic community is facing for offering its support are minimal. Intuitively, when costs to this community rise, it is less likely that the domestic community will be willing to support any organization, even one that could help it achieve its preferred outcome. What are these costs likely to entail? Remember again that advocacy is a global phenomenon. Under the canonical boomerang model, domestic groups work to get others interested in their plight; their costs come from their time and struggle working with a global advocacy network. In order to pressure a state from above, the domestic group needs to aid in the advocacy INGO's work both at the domestic and international levels. In some states, existing connections and information flows would probably lower these costs. In other states, isolation and difficulty transmitting information may exacerbate these costs.

This logic implies two things. First, the domestic community is going to be less likely to support advocacy organizations, even on core issues like the halting of political imprisonment or torture, in states where communication is more difficult and the ability to connect to the outside world is more tenuous. In these situations, the model implies that governments will have less to fear from advocacy INGOs because domestic populations, due to the high costs of transmitting information through and working with INGOs, are effectively too isolated to readily support advocacy INGOs. This logic, although very straightforward, is often missing in the canonical literature, where it could be argued that domestic costs are not sufficiently high to limit support in any situation, since the domestic community is assumed to be calling advocacy INGOs to the state in the first place. This logic would be more in line with Carpenter's (2007) or Bob's (2005) work on how certain issues are missing from the advocacy agenda; these works can serve as a nonformal "reality check" to the result derived here from a formal model. Here, unlike these existing pieces, the logic rests on the idea that certain populations, due to their isolation, face greater costs in support advocacy INGO, effectively lessening the likelihood of a successful advocacy outcome. Second, and more relevant to the role of human security INGOs for advocacy outcomes, this logic implies that domestic information or interaction costs will dictate when and where advocacy INGOs are likely to get measurable results. Since the likelihood of advocacy results depends on domestic community support in the game, this reasoning implies that the costliness of support for the domestic community may limit advocacy INGO results.

Advocacy INGO Hypothesis 4: Advocacy INGOs are likely to have a greater impact in countries with lower information and social contact costs for the domestic population.

Since information access is a type of human right, this hypothesis implies a synergy among rights: certain baseline information rights and globalization levels may be necessary for advocacy INGOs to have any impact on even the most nondivisive human rights issues, like issues relating to bodily integrity. As a "reality check," this hypothesis is in line with even the UN's report on the importance of Internet and other communication tools in human rights advocacy (La Rue 2011).

When we look at situations in which the international community is more likely to support advocacy INGOs, we see similar dynamics. First, as the cost of support for the international community decreases, it is more likely to support any advocacy INGO it comes across. Second, as its value for its preferred advocacy outcome—the extreme outcome advocated by internationally biased INGOs—increases, it is also more likely either to support an organization it knows to be internationally biased based on the signal sent or to support any organization in a world without signals. Taken together, these results from the advocacy INGO model imply, as we discussed with respect to the service INGO model, that the international community should have a great impact on the observable advocacy INGO-induced human security outcomes. The international community is only willing to support organizations greatly when benefits to them are more likely. This leads us to the following.

Advocacy INGO Hypothesis 5: Advocacy INGOs are likely to have a greater impact as support from the international community increases.

This hypothesis definitely has a very clear nonformal counterpart to serve as a "reality check": this is consistent with Keck and Sikkink (1998) and the boomerang model. Actors outside the state can aid in pressuring a government to change its human rights practices.

One of the most interesting implications of the model comes from examining the effect of movement in P, or the chances of the international and domestic communities interacting with a domestically consistent INGO on the behavior of all actors in the model. Remember that the service INGO model implies that an increase in the likelihood of facing a service INGO that is principled and not rent-seeking results in an increased chance that all actors in the model will support the INGO in a scenario where no signals were sent. From the advocacy INGO model, however, we can see that, without signals, as the likelihood of facing a principled, domestically consistent organization increases, the domestic community alone is more likely to support all advocacy INGOs. Because it would actually prefer the extreme advocacy outcome being touted by an internationally biased advocacy INGO, the international community is less likely to support all INGOs as P increases. Again, this is because the international community would prefer to support an outcome that may be more in line with an organization that does not fit the conventional definition of a principled organization because the organization is willing to support international donor issues simply as a way to increase its own private gains.

These dynamics in the movement of P imply that the domestic community is less likely to support INGOs acting on issues where there are lots of internationally oriented INGOs. Thus, on issues where there are lots of internationally oriented INGOs—such as women's rights, for example—the domestic community would be less likely to support all INGOs, even those that share their preference for moderate outcomes, if INGOs cannot send separating signals.

This logic also implies that many INGOs with domestic preferences in a state might actually lessen the support that the international community gives INGOs. In other words, if P is low solely because of a lack of domestically grown organizations, we might see the international community more likely to support all INGOs, even though the domestic community does not prefer the internationally oriented INGOs that would then be present. In other words, in countries or on issues where domestically oriented INGOs are nascent, the international community is more likely to support advocacy INGOs, even putting more money in advocacy projects. As the amount of domestically oriented INGOs increases, the international community is less willing to support any INGO.

Advocacy INGO Hypothesis 6: The international community is more likely to support advocacy INGOs when there are fewer domestically oriented INGOs.

This hypothesis, although pretty straightforward, highlights a very interesting dynamic with regard to the support of advocacy INGOs. Once we relax the assumption that all INGOs are principled and acknowledge that advocacy is often a realm where actors differ in their underlying motivations, it is easy to see that international support for advocacy INGOs is more likely when advocacy INGOs are not homegrown. If there is a rich domestic advocacy INGO sector with preferences for what the domestic community wants, the international community may be less willing to support organizations here. When the international community does offer support, it is likely supporting organizations that do not share the domestic community's underlying preference order, which could limit the overall advocacy results. As a "reality check," this hypothesis is consistent with the nonformal ideas of Goonatilake (2002) and Sundstrom (2006).

CONCLUSION

When and where should we expect human security INGOs to matter on human security–related advocacy and service outcomes? By relaxing—but not abandoning—the underlying assumption that all INGOs are motivated by principles to help the domestic community with what it wants but is not able to achieve on its own, empirical expectations of the conditional effectiveness of INGOs on human security have been derived that speak to many of the recent critiques of the dominant theoretical framework. Not all INGOs share the same preferences, and INGOs can send signals of their underlying preferences to outside actors. Once these dynamics were identified, this chapter has examined when and where support to INGOs is likely, which ultimately matters for their likely overall success on human security outcomes. The empirical implications outlined in this chapter are based on game-theoretic models that reflect on-the-ground differences in the service and advocacy realms, including differences in the motivations of the communities that interact with INGOs.

The theory presented here is novel in many regards in its treatment of INGOs. Most importantly, it stresses that INGOs differ in their motivations: some are similar to the canonical literature and can be categorized as principled actors, while others may not reflect the canonical definition of organizations motivated by principles and shared values. Many of the earlier typologies of INGOs included categories that could be thought of as more likely to have these nonprincipled values (Gordenker and Weiss 1995; Vakil 1997). INGOs' motivations are private knowledge; the international and domestic actors that interact with human security INGOs do not know at the onset whether they are facing a principled organization or one that is motivated mainly by its own materialistic or personalistic agenda. However, INGOs can send signals of their underlying motivations, and the communities they interact with can rely both on this information and on the baseline probability that they are facing an organization with principled motivations when these communities are choosing whether to offer their support.

When we examine INGOs in such a theoretical setup, a few novel things become important. First, and not to belabor the point, the worlds of advocacy and service work are much different. Unlike the conventional INGO literature, we should not assume that similar motivations and behaviors exist across these realms. Our understandings of the likely human security outcomes of advocacy as opposed to service organizations much reflect these differences. Unlike the service INGO realm, where all actors share the same order of preferences to support a non-rent-seeking principled organization, in the advocacy realm, the international community may actually have a strong preference for supporting the nonprincipled internationally biased organization that is willing to work for its extreme outcome instead of what the domestic community actually desires. As a result of the differences in these realms, there will not be one unified reaction of the donor community to the existence of nonprincipled organizations. We are likely to see donors respond to the issue of nonprincipled motivations differently in the service and advocacy realms. Moreover, in the advocacy realm in particular, the congruence of the advocacy desires of the international and domestic communities will influence whether we can see actual advocacy change on a particular issue. Certain advocacy issues, even with much international community support, may not ever see advocated results in even vulnerable states. Reframing and structuring advocacy to reflect domestic community input may help. Understanding these dynamics is critical if we are to make advocacy work effective and donor efforts efficient in gaining actual advocacy results.

Second, and in both realms, because signals can be ways to get organizational support from the international and domestic communities, the signals INGOs send matter for actual outcomes. Although there is a growing cross-disciplinary literature on how organizations can signal their underlying motivations, somewhat surprisingly, this literature has not been extended to what INGOs are actually able to achieve on the ground.

Third, and somewhat missing in the extant literature, the behavior of other actors to the INGO is critical to its success. This idea was built into my theoretical framework at the onset and is not new; for example, we've known for a long time that pressure both "below" and "above" matters for advocacy

INGOs (Brysk 1993). What is novel from the theoretical framework here is the expectation that the costliness of this support for the domestic community and the level of support received from the international community will all matter for human security outcomes. If these implications are supported empirically, INGOs themselves will have to think of ways to eliminate these costs to the domestic community and get international community "buy-in" in the outcomes they are working for.

In short, the model and results presented in this chapter offer a novel approach to understanding the conditional impact of human security INGOs. Underlying the implications presented in this chapter is a more nuanced understanding of INGOs' motivations. Unlike the dominant TAN framework, not all INGOs are predominantly motivated to help a domestic population. It is critical for us to understand how the existence of INGOs with varying motivations complicates when and where these organizations receive support. It is the first step, I contend, to developing a theory of the conditional effectiveness of these organizations on human security.

To be clear, however, this model and results by no means capture all the nuances in the INGO sector. Like any theoretical enterprise, I have had to make sacrifices in favor of parsimony. Some of these nuances could definitely be incorporated into the framework used here. For example, although I do not address it in this book either empirically or theoretically, Sarah Stroup (2012) has shown that organizations differ as a result of their nation of origin. Stroup, and Stroup and Murdie (2012) look at differences in how organizations from various democracies in the Global North interact with governments. An extension of this work could focus on how nation of origin dynamics influence the composition of p. In other words, are organizations from a certain country more likely to be nonprincipled? If so, then examining where these organizations are involved may be important for human security. I do not address this issue in the book mainly because the existing literature has not provided strong theoretical evidence of how nonprincipled organizations vary by country. To the extent that future work addresses these variations, it could be incorporated as an additional empirical test that would be consistent with the theory laid out above.

Likewise, building off Gordenker and Weiss (1995), if quasi-non-governmental and donor-organized organizations are more likely to be nonprincipled, at least for advocacy organizations where international and domestic preferences vary, the nuances of Gordenker and Weiss could be examined from the theoretical lens presented here. For example, if quasi-non-governmental and donor-organized organizations are more likely to be internationally aligned, we should expect more international funds to be geared to them in areas where domestic civil society is nascent, as outlined by Advocacy Hypothesis 6.

Although there are many of the cross-disciplinary nuances of INGOs that could be incorporated into this theoretical model, let me stress again that my theoretical model, like all models, includes simplifications that may not reflect the full complexity in international relations. This is true, of course, of all theoretical models, whether quantitative or qualitative. For example, in the interest of parsimony, I focus on a unified international and a unified domestic community. In reality, however, we do know that these sets of actors often differ in their opinion and views concerning a specific issue. Likewise, these actors could have costs that differ for supporting INGOs. Although, as discussed in Chapter 4, I empirically examine whether there are differences in the influence of aid in the United States and the United Kingdom, two main donor countries, I do not address these dynamics in detail in this model. To the extent that a bifurcated international or domestic community could react to the signals sent by INGOs differently, this is a weakness of my approach that could be addressed by future scholars.

Further, game theory is a great tool to make sure my hypotheses are logically consistent. However, as mentioned above, it does require me to be very rigid about the actors I am including in my model and the assumptions I am making. One nice thing, as a lay out above, is that many of my hypotheses do hold up to a basic "reality check" and are consistent, at least in overall ideas, to thoughts found from case study and practitioner work, most of which does not rely on game theory when deriving hypotheses.

In Chapters 4 and 5, all implications of my theoretical models are empirically tested. Chapter 4 examines the implications from the service INGO model, and Chapter 5 tests the implications concerning advocacy INGOs.

4 INGOS AND HUMAN SECURITY SERVICE OUTCOMES

The Case of Development

LET'S BEGIN THE EMPIRICAL SECTION of this book with an example: Lesotho. In many regards, the country of Lesotho is forgettable. Only 11,000 square miles, the state is completely landlocked, surrounded by South Africa on all sides. Much of the traditional economy is based on subsistence farming in rural areas. Only in the last ten years or so has the country embraced a more export-intensive economy, based mainly on garment manufacturing and diamonds, both of which have taken a hit since the 2008 recession. With the exception of a minor conflict in 1998, Lesotho has managed to avoid widespread political unrest and genocide in its political history. Although droughts are a common occurrence, no CNN-worthy earthquakes or hurricanes have hit the country since its 1966 independence from the United Kingdom.

By all accounts, however, Lesotho is very poor; almost half of the country lives on less than US$1.25 a day. More troubling, perhaps, HIV/AIDS has ravaged the country; almost a quarter of the adult population was infected in 2012. Maternal health is among the worst in the world, and the country is continuing to slip in world rankings of human development (UNDP 2012).

Despite this widespread poverty, several anomalous bright spots in human security outcomes exist in Lesotho. Related to "freedom from want" service outcomes, the country has one of the highest primary school enrollments in all of Africa, in the mid–80 percent range in 2012. Literacy is also extremely high, similar to rates in Syria and Lebanon and higher than the 2012 rate in India. Likewise, basic sanitation rates are reasonable; the percentage of the population with access to potable water in Lesotho is similar to the percentage in the comparatively richer countries of Georgia or Indonesia. Even looking at human security outcomes related to advocacy for the "freedom from fear," Lesotho has a remarkably good record on physical integrity rights and women's rights, higher in recent years on common human rights scales than Turkey and, with regards to physical integrity rights, even the United States. All of these human security outcomes appear somewhat odd and surprising for such a poor state, especially given the lack of democratic institutions in Lesotho until the early 1990s.

Do human security INGOs have anything to do with these anomalies in human security outcomes? Are organizations making a difference in this small state? Although the number of human security organizations in Lesotho is not significantly high—slightly lower in fact than the world mean—their work has long been touted as significant for peoples in the country. For example, as a 2007 report by the Electoral Institute for Sustainable Democracy in Africa remarked:

> NGOs in Lesotho have been involved in areas of service provision such as health and education. They have concentrated on advocacy in terms of the provision of services, evaluating government efforts through access, affordability and efficiency, and establishing health [centers] and ownership of community schools. The NGOs' greatest advantage is their ability to penetrate to areas where government is not able to provide services. (Tsikoane and Mothibe 2007, 72)

Similarly, as another organization concluded:

> Although, non-governmental [organizations] differ in focus, they work together to build strong communities and in assisting people in Lesotho to identify for themselves areas of their lives that are not adequate and on their own develop ways of addressing such problem areas. (TRC 2003, 4)

Since 1990, the work of both domestic and international NGOs in Lesotho has been heralded in particular by the umbrella group Lesotho Council of Non-Governmental Organizations. The group works closely with the government of Lesotho and tries to ensure that all NGO-led projects in Lesotho reflect the desires of the intended beneficiaries of the projects. Any NGO can petition to join the group and must provide a detailed statement of their organizational mission, funding sources, projects, and structure. The organization regularly provides press releases on the successes of INGOs in the country.

Organizations in Lesotho, however, are not without critics. As Matlosa (1999) wrote:

[International and domestic NGOs in the state] have made an appreciable contribution particularly in the social sector and in the area of democracy and human rights; but it cannot be denied that their agenda is also heavily influenced by donor preferences of the day. (24)

William Easterly's 2006 book *The White Man's Burden: Why the West's Efforts to Aid the Rest Have Done So Much Ill and So Little Good* included one such story of international efforts to increase human security that failed in Lesotho. Originally taken from the anthropologist James Ferguson's 1990 book, *The Anti-Politics Machine: "Development," Depoliticization, and Bureaucratic Power in Lesotho*, the story concerns a project that was sponsored by the Canadian International Development Agency and the World Bank and was designed to increase livestock production and market access in a mountain region of the state. The program, however, did not consider the interests of the local people, most of whom had no interest in livestock markets, since they worked in mines, mainly in neighboring South Africa. Ferguson's account of the development INGOs and IGOs in Lesotho in the late 1970s contends that some organizations were not interested beyond their own organizational desires and coffers, "employing expatriate consultants and 'experts' by the hundreds, and churning out plans, programs, and most of all, paper, at an astonishing rate," often without any measurable results (8). However, more recent critiques of Lesotho INGOs as corrupt are rare; in fact, INGOs in the country were critically involved in information production and advocacy concerning an anticorruption case involving the Lesotho Highlands Water Project (Pottinger 2000; Oweyegha-Afundaduula, Afundaduula, and Balunywa 2003).

If INGOs have, especially in recent years, been helpful at human security service and advocacy promotion in Lesotho, can the same be said for INGOs elsewhere? What explains the conditional success of organizations in Lesotho, and, more importantly, under what conditions can INGOs aid human security provision worldwide?

This chapter begins the book's empirical examination of whether and under what conditions INGOs influence human security outcomes across time and across countries. In this chapter, the focus is on only the freedom from want portion of human security. Chapter 5 concerns whether and when INGOs influence the human security outcomes that relate to freedom of fear. I focus here on the effects of INGOs that have mission statements that refer to sustainable development. These organizations often work to lessen "freedom from want" by providing goods and services themselves or working with governments in ways that build government capacity for service provision; they are typically categorized as service INGOs.

To answer whether and under what conditions service INGOs matter for human security service provision, this chapter tests the empirical implications derived from the service INGO game-theoretic model outlined in Chapter 3. The empirical results provide widespread support for the derived hypotheses, indicating that development INGOs can have a powerful impact on human security service provision.

As expected, however, the results also show how tenuous the effects of service INGOs often are. Specifically, reflecting the book's major theme that not all INGOs have motivations for actually aiding the domestic population with what it wants but is not able to achieve on its own, the results here indicate that the whole INGO sector is not likely to have measurable results in situations where nonprincipled rent-seeking service organizations are likely to flourish. However, when I focus only on organizations that send signals that they are not rent-seekers, I do find some positive effects of service INGOs on human security outcomes, even in corrupt countries where more nonprincipled INGOs would likely be located. Other results provided here are also consistent with the expectations derived from the formal game-theoretic service INGO model outlined in Chapter 3 and concern additional conditions influencing the likelihood of service INGO success on human security service provision, including the underlying conditions of the country and the support organizations receive from the international community.

Below, I first briefly review the service INGO hypotheses and the underlying logic of the theoretical argument and then discuss the basic research design utilized to evaluate these hypotheses. After this, the evidence is presented and evaluated. The use of a statistical, global methodology here aids in our collective knowledge of INGOs in many ways. It allows me to explicitly address concerns like self-selection bias and confounding factors. The approach taken here allows us a bird's-eye view of the outcomes of the work of multiple INGOs in multiple countries over a long period of time. However, I hope my approach does not imply that statistical methods are the best or the only way to evaluate the likely effects of INGOs. Much important work has already been done that examines cases of INGO success, as discussed both here and in Chapter 2. In reality, this chapter is choosing "breadth" over "depth," with the idea that existing case study works on INGOs have already captured depth quite nicely.

In order to aid in readability, I have relegated all statistical tables to the chapter's appendix; results are presented only graphically whenever possible. In addition, I have added brief case study examples throughout the chapter that illustrate the empirical models and statistical results. These results serve as an important "reality check" to the quantitative findings.

EXPECTATIONS FOR SERVICE INGO CONDITIONAL EFFECTIVENESS

As Chapter 3 points out, the service INGO theoretical model provides many interesting and testable implications concerning the factors that condition the impact of service INGOs on human security outcomes. The model is structured around the idea that the INGO world is made up of both principled and nonprincipled organizations, with principled service INGOs using donors funds to provide services, while nonprincipled service INGOs simply use the donor funds to fill their own coffers or otherwise engage in rent-seeking behavior. The communities that interact with INGOs, both the domestic groups and individuals to whom service INGOs provide services and training programs, and the international community from which INGOs try to get donations and outside support do not know at the onset what type of organization they are interacting with. In the service realm, however, both the international and domestic communities would like to avoid supporting an organization that is not going to actually use donor funds to provide services; they would like to avoid supporting a rent-seeker. However, these communities do not know for certain at the beginning of their interactions with an INGO whether the organization they are facing shares their motivations. They simply know the underlying percentage of rent-seekers versus non-rent-seekers in the particular state.

Importantly, in the theoretical framework, an INGO can send a signal of its underlying motivations to both the domestic and international communities. If a signal is sent, these communities can observe the signal and then update their beliefs about the type of organization they are interacting with. At the end of the day, the effect of an organization on human security service provision is determined by the support it receives from the international and domestic community, together, of course, with the type of organization it is.

From examining the results of the service INGO game-theoretic model, I concluded Chapter 3 by providing five hypotheses concerning when and where service INGOs will have a likely impact on human security service provision. First, as Service INGO Hypothesis 1 contends, the impact of service INGOs is conditional to the proportion of rent-seeking service INGOs that are active in a country. When this proportion is greater, service INGOs are less likely to get the support of the domestic and international communities and, thus, less likely to have an effect on policy and behavior outcomes. In short, where "bad apples" flourish, the service INGO model predicts that the domestic and international communities do exactly what some in the INGO community fear: they throw out the barrel (Lee 2007).

We don't have a measure, of course, of the exact underlying proportion of rent-seeking service INGOs in a state. Because an INGO's motivations are private knowledge, in fact, it would be difficult if not impossible to get a perfect measure of this proportion. However, anecdotally, many practitioners and academics would contend that there are more rent-seeking organizations in a corrupt country like Haiti or Liberia than in a country with less corruption, like the Philippines or Lesotho. Therefore, I expect that the proportion of rent-seeking service INGOs is higher in states where there is widespread corruption. This is due to the idea that rent-seeking INGOs are less likely to be identified and prosecuted in corrupt states (Lee 2007). If the normal ways to conduct business and governmental affairs include bribes, side-payments, and much rent-seeking, rent-seeking INGOs may be drawn to such places and have little fear of repercussions. Recent reports from Afghanistan also highlight this dynamic (Huggler 2005). As such, Hypothesis 1 contends that the service INGOs' overall impact on human security service outcomes should be greater as corruption is controlled.

Second, the service INGO game-theoretic model results highlight that the international and domestic communities are more likely to support service INGOs who signal their non-rent-seeking motivations; it follows that when there is a greater proportion of service INGOs that signal their motivations, service INGOs will have a greater impact on policy and behavior, as outlined in Service INGO Hypothesis 2. However, also as implied from the service INGO game-theoretic model results, non-rent-seeking INGOs are more willing to send this separating signal as their value of the potential outcomes increases. This implies a potential selection dynamic on behalf of these organizations: they should be more willing to enter into voluntary accountability programs in countries where high outcomes are more likely. Because of this, empirical methodology that accounts for possible self-selection dynamics will have to be utilized when examining the impact of organizations that have sent signals of their underlying motivations. This is discussed in more detail below.

Additionally, as the service INGO model results show, the international community is willing to endure higher costs of support if the effect of the INGO is greater. Therefore, as Service INGO Hypothesis 3 contends, the amount of funds the international community invests should condition the impact of service INGOs.

Finally, the domestic community's support of service INGOs is contingent on the costs it will incur for the support and the values it places on the INGO's services. INGOs typically locate in urban areas within states; as such, states that are in the process of urbanizing could be argued to have fewer costs for the domestic community to interact with service INGOs simply because of lower travel costs for the domestic population. In other words, if the domestic community can readily interact with service INGOs in an urban environment, these interactions are less costly. Thus, in urbanizing states, service INGOs will have a greater impact on policy and behavior outcomes because it is more likely that service INGOs can gain the domestic population's support. This is the logic underpinning Service INGO Hypothesis 4. Additionally, as Hypothesis 5 contends, in states where the domestic population could be argued to place a greater value on the services INGOs provide, the domestic population is more likely to support the organizations, and, therefore, the service INGOs' impact is predicted to be greater.

HUMAN SECURITY SERVICE OUTCOMES: WHAT OUTCOME TO FOCUS ON

To examine the work of service INGOs of "freedom from want," I first must decide on a likely candidate for the dependent variable in the analyses. What human security outcome should be the focus? The service INGOs' work can be diverse; in the name of providing services related to "freedom from want," organizations take a number of different approaches and often have organizational outputs in many assorted areas. For example, the Aga Khan Foundation, a large organizational group with a mission relating to many human security outcomes, has been supporting the restoration of the seawall around Stone Town, Zanzibar, Tanzania, and is working to create a public park in the area. Although the project may seem to be one just for the beautification of the city, the Aga Khan Foundation states prominently on its website that the project is designed to "generate employment opportunities" and promote "socio-economic development" (AKDN 2012). Another development INGO, Global Vision, has been very active recently in documentary film production and, since its inception in the 1970s, has worked mainly to spread the message of sustainability through art. Even very well-known organizations, like CARE International or Oxfam, have projects on everything from climate change to home gardening promotion, with an eye on sustainable development. Despite this diversity, to evaluate the service INGO hypotheses, I need a human security service outcome that both captures what most service INGOs do and is available for as many countries as possible for a long time period. Further, for the first four hypotheses, this outcome needs to be one where it can be assumed that the domestic population and the international community consistently value the service the INGO is providing.

Given this, I focus on the impact that development INGOs have on improving access to potable water (UN 1990, 2005; Ranis et al. 2000; USAID 2006; Nelson 2007). Basic access to an improved water source is critical for a labor force's health and reflects a basic human right (USAID 2006; Nelson 2007). Potable water is often the first project many development INGOs undertake in a state (Gleick 1996, 2000; Fyvie and Ager 1999; Fowler 2002; Ward et al. 2008). Also, it is a project that the majority of development INGOs provide, even if their focus includes other service provisions (UIA 2008/2009). Thus, in the basic statistical models utilized in this chapter, the dependent variable captures the percent of the population with access to an improved water source. This variable comes from the World Bank's (2012) World Development Indicators:

> [The dependent variable is the] percentage of the population with reasonable access to an adequate amount of water from an improved source, such as a household connection, public standpipe, borehole, protected well or spring, and rainwater collection. Unimproved sources include vendors, tanker trucks, and unprotected wells and springs. Reasonable access is defined as the availability of at least 20 liters a person a day from a source within one kilometer of the dwelling.

Do people in recent history really still not have access to potable water? Unfortunately, the answer is "yes." As the UN Development Programme's Human Development Report for 2006 highlighted, "No act of terrorism generates economic devastation on the scale of the crisis in water and sanitation" (3). Robert Buckley (2009) of the Rockefeller Foundation, in an opinion piece for the *Financial Times*, remarked that "lack of clean water and sanitation" kills children at "a rate equivalent to having a jumbo jet full of kids crash every four hours."

If we focus only on developing countries in the lower half of the world's wealth distribution (countries where the GDP per capita is lower than the median GDP per capita in the world in that year) since the end of the Cold War, only about 70 percent of the population of the mean country has access to an improved water source.[1] The variance, however, is pretty great: there are countries like Cambodia in 1996 where only 22.8 percent of the population had access to an improved water source and countries like Belarus in 2003 where 100 percent of the population had access to an improved water source. Many of the observations in the sample are from countries where a slight majority of the population has access to potable water in the given year. However, in most instances, access is still less than perfect; it is obviously less than the 99 to 100 percent scores that are occurring in the United States and the United Kingdom during this same time period.

Also, somewhat surprisingly, the median access to potable water does not change too much in the whole developing world during this time period.[2] Some countries, however, made very significant changes during this time. For example, from 1996 to 2006, Mongolia made a 20-point gain in its percentage of the population that had access to potable water. Burkina Faso had a similar increase of 19 percentage points from 1993 to 2003.

DEVELOPMENT INGOS: LARGE-SCALE DATA SOURCES

For the countries that do improve their access to potable water, what explains the gains they make? I contend that development INGOs can be important actors in this process, especially under certain conditions. To test this argument, obviously, we need a measure of the level of development INGO activity within developing countries. Ideally, we would want a measure of the total activities, writings, specific projects, organizational resources, and staff members active in these countries over a long time span. Unfortunately, this ideal measure does not exist. Organizations are not required, by and large, to release details of their activities and whereabouts. In fact, where organizations are required by law to disclose this information, many often complain that the laws are simply to limit INGO actions that would be contrary to state interests. As discussed in Chapter 2, this is especially problematic for advocacy organizations, like human rights INGOs, which can work specifically through targeting the state government and may not want to release information about their location and activities to a repressive regime. Some development and humanitarian INGOs have recently become very proactive about releasing information about their projects. For example, InterAction, a coalition of US-based INGOs, has prominently released data about their current projects related to food insecurity on the aptly-named website http://ngoaidmap.org/. Similar data for organizations worldwide over a significant period of time, however, do not exist.

As a proxy, and simply as a starting point in this book, I use a variety of measures of the number of development INGOs active in a state. I use data collected from the *Yearbook of International Organizations*, a publication of the Union of International Associations (UIA), an INGO itself whose mission is the "facilitation of the development and efficiency of non-governmental networks" (UIA 2008/2009). The UIA produces a list of all active INGOs in the world by asking other INGOs for new organization information, looking at lists of INGOs produced by donor foundations and international organizations, and original research of newspaper and practitioner reports. The UIA then collects data on all INGOs on its list by sending out information requests to the organizations themselves. The UIA asks these organizations to self-report a plethora of information, including the organization's mission or aims, its services and languages used, main and secondary addresses, structure, staff, and membership details (UIA 2008/2009). It has published its findings in its *Yearbook* every year since 1910.

As discussed more in depth in Chapter 5 with respect to advocacy INGOs, the UIA data are far from perfect at capturing all the activities of all INGOs. For example, the data could not be used to capture the amount of targeted media attention that advocacy INGOs from around the world typically try to get placed in the international press about a particular repressive regime. In other words, the *Yearbook* would not be a good source for "naming and shaming" data about human rights advocacy INGOs. However, with respect to service INGOs in general and development INGOs specifically, data compiled from the *Yearbook* on both the number of issue-specific INGOs with a permanent location in a state and the number of INGOs that have volunteers or members in a state serve as useful proxies for the concept of INGO activities. Unlike advocacy INGOs, such as human rights INGOs, service INGOs, as the category encompassing development INGOs, typically have an active presence in a country in order to provide services. In other words, the service INGO must have an active front on the ground for service provision in the state. Because of this, data taken from the *Yearbook* on service INGOs can serve as a more reliable proxy for service INGO activities than the data from the *Yearbook* on advocacy

INGOs, which often work to impact advocacy outcomes without having an on-the-ground presence in a state.

Therefore, as a reliable proxy on the activities of development INGOs, I can utilize data from the *Yearbook* of the number of organizations with sustainable development goals active in a country in a given year. Luckily, Smith and Wiest (2005, 2012) have coded the *Yearbook* data from 1953 to 2003. Their measure, which records the number of sustainable development INGOs with a volunteer (referred to as a "member" in the *Yearbook*) in a country in a given year, was collected from hard copies of the *Yearbook* every few years. I linearly interpolate the years not coded by Smith and Wiest (2005).

What do summary statistics of this measure tell us? For the post–Cold War time period used in the dataset—1996 to 2003—the median developing country had a little over 120 development organizations active in it. However, this varies widely across countries in the sample. In 1996, Tajikistan had the lowest number of development INGOs active in it, with a very paltry 13 organizations. Compare this with the whopping 342 organizations active in India in 2003.[3]

Both to confirm the validity of the Smith and Wiest (2005) data and to code additional information necessary for this and related projects, I coded similar data on the number of development INGOs that have a permanent location in a state and also coded data on the signals these organizations send, which will be discussed in detail below.[4] Worth noting, when my self-coded data on the number of development INGOs that have a permanent location in a state is substituted for the Smith and Wiest (2005) data utilized here, which captures, again, the number of these organizations with volunteer/members in a state, the empirical results in this chapter are substantively and statistically very similar.

STATISTICAL MODELING DECISIONS

Many potential variables can be correlated with both the dependent variable and the key independent variables used in this study and, thus, must be controlled for across the various empirical models. First, as Baum and Lake (2003) point out, democracies are often better at human capital provision. Regime type could also be correlated with the number of development INGOs active in a state. Thus, I account for regime type in the statistical models in this chapter by including as a control the revised consolidated polity index, which ranges from −10 for strongly autocratic to +10 for strongly democratic regimes (Marshall and Jaggers 2010).

Additionally, many have contended that larger populations impact both service provision and civil society (Boli and Thomas 1999; Baum and Lake 2003; Smith and Wiest 2005). Therefore, I include a control for the natural log of population in all models (WDI 2012). Finally, because of the impact that higher levels of economic development have on service provision and on civil society, I include a control for gross domestic product (GDP) per capita (ln) in constant US dollars in all statistical models (WDI 2012).[5]

Finally, due to the time series, cross-sectional nature of the dataset, I use models that include Newey-West standard errors. Newey-West standard errors are consistent to both unequal variance across cases (heteroscedasticity) and "stickiness" across time (autocorrelation) without introducing bias in my point estimates (Wooldridge 2006).

Beyond these uniform modeling decisions, the various statistical models used in the chapter are somewhat different, reflecting, of course, the differences in the hypotheses they are testing. Below I outline the various models and statistical results in the order in which they were given as hypotheses, paying special attention to what these results mean substantively.

1. The Impact of Development INGOs Is Conditional on a State's Control of Corruption

To support Service INGO Hypothesis 1, development INGOs' impact on the percent of the population with access to an improved water source must be conditional to the state's level of corruption. Again, this reflects the idea that the underlying proportion of the type of organization in a country— rent-seeking or not—will move with the level of corruption in that country. When a country is corrupt, service INGOs in the country are likely corrupt as well, limiting the overall impact of the service INGO sector on human security outcomes.

To examine the validity of this hypothesis, the key independent variable is an interaction term of the number of development INGOs variable, discussed above, and the World Bank Governance indicator of control of corruption.[6] This corruption control indicator is a measure of the perceptions of state corruption, defined as the use of public power for private gain (Kaufmann et al. 2006). This indicator is based on a compilation of dozens of different variables measuring perceptions of corruption, combined using an "unobserved component model" (Kaufmann et al. 2006). The indicator ranges from −2.5, indicating widespread corruption, to 2.5, indicating little to no corruption, with a mean of about 0 for the full dataset (i.e., both developed and developing countries). Although the indicator goes up to 2.5 in the full dataset, within the sample of developing countries used in the model, corruption control is not as extensive, topping out at around 0.5 for Lesotho in 2000. The mean country in the sample has a control of corruption score of −0.725.

Again, the focus is on the impact of development INGOs in developing countries, defined as countries in the lower half of yearly GDP per capita levels. Because I am interested in the effect development INGOs have on future access to an improved water source, I measure the independent variables at one year prior to the dependent variable. When the necessary control variables were included, I have a data set of roughly 71 states and a total of 515 observations for the years 1996 to 2003.

What do the results of this statistical test indicate? As expected, development INGOs only have a positive and statistically significant impact on access to an improved water source when corruption is controlled.[7] This is evident in Figure 4.1, which plots the marginal effect of development INGOs as control of corruption increases in a country. As shown, when corruption is not controlled,

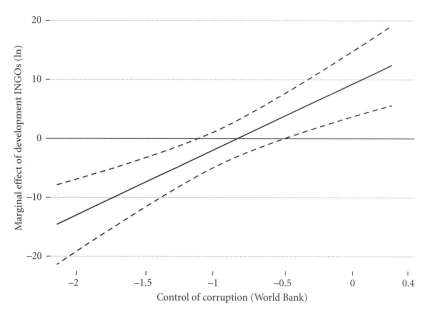

Figure 4.1 Marginal effects of development INGOs (ln) on access to improved water source as control of corruption increases

like in the far left-hand side of the graph, more development INGOs can actually have a negative impact on access to potable water. I argue that this is due to the high percentage of rent-seeking organizations in states where corruption is not controlled; these rent-seeking organizations only take money for their own purposes and do not provide any human security output. For example, if corruption within a country is among the highest levels in the sample, as indicated by a World Bank Governance control of corruption indicator of about −0.7 or lower, more INGOs actually have a negative effect on service provision. Countries with this level of corruption would include places like Haiti in 2002 and 2003, the Democratic Republic of Congo for most of the late 1990s, and Liberia from 1996 to 1998.

However, as corruption becomes controlled, the marginal impact of development INGOs becomes positive, as evident on the right side of the graph in Figure 4.1. I argue that this is due to less of a presence of corrupt, rent-seeking INGOs in a state where corruption is controlled. In these countries, rent-seeking INGOs fear prosecution or attention for their corrupt practices and are less likely to be present, leaving the proportion of rent-seeking to non-rent-seeking INGOs heavily swayed in favor of the non-rent-seeking organizations. As such, the domestic and international populations in states with a greater percentage of non-rent-seeking organizations are more likely to support any organization they are facing, leading to a more likely effect on the ground.

One thing worth mentioning is that this effect of development INGOs in developing countries where corruption is controlled could be argued to be somehow linked to just an overabundance of organizations in noncorrupt versus corrupt countries. However, as Figure 4.2 illustrates, if I divide the sample into just cases below and above the mean in the control of corruption variable, it is pretty evident that both corrupt and noncorrupt states have similar levels of total development INGOs active within them. In fact, there is no statistically significant difference between these two cases. Corrupt countries have an average of around 128 organizations active within them (95% confidence interval between 123 and 134), while noncorrupt countries have an average of 114 organizations (95% confidence interval between 100 and 127); this is not a significant difference using conventional t-tests.[8] In line with my baseline argument, however, what is different among these groups is the proportion of organizations that would be rent-seekers. In the noncorrupt countries, where the proportion of rent-seeking INGOs could be argued to be lower, the effect of the organizations that are present within the country is positive; they actually deliver on

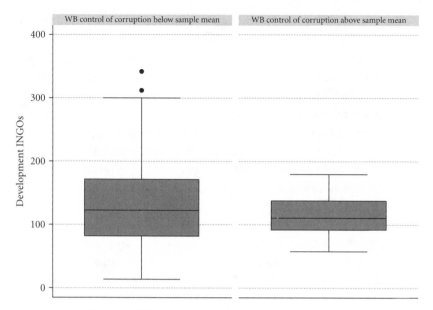

Figure 4.2 Distribution of development INGOs in corrupt and noncorrupt countries

human security service provision. In corrupt countries, however, as shown in Figure 4.1, the likelihood of the overall development INGO community having a positive impact on development outcomes is slight. In fact, if corruption is bad enough, more development INGOs can actually harm service provision in a state.

As a "reality check," some qualitative examples might help provide some context for this quantitative finding. Let's compare the cases of Burkina Faso and Nigeria, two developing countries in West Africa, in the early 2000s. Neither one is extremely wealthy. The GDP per capita in Nigeria was slightly higher than the GDP per capita of Burkina Faso in 2000. Nigeria is larger and has access to the Atlantic Ocean, something landlocked Burkina Faso does not have. Neither country was a consolidated democracy in 2000, but Nigeria started off the decade as much more democratic than Burkina Faso and has continued to fall right on the cusp of the common cut-point for democracy, according to the revised consolidated polity index (Marshall and Jaggers 2010). Armed conflict in either country is relatively rare. Nigeria did have a minor conflict in its borders in 1996, according to the UCDP/PRIO Armed Conflict dataset, but neither country had any other conflicts after this.

Both Burkina Faso and Nigeria have established service INGO sectors. According to the data from Smith and Wiest (2012), coded from the *Yearbook of International Organizations*, Burkina Faso had 142 sustainable development INGOs with volunteer/members active within its borders in 2000. Nigeria had 219. Even adjusted for population size, Nigeria still had a stronger sustainable development INGO sector than Burkina Faso.

Given these figures, it could easily be anticipated that Nigeria will be the state with the better provision of human security outcomes. It is larger, slightly wealthier, and slightly more democratic, and it has a larger sustainable development INGO sector. By all accounts, these factors should make access to potable water almost a given in Nigeria. We could expect the background characteristics to provide some basic level of access to potable water and then expect this established INGO sector to improve this human security outcome in a very concrete way in Nigeria. Burkina Faso should have a population with a similar, albeit slightly lower, access to potable water, since it has the smaller development INGO sector.

However, as my argument contends, this conclusion about the relative human security goods provision in Burkina Faso and Nigeria would require us to assume that all sustainable development INGOs were actually motivated to provide services that aid the domestic population. If that was the case, then a higher number of organizations, all else being equal, should equate to more goods provision. In actuality, however, this conclusion is far from accurate: although Nigeria started the 1990s with slightly better access to potable water, by 2003, this pattern had reversed, and Burkina Faso's access to potable water is now more than 20 percentage points higher than Nigeria's access to potable water.

What explains the success of Burkina Faso in terms of this human security outcome and the relative failure of Nigeria on this outcome? Instead of all INGOs having the same motivations to provide human security goods, I contend that some organizations want to simply rent-seek and will use donations to line their own pockets. In countries with higher levels of corruption, we should expect more INGOs to behave in this corrupt manner. This idea is important to understanding the limitations of the INGO sector in Nigeria and the relative success of the INGO sector in Burkina Faso. Although these countries look similar in many regards, when it comes to corruption, Nigeria definitely has a pattern of being much more fraudulent. On the World Bank scale of corruption control used in the statistical analysis, Nigeria is among the lowest

20 percent of countries in terms of controlling corruption; Burkina Faso is in the top 20 percent.

Accounts of the corruption in Nigeria are widespread and permeate every aspect of society. Former secretary of state Colin Powell famously remarked that the country is a "nation of scammers" (as quoted in French 1995; Glickman 2005; and Hagher 2011). Of course, many throughout the world can attest to the corruption in Nigeria's business practices; the common practice of "advanced fee" email or letter scamming has been so commonly associated with Nigeria that it is often talked about as a "419" scam, referring to the Nigerian criminal code number 419, against "impersonating officials for financial gain" (Glickman 2005, 461).

Stories of government corruption are also widespread in Nigeria. In 2006, Alex Last of the BBC wrote that government corruption, even corruption among low-level bureaucrats and police officers, was so widespread that it was "visible on the street." Even the president of Nigeria from 1999 to 2007, who ran on an anticorruption campaign in 1999, has had members of his staff accused of corruption (Falola and Heaton 2008; Ojukwu and Shopeju 2010). Many stories abound of his corrupt practices, including awarding "[US$]2.2 [billion] worth of Nigerian energy contracts . . . without a bidding process" (BBC, "Nigerian Deals 'Wasted Billions,'" March 14, 2008). Public perception of government corruption in Nigeria continues to rise; according to Gallup surveys taken between July and August 2011, 94 percent of citizens in Nigeria think that "corruption [is] widespread throughout the government" of Nigeria (Crabtree 2012).

Perhaps because of the corruption in the business and government sectors, it is no wonder that accounts of corruption among domestic and international NGOs in Nigeria are so prevalent. Anthropologist Daniel Jordan Smith has written extensively on this, both in his 2008 book, *A Culture of Corruption: Everyday Deception and Popular Discontent in Nigeria*, and in a series of articles. Smith contends that development NGOs are a "common cover for some of the most venal forms of corruption" (88) and that corruption among "Nigerians running development NGOs" has been refined to an "art form" (89). He relays many stories of corrupt organizations and individual members of organizations, including cases of "PONGOs (short for post office box NGOs) [and] "E-NGOs" (short for email NGOs)" (Smith 2010, 250–251). The cases are not unique to just development organizations; later work by Smith (2012) also highlights the same sad tales in the HIV/AIDs sector, where leaders of NGOs often took international donor funds and used them to purchase extravagant cars, homes, and "chieftancy titles" (478). Although many of the cases in Smith's work are of organizations that could be thought of as domestic, they are taking international donations and responding to international calls for aid; it is likely that similar patterns exist among organizations involved in multiple countries, which Smith (2008) calls as "complicit" in even the local-level corruption (88). Thus, even though there are many INGOs in Nigeria, as Smith (2008) put it, "a large proportion of the NGO sector in Nigeria, however, was created solely in response to the awareness that donor monies were available" (102). If these organizations are supported, they will not likely use the funds to increase access to potable water. If corruption becomes a significant problem, the donor community is unlikely to provide support to the general INGO community without some sort of signal that the organizations they are supporting are going to be those motivated to actually help the domestic population.

Contrast the dire situation in Nigeria with the case of Burkina Faso. As mentioned, corruption in Burkina Faso is not as rampant, although it does exist and did briefly increase in the latter years of the first decade of the twenty-first century. Accounts of corruption in the local governmental sector and in the business sector in Burkina Faso are the most prevalent. For example, in January 2012, the head of the customs service in the country was arrested with €3 million packed in suitcases (Africa Research Bulletin 2012). According to researchers at the Afrobarometer, in 2008, the majority of individuals thought that only "some" or "none" of various government officials were involved in corruption. However, almost half reported having to pay a bribe at some point in the past year.

Among NGOs, however, widespread evidence of corruption in Burkina Faso just does not exist. To the best of my knowledge, there are not any scholarly or journalistic accounts of corruption in NGOs in Burkina Faso. In fact, most of the literature that does exist concerning corruption and NGOs in Burkina Faso actually chronicles the work that both domestic and international NGOs have taken to aid in recent government crackdowns of corruption in the country. Both Amnesty International and the National Democratic Institute have worked with other NGOs in the state on anticorruption efforts (AI 2009b; NDI 2012). The organization National Network of Fight Against Corruption (Réseau National de Lutte Anti-Corruption, or REN-LAC) has been among the most active critics of corruption in the country; its work has been highlighted in US State Department and Freedom House reports (USDoS 2007; FH 2011). In short, corruption, although still problematic in Burkina Faso, permeates society at a much lower level in Nigeria. This is likely reflected in the lower number of corrupt INGOs in Burkina Faso.

The cases of Burkina Faso and Nigeria illustrate that the effect of INGOs on human security outcomes is not just a "more means more" situation. INGOs do not all share the same motivations to help a domestic population. Some INGOs that are supposed to be motivated to help provide human security services to a developing country's population actually are motivated by private greed. If a country is likely to have its INGOs sector full of these corrupt "types," like in Nigeria, it is likely that the whole sector will not be effective at improving human security. As this proportion of corruption INGOs decreases, like in Burkina Faso, it is more likely that service INGOs will actually be successful at providing human security outcomes, as is the case with access to potable water.

Beyond the focus on domestic levels of corruption, are there other domestic characteristic or political structures that make it less likely for rent-seekers to flourish? In a series of robustness checks,[9] I examined various additional domestic conditions and political structures that could also be associated with an increase in the proportion of rent-seeking service INGOs active within a country. In particular, I focused on interactions of development INGOs with (a) the revised consolidated polity score, (b) the World Bank's political stability indicator, (c) the World Bank's indicator for voice and accountability, (d) the World Bank's indicator for regulatory quality, (e) a similar indicator for political fragmentation (Kaufmann et al. 2009), and (f) Cheibub, Gandhi, and Vreeland's (2009) measure of regime type. All of these indicators reflect additional political structures and conditions that could be thought of as also reflecting controls on the proportion of rent-seeking organizations within a country. For example, a country with a democratic political structure or much voice and accountability for citizens would have a domestic population that might serve as whistle-blowers to corrupt INGOs.

Worth noting, within the sample of developing countries used here, the correlation between regime type, as measured by the revised consolidated polity index, and the previously used control of corruption measure, which is still included as a necessary control, is less than 0.10. Similarly, Cheibub, Gandhi, and Vreeland's (2009) measure of regime type is only correlated with the control of corruption measure at 0.14. For the World Bank's various measures, no measure is correlated with the control of corruption measure at over 0.58, all of this indicating that these additional measures are capturing conceptually distinct domestic political structures and conditions. In short, these measures are a good way to reinforce how domestic political conditions can influence development INGO success. As I argue here, these conditions are important because they reflect ways in which the proportion of rent-seeking INGOs may vary across countries.

The results of these robustness checks all reinforce the main point from the control of corruption model: when domestic political structures are such that (a) citizens have a voice to combat corruption or (b) domestic political structures have checks that limit corruption, it is more likely that development INGOs will be successful in improving human security. For all variables except for the political fragmentation indicator, the domestic political conditions and structures outlined above interact with development INGOs to influence human security. This makes much theoretical sense: political fragmentation, although an interesting domestic condition that could influence the work of INGOs, is not necessarily connected to the concept I am trying to capture: the domestic structures that limit nonprincipled INGO behavior. For the other indicators, however, these measures reflect checks on rent-seeking writ large and conditions where citizens can voice their concerns about rent-seeking. In other words, when domestic structures and conditions limit the propensity of rent-seeking by INGOs, it is more likely that development INGOs will improve access to potable water.

As an added check on the results presented here, I also focused on whether the interaction between control of corruption and development INGOs continues to hold in nondemocracies. In short, it does. Even in dictatorships, development INGOs can continue to have a positive influence on potable water when corruption is controlled. Looking between various types of dictatorships, this result appears to be driven by military dictatorships. In other words, the interactive relationship between control of corruption and development INGOs continues to hold in dictatorships, mostly driven by the strength of the relationship in military dictatorships. This finding actually follows much research on rent-seeking in authoritarian regimes: in general, as Chang and Golden (2010) point out, military dictatorships are less likely to be corrupt when compared to other types of authoritarian regimes. If military dictatorships are not prone to overall corruption, it makes sense that, within regimes that are military dictatorships, development INGOs would be most effective when corruption is sufficiently controlled.[10]

So what does all of this mean? First, the results presented here support Hypothesis 1: service INGOs are more likely to have a positive influence on human security service outcomes as corruption becomes controlled. Although this seems like a pretty straightforward finding, it stresses a real limit in the ability of the whole of the service INGO sector to provide services where they are needed the most. Once we acknowledge that not all INGOs are motivated primarily by shared values or principles to help a domestic population with what it wants but is not able to achieve on its own, we can then examine situations where nonprincipled organizations are likely to flourish, like in corrupt countries. Given this, aid programs designed to bypass corrupt governments in favor of funding to INGOs must be extremely careful in their administration (Dietrich 2013). If not carefully designed to only or predominately support organizations that have sent signals of their underlying non-rent-seeking motivations, supporting INGOs in corrupt countries will not lead to actual service provision. Instead, it is likely that support will go to INGOs just as corrupt as the government that was bypassed. These results highlight the need to relax the assumption that all INGOs have similar motivations and would support efforts by the INGO community to control and monitor rent-seeking INGOs, especially in states with little overall control of corruption (Ben Attia 2004).

Despite this somber situation, the results here also support the idea that service INGOs, in states where corruption is controlled, can actually be powerful conduits for service provision. As a greater percentage of INGOs active within a state actually have motivations to use their donor funds for service provision, service INGOs can provide services that governments have not been able to, ultimately improving human security.

2. The Impact of Development INGOs Is Conditional on the Number of INGOs Belonging to Voluntary Accountability Programs

The above results concerning how the impact of the overall INGO sector is conditional to a country's level of corruption could be somewhat disappointing for human security supporters. In the worst of the worst cases, where corruption is widespread, we cannot depend on the service INGO sector to provide services. Too many of them will be too busy lining their own pockets. In such a situation, what can the "good guys," the principled organizations, do? Is there still a silver lining? Remember again that Service INGO Hypothesis 2, if supported, concerns a bit of good news for human security: there is likely to be an impact of service INGOs on service delivery human security outcomes when more service INGOs have signaled their underlying motivations. This result should hold even in countries with widespread corruption and even when I pay attention to self-selection dynamics.

To test this hypothesis, I first needed data on the number of development INGOs that have signaled their underlying motivations as a non-rent-seeker. For this, I use newly coded data on the number of development INGOs with consultative status in the United Nations Economic and Social Council (ECOSOC). To code this data, I use the *Yearbook of International Organizations* myself and tried to utilize a similar coding procedure as Smith and Wiest (2005) and Smith and Wiest (2012) but relied on both the *Yearbook* online during the fall of 2008 and the hard copies of the *Yearbook*. As mentioned in Chapter 3, UN ECOSOC is arguably one of the most well-known and prominent signals that an INGO can send and has resonance both with the domestic and the international communities.

As mentioned, principled service INGOs are more likely to send signals of their underlying motivations in "easy" states, where they a priori expect a higher outcome. Thus, empirically, testing this hypothesis requires the use of a simultaneous equations approach, where the first stage predicts the number of development INGOs that have sent these signals and the second stage then focuses on the impact of these INGOs on the policy and behavior outcomes in question.

To statistically model this, I run a two-stage least squares regression with robust standard errors, clustered on country, and a lagged dependent variable. The first stage-dependent variable is the newly coded data on the number of development INGOs with consultative status. The second stage-dependent variable is access to an improved water source. The two-stage approach lets me utilize a version of the key independent variable (number of development INGOs with consultative status) that has been corrected for self-selection in the second stage.

To use this two-stage model, however, I need variables to include in the first stage model that can be argued to matter for the number of development INGOs with consultative status active within a country but are exogenous to the second stage-dependent variable of access to an improved water source. These variables, referred to as *instruments*, help correct for the self-selection in the key independent variable in the second stage. For instruments, then, first I draw on sociology literature and use the natural log of tourism arrivals to the country (Boli and Thomas 1999; Zinnes and Bell 2002; Tsutsui and Wotipka 2004; WDI 2012). This variable captures the idea that countries with more tourists generally have more INGOs involved within them and are places where INGOs are simply more likely to flourish (Boli and Thomas 1999; Zinnes and Bell 2002; Tsutsui and Wotipka 2004; WDI 2008). Second, consistent with the argument that INGOs are more likely to enter into these programs in "easy" states, I need a variable that captures the assured nature of an "easy" effect on the development outcome and yet is still properly exogenous. For this, I use the previous year's change in access to an improved water source. In using this variable as an instrument, I am capturing something that, theoretically, might make a higher outcome the next year more likely in the calculations of the INGO and thus might make the INGO more likely to signal its underlying motivations. Importantly, both of these variables are statistically established to be properly exogenous to the current year's access to an improved water source (Dhrymes 1994; Wooldridge 2006).

In addition to the controls outlined in the previous section, I include a control for the number of development INGOs that do not have consultative status that are active within the country. I also run models both with and without the control for corruption indicator discussed above. The inclusion of these variables does not change the statistical results.

What do the results of this test imply? In general, as shown in the table in the chapter appendix, when I focus only on the organizations that have sent a signal of their underlying non-rent-seeking motivations through registering with UN ECOSOC and account for issues of self-selection, I find that these organizations do have a positive and statistically significant effect on access to an improved water source. Importantly, this result holds even if I restrict the sample of only corrupt countries, defined here as those below the sample median World Bank control of corruption indicator provided above.[11]

This result should be a silver lining for the results provided for Hypothesis 1. Once we relax the assumption that all INGOs share the same principled motivations, it is easy to see that not all situations will be ones where the whole of the INGO community will have a positive impact. Some countries will have a higher proportion of organizations that are not principled, limiting the overall human security effect. In certain scenarios, the situation is so dire, with the proportion of nonprincipled organizations being so high, that the overall human security effect of service INGOs could be actually negative, as was shown in the previous results.

However, service INGOs can send signals of their underlying motivations and, as the service INGO formal model showed, service INGOs with principled motivations often signal these motivations, gaining the support of the international and domestic communities. When we only focus on these organizations, their positive impact on human security outcomes is quite clear. As predicted by the theoretical model, though, there is self-selection of INGOs when they signal; in "easier" states, more development INGOs will signal their underlying motivations. Once this self-selection is accounted for, however, these organizations still have a significant impact on access to an improved water source in developing countries. When self-selection is accounted for, holding everything else at its mean value in the sample, the substantive effect of an increase from the 25th to the 75th percentile of the number of development INGOs with consultative status in the sample equates to over a 6 percent increase in the percent of the population with access to an improved water source (95% confidence interval from 5.49 to 6.50).[12] This effect is larger than is estimated to occur if GDP per capita within the country was to raise similarly from the 25th to the 75th percentile in the sample; that effect would only increase access to potable water by a little less than 1 percent (95% confidence interval from 0.89 to 0.98).

Also, the effect of service INGOs with UN ECOSOC status on access to potable water is not dependent on the levels of corruption within a country. I ran additional models, also available in the chapter appendix, where I divided the sample of countries into those that are not corrupt and those that are corrupt. The positive and statistically significant effect of service INGOs that have sent this separating signal continues to hold in both samples, reiterating the idea that principled INGOs are able to work in complex, corrupt environments and still produce measurable results.

The qualitative record on development INGOs and donor support provides a much-needed "reality check" of this quantitative finding. Donors often have to rely on signals of NGO motivations in corrupt countries and often only support organizations that have sent signals that they are not rent-seeking. In Smith's (2008) account of the problem of corruption in the Nigerian civil society sector, for example, he contends:

> Donors faced great challenges in figuring out which NGOs were legitimate institutions of civil society that might really contribute to democratic and development ideals and which were created simply to tap into the flow of international aid. (102)

Similarly, the United Kingdom's International Development Committee concluded that they should take NGO work on "principles and standards" into account when determining which NGOs to fund in disaster relief (UKIDC 2006).

Even in the case of the relatively corrupt country of Nigeria, there are examples of individual NGOs who have (a) signaled their underlying preferences through registration in UN ECOSOC, (b) received donor support, and (c) actually provided human security output in the state. For example, the organization Engender Health, which has had consultative status with UN ECOSOC since 1979, has been active in Nigeria since 1985. The organization focuses mainly on providing contraceptives and fistula repair, including training local doctors to treat and prevent fistulas that result from childbirth (Engender Health 2012). Likewise, the organization Leadership for Environment and Development (LEAD), a special member of UN ECOSOC since 2002, has been active in training leaders from Nigeria to carry out internationally funded programs on agricultural development, alternative energy sources, and microcredit programs, among others. Many other examples exist of the human security output of UN ECOSOC organizations in Nigeria, including the work of well-known organizations like CARE International and the Society for International Development and organizations that operate under the Medicus Mundi umbrella network.

Beyond the signal sent through registration in UN ECOSOC, there are many other possible signals that NGOs send to indicate their underlying motivations and separate themselves from corrupt organizations. Mary Kay Gugerty's (2009, 2010) work on NGO self-regulation in Africa provides several examples of this practice. Organizations, both domestic and international, often have created their own regulating bodies or "clubs" and require that certain information is reviewed before an NGO can have accreditation with this body. As Gugerty (2010) contends, many recent examples of this practice are "intended to distinguish high-quality NGOs from low-quality or illegitimate counterparts" (230). The umbrella organization in Lesotho that was referred to in this chapter's introduction, the Lesotho Council of Non-Governmental Organizations, is one example of this phenomenon. Although Gugerty (2010) places this body in the "relatively weak" category, it does require an application procedure where the funding and decision-making structure of any applicant organizations are reviewed.

Instead of just enumerating or discussing the growing existence of such programs, however, the results should here illustrate that these programs, as proxied by the signal of UN ECOSOC consultative status, actually do matter for human security outcomes. These organizations, because they have signaled their underlying motivations, are better able to get the support necessary to provide goods and services and, unlike their counterparts, actually use donor funds on service provision. In short, these results would support moves by the donor community to require some sort of costly signal of underlying motivation, like registration with UN ECOSOC, before offering their support to service INGOs. These results may also serve to show INGOs themselves that these signals, although costly, are important for their support and their overall impact related to human security. Although not all INGOs will matter for human security service provision in corrupt countries, those that signal their motivations through registering with UN ECOSOC can still be powerful conduits of services related to the freedom from want, regardless of the level of corruption within the state.

3. The Impact of Development INGOs Is Conditional on Support from the International Community

Beyond the issue of INGO motivations, the service INGO model predicted several things with respect to where and on what issues service INGOs will have the greatest impact. As an example, the third hypothesis of this chapter predicts that service INGOs will have a greater impact on human security service outcomes when support by the international community increases. Because the international community is likely to rely on signals sent by INGOs themselves, as mentioned above, these results should hold for the entire INGO sector and not be dependent on the level of corruption within a state.

To test this hypothesis, I again use access to potable water as the dependent variable in the statistical model. I create a key independent variable that is an interaction term between the number of development INGOs measure used in the model for the first hypothesis and a measure, in millions of constant US dollars, of the Official Development Assistance (ODA) from states that are in the Organization for Economic Cooperation and Development (OECD) to NGOs, mostly international by definition, in the particular developing country. The OECD is an organization of the richest, most developed countries that are likely aid providers to the developing world. Because it could easily be assumed that this aid is used to increase service provision from one year to the next, the ODA aid to NGOs variable is lagged one year in the statistical analysis.

The same modeling decisions and control variables used in the previous statistical models are included here. I also include a control for the natural log of overall bilateral ODA Aid; this is to account for any correlation between general ODA aid and either my key independent or dependent variables.

Results of this statistical model support my hypothesis.[13] Service INGOs do not operate in a vacuum and are not magicians; they need funds, typically from the international community, to carry out their service projects in ways that actually result in measurable outcomes for human security. Figure 4.3 provides a graphical representation of the findings for all countries in the sample. As shown on the far left of this figure, when INGOs are active in a country with no aid from the donor community, they may not have any measurable results. However, as ODA aid to the NGO community grows, as shown in Figure 4.3 as you move to the right on the x axis, the marginal effect of development INGOs on access to an improved water source quickly increases substantially. In the murky world of foreign aid, where much evidence points to very little measureable results (Easterly 2006, for example), the results here—that aid increases the marginal effect of development INGOs on human security outcomes—is pretty astounding. And for the reasons described above, the result continues to hold only if we look at corrupt countries. Tables where the sample of countries has been divided to those above and below the mean World Bank control of

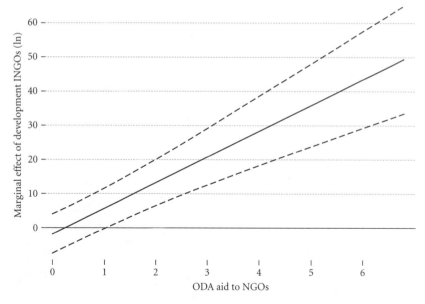

Figure 4.3 Marginal effects of development INGOs (ln) on access to improved water source as ODA aid to NGOs increases

corruption score are provided in the chapter appendix. If sustainable development INGOs receive necessary funding, they are successful at delivering measurable results for human security.

What about variations in funders? Are certain funders more likely to improve the success of development INGOs? In general, this is somewhat beyond the theoretical focus on this book. However, to the extent that (a) certain funders rely on signals more than others or (b) certain funders value potential high human security outcomes more, examining variations in the conditional influence of different countries' aid on development INGOs could be interesting. As a first step in this useful expansion of the framework developed here, I focused particularly on differences between two major donor states: the United States and the United Kingdom. These states have been the biggest aid providers in raw monetary amounts (Provost 2011; Dixon 2013). The states also have very different policies for INGOs and aid in general. At the onset, as Stroup and Murdie (2012) point out, the US government funnels a greater percentage of aid to the [I]NGO sector than the United Kingdom does. This, at the very onset, could mean that US monies may be subject to more potential for rent-seeking. Historically, Britain bureaucrats have also been more separated from INGOs than their US counterparts (Stroup 2012). This may make UK aid more likely to go to organizations that have had to provide rigorous signals of their principled motivations. Additionally, many have lamented that US aid in particular is likely to go to corrupt governments for geopolitical reasons (Alesina and Weder 1999). For these reasons, when comparing the interaction of US and UK aid with development INGOs, it follows that UK aid in particular will help improve human security outcomes. What does this robustness test show? As expected, I find that the overall amount of UK aid to a country interacts with development INGOs to improve human security outcomes. For US aid, however, I find no statistically significant relationship; although the coefficient on the interaction term is positive, it does not reach standard levels of statistical significance. In general, this result highlights a fruitful area of future research—differences among donor countries and their influence on development INGO outcomes—and all serves to reinforce the basic dynamics of the theoretical framework. International aid can be necessary for the work of service INGOs but, if not going to principled organizations, can be wasted in the struggle to improve human security.

Do these results hold up to reality? The results, although they speak of the potential of service INGOs when adequately funded, also stress some real limitations to the INGO sector. First, at times, INGOs themselves have high-lighted how their biggest strength comes from the fact that they are separate from state apparatuses (Edwards and Hulme 1996; Clark et al. 2006). Even though this might be the case in much of their decision-making structure, to the extent that INGOs get their funding from state actors—or to the extent that nonstate or private donors follow the same patterns of states in aid alloca-tion to NGOs—INGO success is still dependent on a few donor countries. If INGOs are somewhat beholden to state interests when it comes to public fund-ing to NGOs, then changes in state funding patterns or constrictions on NGO-earmarked aid will definitely harm the work of the INGO sector. As Clark and colleagues (2006) point out, this was definitely a problem for women's rights groups, even in the area of development:

> The most prominent supporters of women's rights groups have traditionally been development aid agencies, large independent foundations and public foundations. . . . Bilateral and multilateral aid agencies that were once strong supporters of women's rights organizations are cutting back their levels of funding for women's organizations and are directing more funds through na-tional governments rather than to NGOs. (2)

Clark and colleagues cite many reasons for the decrease in women's funds, in-cluding "few successes on the ground" in the eyes of the donors and "grow-ing conservatism within many donor countries" (2). In short, if dependent on public funding, women's rights organizations faced funding constrictions due simply to changes in donor priorities, some of which may have been driven by a perceived lack of progress.

Similarly, if an INGO is beholden to private endowments or donations and does not have many reserves, changes in private donation patterns can also influence their work. This was definitely the case for both domestic and in-ternational NGOs during and immediately after the 2008 constriction of the economic markets. For example, as the *Times* of South Africa quoted David Barnard of The Southern African NGO Network, "The substantiality of NGOs ultimately relies on other people's money. If people and businesses don't have money, NGOs suffer" (Evans 2009). Similarly, the organization OneWorld South Asia reported on how the economic downturn was affecting INGOs in early 2009; other media reports spoke of cutbacks in donations (IRIN 2008b; McCoy and Dorell 2008; Peters 2008). In an unpublished paper, however, Ma-tos (2009) reported that the recession was a "mixed blessing for NGOs," with some NGOs "receiving more volunteers" as a result of the recession. Thankfully, although some countries did restrict their ODA aid to the NGO sector in the immediate aftermath of the 2008 recession, including disbursements by Germany in 2010, Belgium in 2011, and Norway in 2010, among others, the total aid to the whole NGO sector by OECD countries did increase in the two years after the 2008 recession. As expected, however, there were some changes in how this aid was allocated, including a slight decrease in funds disbursed to NGOs for "basic drinking water supply and basic sanitation" from 2010 to 2011.

Worth mentioning, another potential problem related to INGO funding comes from too much economic growth. Zara Nicholson of the *Cape Times* in South Africa reported in 2012 that two organizations active in South Africa had to close their doors because the country "was no longer seen as being among the poorer countries." Additionally, the article mentions that donors, both public and private, were changing funding strategies. As one official from the NGO Molo Songololo, an organization specializing in children's rights, said, "Donors are moving their funds to poorer countries or countries in conflict. Corporates are also not easily giving money for things like the daily operational costs of an organization. They only fund certain projects" (Nicholson 2012).

A recent scholarly article by Büthe, Major, and Souza (2012) looks at the pattern of private aid allocation by 40 of the major INGO donors based in the United States—organizations that routinely aid other INGOs and NGOs in the field, like the US chapters of Oxfam and Doctors Without Borders. The study concludes that private aid by these organizations goes to the "neediest within the recipient countries" and is not influenced by country characteristics like corruption or media coverage (599).

Given these results and the anecdotes above, together with my findings on the necessity of donor aid for project success, a secondary question of concern both to human security advocates and INGOs may be as follows: which countries are most likely to receive ODA aid directed to the NGO community? Unfortunately, there is not a lot of academic literature on the topic. Dietrich (2013) is a notable exception, finding that any decision to bypass the state in favor of any nonstate development actor (multilateral, private, or NGO) is typically dependent on corruption and other problems with governance in the recipient state.

For ODA aid directed at the NGO community in particular, regardless of whether this is a decision to bypass the recipient government or just direct monies to NGOs in addition to the government, I ran an auxiliary statistical model on a sample of lower-income countries where the dependent variable was the amount of aid ODA countries gave to NGOs, as discussed above, and the independent variables were lagged measures of (a) GDP per capita, (b) access to an improved water source (c) regime type, (d) World Bank control of corruption, (e) all ODA aid, (f) the number of development INGOs, (g) tourism arrivals, (h) whether the country was a location of a major or minor armed conflict, and (i) the natural log of the total mentions of the country in Reuters Global News Service. Many of these variables were the same indicators discussed above. I include GDP per capita and access to an improved water source to account for whether NGO-earmarked aid is flowing to areas with the most need, as Büthe, Major, and Souza (2012) found with respect to private US INGO aid flows. I include the indicators for regime type and corruption control to test whether aid is being earmarked to NGOs because of worries about corruption or dictatorial cronyism in bilateral aid flows (Dietrich 2013). The indicator for overall ODA aid was to control for the amount of bilateral aid flow and the number of development INGOs was to, likewise, account for whether money was directed to those states with vibrant (or, conversely, nonexistent) civil society sectors. I include tourism arrivals to account for whether aid to NGOs was directed to states that are more popular destinations or tourists and volunteers, as discussed more in depth in Chapter 5, and include the control for conflict to account for whether, like some reports discussed above have mentioned, aid is routinely given to only countries in the midst of conflict. I follow Büthe, Major, and Souza (2012) in including an indicator of media coverage, here using an indicator from the international news source Reuters. The idea here would be to see whether ODA aid to NGOs is being driven by media attention.[14]

The results of this analysis on the same sample of country-years used in the baseline model for this section are provided in the chapter appendix and, on the whole, show a somewhat complimentary pattern for ODA aid to NGOs that the Büthe, Major, and Souza (2012) paper showed for private aid from large US-based INGOs.[15] First, while I find that the indicator for GDP is not statistically significant, the indicator for access to potable water is and the coefficient is negative, indicating that OECD countries give more money to NGOs in countries with lower access to this basic human security service. This is, like Büthe, Major, and Souza (2012) contend with respect to private aid by US-based INGOs, potential good news for human security and development outcomes. As a country drops from the mean score in the sample on access to an improved water source to one standard deviation below the mean, ceteris paribus, there is expected to be US$306,581 more (constant) for NGOs (95% confidence interval from $58,498 to $562,900). Given that my results show that these funds have a latter effect on helping INGOs improve access to potable water, this type of targeted aid could be very beneficial. Like could be expected, I also find that more ODA aid to NGOs is likely in countries that are just receiving more ODA aid overall.

Although I find no distinguishable pattern with respect to control of corruption, I do find that the combined revised polity scale—the -10 to $+10$ indicator of a country's regime type—is positive and statistically significant, indicating that a more democratic country is going to get more ODA aid to NGOs. This is somewhat consistent with the underlying logic of Hypothesis 1 and the service INGO game-theoretic model implications: international donors are more likely to be willing to give more money to a country if they feel they are more likely to face an INGO that will use this money to provide services. Since democratic states are generally thought of as being more transparent and with a better functioning judiciary, that could be more willing to crack down on corruption among NGOs, it follows that more money should be given to these states. As a country moves from the mean score in the sample to one standard deviation above the mean holding all other variables to their means, there is an expected increase in ODA aid to NGOs of US$179,220 (95% confidence interval from $27,471 to $336,887). Again, this might sound like a small amount, but remember again that the above results indicated that small increases could have measurable effects on the percentage of a country's population that has access to potable water.

Unlike Büthe, Major, and Souza (2012), I find that media attention for a country makes more aid to NGO likely, reflecting the idea that some aid could be a result of the often mentioned "poverty porn," or vivid attention to the plight of those suffering (Buckley 2009). Academically, there is a large literature on how the "CNN effect" could drive foreign policy, often with mixed empirical results when the focus is on whether the media drives very costly military endeavors (Gilboa 2005; Robinson 2011). Here, however, I find that media coverage may drive comparatively minor foreign policy decisions, like the amount of funding to NGOs in a developing country. Even if this evidence of the "CNN effect" does not amount to "boots-on-the-ground," it is a substantial amount of funds; as the number of Reuters media reports about a developing state grows from its mean in the sample to one standard deviation above the mean, there is an expected increase in ODA aid to NGOs of US$309,069 (95% confidence interval from $9,134 to $607,884).

Taken together, the results presented here indicate that INGOs need funds for service delivery outcomes and that, at least for ODA aid to NGOs, these funds are going to those most in need. When supported, INGOs are able to produce measurable results in access to potable water. These results would support policy positions arguing for increasing aid to civil society actors for its developmental benefit.

4. The Impact of Development INGOs Is Conditional to Factors That Make It Easier for Domestic Populations to Work with Organizations

In states where it is less costly for the domestic population to interact with service INGOs, the effect of service INGOs on policy and behavior will be greater. This is the logic underlying Service INGO Hypothesis 4, which contends that the impact of development INGOs on development outcomes will be more likely in urbanizing states. This is not to say, of course, that travel in urban areas is necessarily a cakewalk; the logic underlying this hypothesis is just based on the idea that, on average, the costs of working with an INGO for a domestic population will be lower when the domestic population and the INGOs are in closer proximity. To the extent that INGOs often locate first in urban areas within a country, it can be more costly, in terms of lost time and transportation costs, for a nonurbanizing population to work with INGOs. This, it follows, lowers the necessary support INGOs receive from the domestic population, limiting their overall effect on human security outcomes.

This is a general hypothesis; it should apply even when we are focusing on all organizations, regardless of their signal sent. Any effect that the general INGO sector has should be conditional on the costs a domestic population faces to interact with service INGOs. Here, of course, I proxy that cost by the country's urbanization status. As such, to test this hypothesis, I again use an interaction term, this time between the number of development INGOs measure used above and a measure from the World Bank's World Development Indicators of a country's annual urbanization growth rate. I use the annual growth rate in a country's urban population because it is stationary and reflects the concept of interest; it captures the idea that if it is becoming easier for the domestic population to interact with INGOs in time t, the impact of development INGOs will be greater in time $t + 1$. I rely on similar control variables and modeling structures as were used before.

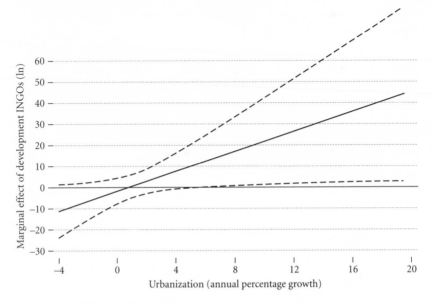

Figure 4.4 Marginal effects of development INGOs (ln) on access to improved water source as urban population (annual growth rate) changes

Figure 4.4 illustrates the results of this statistical model. Again, only in states with sufficiently high levels of urbanization growth rates do development INGOs have a positive and statistically significant marginal effect on access to potable water.[16] In states that are not urbanizing, where it could be argued that the costs of supporting development INGOs are greater simply because of travel costs from rural areas, there is no discernible effect of development INGOs on this human security outcome.

Do these findings hold up to a "reality check"? Although, as the graph shows, there is some statistical uncertainty over the actual size of this positive conditional effect, there is much anecdotal evidence that the majority of INGOs are located in urban areas within a country, even if this is not where the domestic need for human security service provision is. For example, in a 2010 article in Nepal's *Kathmandu Post* about the district of Dailekh in western Nepal, the paper reported that the "majority of the NGOs . . . are town centered" (Adhikari 2010). The article quoted development officials as saying that "donors prefer" the urban areas, even if it could lead to some redundancies. Similarly, a 2001 report by the INGO Aga Khan Foundation said that 70 percent of organizations in Pakistan were in the urban areas, not reflecting the "population that is 65 percent rural" (Baig 2001, 7). The report attributed the divide to "class structure" and "logistical difficulties, widespread illiteracy, limitations on women's mobility, and the tribal/feudal system that frowns upon efforts for social change" (7). In Tanzania, a 2003 UNAIDS project on HIV/AIDS service organization reported that a major problem for NGOs was that "most of the NGOs prefer to work in urban areas, and most of their programs and activities do not reach the rural areas and the rural areas are left behind in efforts against HIV/AIDS" (EANNASO 2003, 6).

This division between where INGOs are often located and where domestic populations often live can create difficulties in getting those most in need of the services access to the INGO's provisions. Some organizations, however, have taken important steps to help reach people in rural areas. To the extent that this practice increases, it would lessen the conditional statistical effect shown in Figure 4.4, albeit in ways consistent with the underlying logic of the hypothesis. In other words, because costs for the domestic community can limit their work with INGOs, some INGOs have already taken steps to lower these costs. For example, the Engender Health INGO, active in Nigeria and other parts of the developing world, worked with the Nigerian government to establish a mobile maternity clinic in an extreme rural part of northern Nigeria (2012). Likewise, the Canadian-based INGO Anderson Association (2012) established a clinic in rural Rwanda and explains:

> [It is] the only clinic easily accessible to local residents who are sorely in need of medical attention and do not have the time or money to travel to faraway clinics. Since there are no ambulances, or any other forms of transportation, without our assistance sick or pregnant individuals have to get themselves to the nearest clinic, a two-hour walk down the mountain before catching a public bus to the nearest medical facility.

In short, many organizations are operating in ways that limit the travel costs for domestic populations. As more organizations adopt similar practices, this conditional relationship might lose importance, perhaps improving overall service delivery.

To reiterate, however, the game-theoretic model finding that underlies this hypothesis was very general: as the cost of supporting the service INGO increases for the domestic community, it is less likely that the INGO will be able to provide noticeable outcomes related to human security. In the empirical implication I test here, I focused on travel costs for a rural population to interact with the more likely urban-based INGO. Another plausible proxy for these costs comes from examining any restrictions on association, movement, and other empowerment rights: if the government within a country increases the costs citizens face for moving within their state and working with organizations, it is likely that this will heighten the costs the domestic population would face for interacting with development INGOs. Thus, in states where these empowerment rights are not protected, it is less likely that development INGOs will get the domestic population support necessary for their success, lowering their overall impact on human security service outcomes.

This logic, which is an alternative way to proxy for the general idea of domestic costs, can serve as a robustness test for this hypothesis. In line with this, I run a statistical model similar to the rest of the models in this chapter where the key independent variable is an interaction term between the development INGO measure and the Cingranelli-Richards (2010) empowerment rights index. The Cingranelli-Richards (CIRI) empowerment index is a 0 to 14 measure of a government's respect for "foreign movement, domestic movement, freedom of speech, freedom of assembly and association, workers' rights, electoral self-determination, and freedom of religion" (4). A higher score on this index indicates more respect for these empowerment rights. The rights included are all the rights that, if protected, may make a domestic population more willing to support a service INGO they are interacting with simply because the domestic population does not fear government reprisal. For example, the freedom of domestic movement component of this indicator captures whether citizens of a country have "freedom to travel within their own country" (Cingranelli and Richards 2010, 5). The freedom of assembly and association captures whether citizens can "assemble freely and . . . associate with other persons in political parties, trade unions, cultural organizations, or other special-interest groups" (Cingranelli and Richards 2010, 4). Other rights on this index also represent rights that, if protected, could increase the general sentiment in the domestic population that working with service INGOs is not something that would incur reprisal by the government.[17]

Figure 4.5 provides the marginal effects of this test: as empowerment rights become more respected, development INGOs are more likely to have a positive and statistically significant effect on access to potable water.[18] When these rights are not protected, like in the far left-hand side of the figure, development INGOs will not have a positive effect on access to potable water; in fact, the effect could be negative overall. As protection for these rights increases, however,

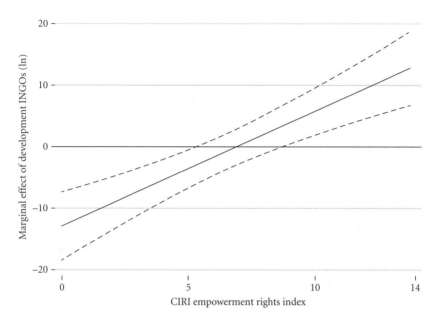

Figure 4.5 Marginal effects of development INGOs (ln) on access to improved water source as CIRI empowerment rights index changes

development INGOs are more likely to have a positive and statistically significant marginal effect on access to potable water, arguably because the domestic costs of supporting the INGO are diminished in these scenarios. What level of rights is necessary for this effect? As the graph shows, a positive marginal effect of development INGOs is unlikely to happen until the score on the CIRI empowerment rights index is around a 6. Within the sample of developing countries used in this chapter, the median index value is 7, indicating that many countries would be places where domestic populations are not unduly burdened in this way in their support of development INGOs.

These results, which serve as a robustness test to the results on how the effect of development INGOs is conditional to a country's urbanization status, are interesting in their own right in that they highlight the interconnected nature of the "freedom from want" and the "freedom from fear." If rights related to "freedom from fear" are not protected, as would be the case in a country with a low score on the CIRI empowerment index, development INGOs have a much more difficult time getting the domestic support necessary to make measurable improvements in "freedom from want" service provision, like access to potable water.

5. The Impact of Development INGOs Is Conditional to the Preexisting Value the Domestic Community Places on the Service Provision

The final hypothesis of this chapter concerns the value that the domestic community places on the services the INGO is providing. If, at the start of their interaction with the INGO, the domestic community greatly values the outcome that the domestic community is providing, it is more likely to support the service INGO, leading to a more likely effect on the ground. Conversely, if the domestic community sees little benefit in what the service INGO is trying to do, there are fewer scenarios where the domestic population would be willing to offer their costly support to the organization, limiting any overall improvement on human security outcomes.

On one hand, this hypothesis is very simple: service INGOs are more likely to be successful when the domestic community values what they are doing. If the domestic community sees little benefit from the service provided, the effort of the INGO will likely not be successful. On the other hand, however, this hypothesis concerns a very real constraint on the ability of organizations to enact drastic changes in the short run. If the preexisting value that the domestic community puts on what the service the INGO is providing is sufficiently low, the project in less likely to be successful. This hypothesis, of course, says nothing about the potential for a long-term program that is designed to first change preferences about the services that the INGO wants to provide and then designed to try to get domestic community support in supplying those services. This type of long-term scenario may be successful if the focus on service provision does not start until after domestic preferences have been changed. If started too soon, however, the hypothesis here would suggest that service provision will not make a measurable impact on human security outcomes.

At the very least, this hypothesis, if supported, would echo calls for domestic stakeholder buy-in in the projects that the organizations are working toward. This idea is not new; as Banks and Hulme (2012) point out, service INGOs have long been thought to be at an advantage in the development sector because of their "grassroots" connections to the populations they are working on behalf of. However, as the industry grew, donor pressure, according to Banks and Hulme, drove some organizations away from what their domestic clients wanted to do and toward projects that were related to the buzzwords that IGO and donor states were funding at the time. Banks and Hulme argue that many are now calling on INGOs to "reorient themselves with their grassroots-roots" (6). They believe that unlike the common view of INGOs as well-connected voices of the poor, the funding environment can cause organizational drift away from what domestic populations actually want:

> Contrary to popular perceptions, therefore, NGOs face significant difficulties tailoring programmes to local needs and realities, incentivized, instead, in a competitive and donor-driven funding environment, to formulate their strategies and policies in line with donor priorities and interests. (12)

To test this hypothesis, I need a dependent variable where a domestic community's preexisting utility for the service provision could be argued to vary. Ideally, I want a human security outcome that reflects a service provision that some domestic populations could be argued to desire, even before the presence of INGOs, while domestic populations in other countries could be argued to be less likely to have a preexisting desire for the service. I further need this service outcome to be something for which large-scale data across time and space exist and that are something many INGOs, across various countries, are actually working to provide.

Given these various constraints, I use the prevalence of contraceptives (birth control) use as my dependent variable in this model. This variable comes from the World Development Indicators (2012) and is a measure of "the percentage of women who are practicing, or whose sexual partners are practicing, any form of contraception. It is usually measured for married women ages 15–49 only." The variable is only available every few years for most of the countries in the sample but starts in 1980. I run models on only the post-1995 time period, including the variable for control of corruption, and on the full sample until 2003, the last year I have data on the key INGO variable. Results are substantively and statistically similar.[19] Birth control prevalence varies widely in the sample of developing countries used here; Mauritania had a birth control prevalence rate of less than 1 percent in 1981, while China, not surprisingly, had a prevalence rate above 90 percent in 1995. Other countries with very high birth control prevalence rates in the sample include Bulgaria and Iran, both with rates above 70 percent for certain years in the sample.

Many development INGOs provide contraceptives in the countries where they are working and see this as part of fulfilling their development mission. Sometimes birth control is seen as part of an INGO's efforts to reduce the spread of HIV/AIDS. Other times, it is seen as a way to improve infant health, help women stay in school and career training programs, and enter the workforce. For example, Ashley Judd, an American entertainer, wrote a 2009 editorial piece in *USA Today* as part of her role in the INGO Population Services International, where she heralded the many benefits of improving access to contraception:

> In my work around the world with [Population Services International] and our many partners, I have seen irrefutable evidence that unregulated fertility undermines every other effort to improve health, living standards, the economy, and the environment. Thus, empowering reproductive health is low-hanging fruit. In helping women and their families prevent unintended pregnancies and space out births, we improve outcomes in every area of human endeavor. (A11)

Some donors, both governments and private foundations, largely support INGO efforts to provide birth control and see it as part of the development mission. For example, Melinda Gates, co-chair of the Bill and Melinda Gates Foundation, arguably the largest private donor in the development arena, recently remarked that birth control access starts a "virtuous economic cycle" and that the Gates Foundation would be working to increase access to birth control in sub-Saharan Africa and South Asia (Smith 2012). Other donors, however, have been hesitant to support INGOs that are active in birth control services for mainly domestic partisan or ideological reasons. Some have restricted services only for INGOs providing or counseling in favor of abortion; other restrictions have been more widespread. For example, in 2003, President George W. Bush restricted INGO funding for birth control in sub-Saharan Africa; many contend that the restriction "contributed to Africa's epidemic population growth by undermining efforts to help women in some of the world's poorest countries exercise greater control over their fertility" (Bengali 2009).

Like variance in donor preferences for birth control funding, a domestic population's desire for birth control provision by INGOs appears to vary greatly over time and space. In some locations, there is evidence that the domestic population within a country desperately wants better access to birth control. For example, the INGO Women's Commission for Refugee Women and Children released a 2007 study entitled "We Want Birth Control: Reproductive Health Findings in Northern Uganda," where they reported on a series of interviews they had conducted with the population displaced by the most recent Ugandan conflict. From their interviews, the organization concluded that the Ugandan population wanted better access to contraception, saying that the "sexual and reproductive health needs of the displaced population have been largely overlooked" (2). Similarly, in Ghana, where maternal mortality has been declared a "national emergency," many organizations, like Marie Stopes International, have reported on widespread domestic need for contraceptive services (MoH 2011; Roth 2013).

On the other hand, in some countries and during some time periods, many have contended that the domestic population the INGO is working with does not want INGO birth control programs and that they are instead the result of donor initiatives. For example, in 1989, a local health worker in Peru wrote a poignant letter to the editor of the *New York Times* in 1989 in which she remarked, "We don't need birth control. We need to end our poverty. . . . At times, I view with sadness that many women bring their children with an injury or a burn to health centers that don't even have gauze or antiseptics but shelves filled with birth control pills" (Ccocllo 1989). Instead of a birth control service programs, the letter writer urged donors to "think about what we want and need," which she says includes "technical and economic assistance to make progress." Brown and Moore (2001) also write that sometimes these programs are unwanted and "clients would prefer food or income assistance" (508). A 2000 article in the *Economist* echoed this sentiment writ large: "Groups that carry out population or birth control projects are particularly controversial; some are paid to carry out sterilization programmes in the poor parts of the world, because donors in the rich world consider there are too many people there" (27).

Which populations are more likely to have a preexisting favorability for INGO birth control services? Consistent with literature on contraceptive prevalence rates in married women of childbearing age, women who already work outside the home are more likely to want access to contraception (Bankole and Singh 1998; Bawah et al. 2005; WDI 2008). Therefore, in states where the existing percentage of women in the labor force is greater, the future effect of development INGOs on contraception prevalence should be greater.[20]

To test this argument, my key independent variable is an interaction term between the number of development INGOs measure used in this chapter and the percent of female labor force participation from the World Development Indicators (2012). Consistent with the literature, I include additional controls for Latin America and sub-Sahara Africa locations; it is argued that countries in these regions have less contraceptive prevalence due to cultural or historical reasons (Bankole and Singh 1998).

What do these results indicate?[21] As shown in Figure 4.6, as the percentage of females in the workforce increases, it becomes more likely that development

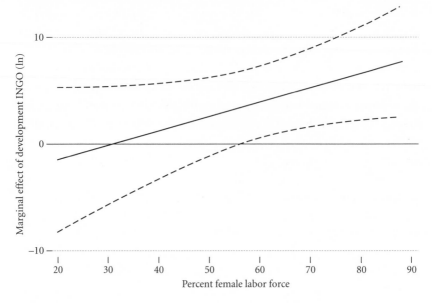

Figure 4.6 Marginal effects of development INGOs (ln) on contraceptive rate as percent female labor force changes

INGOs will have a positive marginal effect on the contraceptive rate in a country. This result holds both in the larger sample of all available country-years from 1980 to 2003 and in the more restricted post-1995 sample that all accounts for a country's control of corruption.

This finding would support efforts by service INGOs to tailor their service provisions to reflect the desires of the domestic population where they are located; the likelihood of short-term success depends on making sure a domestic population values the services that are being provided. If not, service INGOs may first have to become advocates, trying to change the preexisting value that a domestic population puts on a particular good or service. This finding is consistent with earlier, nonformal work on issue salience: there must be some domestic buy-in in order for organizations to get the domestic support necessary for actual change in human security outcomes (Risse 2002).

This result would also highlight a potential problem with donor aid: although, as shown with the support for Hypothesis 4, donor aid is important for success on goods and services that are generally valued by the population where the INGO is working, if the donation is earmarked for services that are of little value to the domestic population, it is unlikely that the INGO will be successful. This presents somewhat of a problem for the INGOs themselves: aid is necessary, but it is often difficult to juggle donor demands and domestic stakeholder desires. Banks and Hulme (2012) contend that organizations must not rely on only a few donors who earmark aid for specific purposes and must "start taking participatory design and implementation seriously" with an eye toward grassroots support (14). When this is done, it is more likely that there will be measurable successes in a shorter time period.

CONCLUSION

Do service INGOs matter for human security outcomes related to the "freedom from want" in the developing world? Focusing on organizations with a development mission, as an important subset of service INGOs, the results of this chapter highlight the dramatic potential these organizations have for improving access to potable water, both a basic human right and a Millennium Development Goal of the United Nations (Nelson 2007). Because access to an improved water source is such a crucial component to improvements in health, well-being, and economic growth, the potential impact of development INGOs in developing countries could be argued to be a critical link in the development puzzle.

Nonetheless, the results here further show the conditional nature of the impact of development INGOs and, moreover, stress the need for our theoretical understanding of service INGOs to account for the existence of both principled and rent-seeking organizations. First, the overall effect of service INGOs can be dampened in areas where rent-seekers are allowed to flourish, as proxied by a country's overall corruption levels. Where corruption is not controlled, and, thus, where rent-seeking INGOs are more likely to flourish, development INGOs will have little effect on development outcomes. This result supports arguments for the importance of accountability for INGOs; these arguments come from both within the INGO community and within the theoretical literature (Brown and Moore 2001; Grant and Keohane 2005; HAI 2008).

Further, the results presented here serve as the first evidence of the effect of the signals that INGOs send on service outcomes and add to the cross-disciplinary theoretical literature on their utility by highlighting the factors which influence an organization's self-selection into these programs (Gibelman and Gelman 2001; Grant and Keohane 2005; Gugerty and Prakash 2010).

Additionally, the potential role the international community has in aiding development INGOs is shown in the results presented here. International community support to development INGOs may be an effective strategy for the fulfillment of Millennium Development Goals (Ahmed and Potter 2006; Nelson 2007).

Finally, the results here stress the need for development INGOs to work to limit the costs that domestic communities face for interacting with their organizations and, moreover, show the need for INGOs to structure their service provision to reflect the preferences of the domestic population. When these practical implications are utilized and, moreover, when development INGOs do not rent-seek, these organizations seem to deliver on their promises and aid in poverty relief and development in poor countries.

This chapter used a large dataset of development INGO activities and cross-national indicators of governance and development outcomes. Of course, there are downsides to such an approach, including the inability to get at many of the nuances in on-the-ground development INGO work. In reality, the results presented show that hypotheses are supported "on average" throughout the developing world. That said, as shown in the section above, the findings seem to be supported with anecdotal "reality checks" from many areas of the world, indicating that these dynamics appear at both the micro and the macro levels.

The findings in this chapter provide much support for the overall theoretical framework outlined in Chapter 3. As mentioned, however, the framework here only presents a very broad-based look at the basic tensions and dynamics underlying the service INGO world and how these tensions matter for human security outcomes. By no means is this theoretical framework supposed to be exhaustive about the particularities that explain any one situation. Instead, the theoretical framework is intended to represent a simplified view of the way service INGOs operate in a world where their motivations differ and are not common knowledge. Future work that focuses on additional divisions among the various key actors could be particularly useful at extending the theoretical logic. If certain international actors face significantly different costs and benefits for supporting service INGOs, understanding this variation could add to our overall understanding of when and where services will be provided that improve human security.

APPENDIX

Table 4.1 Impact of development INGOs on access to an improved water source, conditional on control of corruption

Variable	(1) *Access to an improved water source*
Interaction term of development INGOs (ln) and control of corruption score$_{t-1}$	11.22961*** (3.207)
Development INGOs (ln)$_{t-1}$	9.21968** (3.582)
Control of corruption$_{t-1}$	−49.04357*** (15.660)
Population (ln)$_{t-1}$	0.50871 (0.638)
Revised combined polity index$_{t-1}$	0.01183 (0.166)
GDP per capita (ln)$_{t-1}$	14.47769*** (1.042)
Constant	−67.94384*** (14.628)
Observations	515

NOTE: Newey-West standard errors (lag of 1) in parentheses.
$^*p < 0.1$, $^{**}p < 0.05$, $^{***}p < 0.01$.

Table 4.2 Impact of development INGOs with ECOSOC consultative status on access to an improved water source

Variable	(1) Access to an improved water source	(2) Access to an improved water source (corrupt countries)	(3) Access to an improved water source (noncorrupt countries)
Development INGOs with UN ECOSOC consultative status (instrumented)	0.81361*** (0.173)	0.60688*** (0.218)	0.55731*** (0.130)
Lagged access to an improved water source	0.94195*** (0.013)	0.95288*** (0.016)	0.98108*** (0.011)
Aid per capita (ln)	−0.04874 (0.198)	−0.29804 (0.234)	0.71857*** (0.242)
Control of corruption	−0.46229 (0.400)	−1.75079** (0.837)	0.07613 (0.454)
Development INGOs without consultative status (ln)	−6.30117*** (1.340)	−4.68324*** (1.580)	−5.81741*** (1.447)
Population (ln)	−1.80139*** (0.437)	−1.37924*** (0.518)	−0.69660*** (0.239)
GDP per capita (ln)	0.83208*** (0.291)	0.45292** (0.225)	0.46703* (0.280)
Revised combined polity index	−0.02559 (0.028)	0.07244** (0.037)	−0.07030** (0.029)
Constant	47.60153*** (10.237)	36.69209*** (12.841)	28.19821*** (6.930)
Observations	450	247	203
R^2	0.977	0.988	0.990

NOTE: Robust standard errors (clustered on country) in parentheses.
*$p < 0.1$, **$p < 0.05$, ***$p < 0.01$.

Table 4.3 Impact of development INGOs on access to an improved water source, conditional on ODA aid to NGOs

Variable	(1) Access to an improved water source	(2) Access to an improved water source (corrupt countries)	(3) Access to an improved water source (noncorrupt countries)
Interaction term of development INGOs and ODA aid to NGOs (committed)$_{t-1}$	7.51746*** (1.177)	6.98689*** (1.285)	6.85049*** (2.467)
Development INGOs (ln)$_{t-1}$	−1.69865 (2.064)	−3.62465 (2.238)	7.30503* (3.801)
ODA aid to NGOs (committed)$_{t-1}$	−38.28866*** (5.904)	−34.89451*** (6.303)	−35.94447*** (12.493)
Control of corruption$_{t-1}$	4.65474** (1.834)	10.88618** (4.570)	−4.27089 (3.398)
ODA aid (ln)$_{t-1}$	−0.50061 (0.970)	−2.01593* (1.198)	−0.38709 (1.579)
Population (ln)$_{t-1}$	0.93622 (0.689)	0.78368 (1.236)	−0.04930 (0.715)
Revised combined polity index$_{t-1}$	−0.01682 (0.168)	−0.27564 (0.245)	0.07064 (0.195)
GDP per capita (ln)$_{t-1}$	13.23916*** (1.089)	13.31475*** (1.411)	13.10648*** (1.593)
Constant	−12.38770 (10.831)	12.89087 (18.977)	−41.86522*** (13.742)
Observations	487	265	222

NOTE: Newey-West standard errors (lag of 1) in parentheses.
*$p < 0.1$, **$p < 0.05$, ***$p < 0.01$.

Table 4.4 Determinants of ODA aid to NGOs (committed)

	(1)
Variable	*ODA aid to NGOs (committed)*
GDP per capita (ln)$_{t-1}$	0.06483 (0.130)
Percent of population with access to improved water source$_{t-1}$	−0.01795** (0.007)
Revised combined polity index$_{t-1}$	0.03116** (0.013)
Control of corruption$_{t-1}$	−0.00581 (0.122)
ODA aid (ln) (committed)$_{t-1}$	0.18882*** (0.068)
Development INGOs (ln)$_{t-1}$	−0.28834 (0.337)
Tourism arrivals (ln)$_{t-1}$	0.08242 (0.090)
Conflict location$_{t-1}$	0.05162 (0.101)
Media coverage (ln)$_{t-1}$	0.18463** (0.092)
Constant	−1.20234 (1.233)
Observations	428
R^2	0.266

NOTE: Robust standard errors in parentheses; yearly fixed effects included (not shown).
*$p < 0.1$, **$p < 0.05$, ***$p < 0.01$.

Table 4.5 Impact of development INGOs on access to an improved water source, conditional on urban population growth (annual %)

Variable	*(1)* *Access to an improved water source*
Interaction term of development INGOs and urban population growth (annual %)$_{t-1}$	2.47236** (1.087)
Development INGOs (ln)$_{t-1}$	−2.37165 (3.096)
Urban population growth (annual %)$_{t-1}$	−13.13025*** (4.986)
Control of corruption$_{t-1}$	4.99263* (2.543)
Population (ln)$_{t-1}$	0.45870 (0.889)
Revised combined polity index$_{t-1}$	−0.13530 (0.231)
GDP per capita (ln)$_{t-1}$	11.89417*** (1.735)
Constant	8.71546 (14.813)
Observations	515

NOTE: Newey-West standard errors (lag of 1) in parentheses.
*$p < 0.1$, **$p < 0.05$, ***$p < 0.01$.

Table 4.6 Impact of development INGOs on access to an improved water source, conditional on empowerment rights

	(1)
Variable	*Access to an improved water source*
Interaction term of development INGOs and CIRI empowerment$_{t-1}$	1.86203*** (0.425)
CIRI empowerment$_{t-1}$	−9.72965*** (2.150)
Development INGOs (ln)$_{t-1}$	−12.92602*** (2.978)
Control of corruption$_{t-1}$	5.79858*** (1.942)
Population (ln)$_{t-1}$	0.13071 (0.770)
Revised combined polity index$_{t-1}$	0.44402** (0.197)
GDP per capita (ln)$_{t-1}$	13.67117*** (1.141)
Constant	55.56191** (21.896)
Observations	502

NOTE: Newey-West standard errors (lag of 1) in parentheses.
$^*p < 0.1$, $^{**}p < 0.05$, $^{***}p < 0.01$.

Table 4.7 Impact of development INGOs on contraceptive use rate, conditional on percent female labor force

Variable	(1) Contraceptive use rate
Interaction term of development INGOs and percent female labor force$_{t-1}$	0.13587** (0.066)
Development INGOs (ln)$_{t-1}$	−4.17744 (4.722)
Percent female labor force$_{t-1}$	−0.21458 (0.299)
Latin America	−7.67775** (3.869)
Sub-Saharan Africa	−26.01746*** (2.809)
Population (ln)	2.49824*** (0.934)
Revised combined polity index	0.06333 (0.192)
GDP per capita (ln)	13.78042*** (2.000)
Constant	−84.87404*** (25.073)
Observations	241

NOTE: Standard errors in parentheses.
$^*p < 0.1$, $^{**}p < 0.05$, $^{***}p < 0.01$.

5 INGOS AND HUMAN SECURITY ADVOCACY OUTCOMES
The Case of Human Rights

AT THE BEGINNING of the twenty-first century, no one, except perhaps the staunchest of regime supporters, would deny that the human rights situation in Colombia was abysmal. The South American country was riddled with accounts of government violations of physical integrity rights. For example, in 1999, Colombian armed forces, in the midst of a long-standing civil war with the FARC (Revolutionary Armed Forces of Colombia) and the National Liberation Army, carried out "selective killings of people considered to be guerrilla sympathizers or collaborators" (AI 2000, 1), while "police-backed" "death squads" were responsible for "social cleansing" killings of vulnerable populations. Although there were many atrocities attributed to paramilitary and opposition groups, "all parties" were responsible for violations. In the next few years in Colombia, things certainly got worse. In August 2002, a new head of state, Álvaro Uribe, took office, ushering in a new era of heightened and widespread killings, disappearances, kidnappings, and torture, often under the guise of the "war on terror."

On the typical scales used to measure human rights performance, the situation in Colombia for most of the 2000s continued to be among the worst in the world. Widespread violence against civilians was heightened, albeit typically perpetrated by rebel groups instead of the government. Government abuses under Uribe were also abundant, especially abuses by military forces under his command. In addition, Uribe was responsible for a tremendous increase in violations of privacy and association rights. Unlawful wiretapping was widespread, as was outright intimidation of human rights advocates. Uribe went as far as branding "human rights advocates in Colombia as terrorist sympathizers and has insinuated that illicit connections exist between human rights NGOs and illegal armed groups" (HRF 2005, 1).

As time marched firmly into the second decade of the 2000s, however, government protection of physical integrity rights in Colombia appear to be changing, remarkably, for the better. A new president, Juan Manuel Santos, was elected in August 2010, and since then, many have been observing how Colombia appears to be at a precipice for drastic human rights improvements. For example, the head of the Americas division of the human rights INGO Human Rights Watch, José Miguel Vivanco, reported in 2011 that "the country has improved its political climate, public debate, in all manner of things . . . in the subject of human rights" (quote in Peters 2011). Similarly, the US State Department (2012), in its annual report on the human rights situation in 2011, singled out Colombia as an exemplar of progress:

> In Colombia, the government worked to address the climate of impunity with respect to harassment, intimidation, and killings of human rights workers, journalists, teachers, and trade unionists. Extrajudicial killings declined in large measure due to efforts by the government to stop such crimes. (2)

The changes in Colombia, albeit impressive, are still just beginning. Some, including the human rights INGO Amnesty International, have remarked that the expressed "commitment" of the Colombian government has thus far produced "few tangible improvements in the overall human rights situation" (AI 2012, 1). Powerful paramilitary and guerilla groups still threaten violence against civilians, despite Santos's proposed changes. As Vivanco of Human Rights Watch remarked to the US House Ways and Means Committee in 2011:

> It is encouraging that the Santos government has stated its commitment to pursuing new strategies to address the threat posed by successor groups to paramilitaries. But these steps have not yet been fully implemented, and they face powerful opposition from the armed groups and their political supporters. And as these successor groups continue to operate throughout Colombia, levels of violence against trade unionists remain alarmingly high. (3)

In short, although far from a panacea for rights protection, Colombia, at the end of a civil war and with group violence still at high levels, appears to be making some improvements in government respect of physical integrity rights. These government changes have continued in the face of paramilitary and group opposition.

What explains the human rights trajectory of Colombia? Why is Colombia's government appearing to improve its human rights practices? Looking within the country, explanations appear mixed. For all of the 2000s, Colombia was technically a democracy. Its financial situation has not changed much, and it is not as globalized as its neighbors. Although the end of the Colombian civil war could definitely lessen abuses perpetrated by guerrilla groups and paramilitary forces, the tenuous security situation could have made Colombian governmental officials more willing to undertake repressive actions in the name of crushing possible descent. The poor, rural population lacks many of the tools through which to demand improvements in human rights themselves.

Given these ambiguous domestic conditions in Colombia, with very few changes in clear pathways for improvements in human rights, did actions by actors outside of the state influence the protection of human rights? The historical record shows very few actions by many conventional international actors directed at Colombia for primarily human rights purposes during the 2000s. There were no armed humanitarian interventions by state or intergovernmental actors; no sanctions were imposed with the purpose of improving human rights. Colombia did receive a free trade agreement with the United States in 2011, an event that many advocates used to bring attention to the Colombian situation.

One thing that did increase in Colombia during the 2000s was the amount of work by human rights organizations, both internally and internationally, that were concerned about the state. The work of organizations in Colombia was extremely dangerous during this time period; Uribe was accused of abuses against advocates; paramilitary groups also carried out violence (HRF 2005). Nonetheless, Colombia had 10 percent more human rights INGOs active within its borders in 2003 than its neighbors had; in the 2000s, human rights INGOs also publicly attacked the government of Colombia 40 percent more times than its neighbors. Perhaps it was due to its abysmal rights situations or perhaps to the attention Colombia had received from its long-standing civil war. Perhaps it was just the outcropping of a much more vibrant historical civil society sector in Colombia. Regardless of what explains the increased advocacy human rights INGO movement in Colombia, the work of the organizations during this heightened movement has been heralded for its impact on the human security "freedom from fear" situation in the state. Even back in the 1990s, the short-term successes of truth and reconciliation processes in Colombia were explained by the work of human rights NGOs:

In particular, Colombian NGOs have been especially effective in invoking international oversight mechanisms and procedures and in reinforcing their pronouncements on the ground. (Carrillo 2009, 149)

More recently, US State Department cables from 2005, leaked as part of the "Wikileaks" scandal, even highlighted how "human rights organizations in Colombia" were an "important part" of the effort for the "advancement of a strong democracy to improve the human rights situation" in the state (E.O. 12958).

Further, as the organization Fellowship of Reconsolidation (2010) reported:

After November 2008, the number of reported killings of civilians by the Colombian armed forces dropped precipitously, apparently due to an institutional decision to address the practice. In this respect, the work of human rights advocates in Colombia and the international community seems to have had a substantial and material impact. (9)

Even recent changes designed to reduce violence against human rights organizations in Colombia can be explained by advocacy by the organizations themselves. As Lisa Haugaard (2012), executive director of the Latin America Working Group Education Fund, remarked in testimony to the Tom Lantos Human Rights Commission of the US Congress in May of 2012:

Colombian human rights organizations, through an organized campaign on the right to defend rights, have awakened a greater acknowledgment in Colombian media and society about the role human rights defenders play. (14)

If human rights organizations, both international and domestic, have been crucial in the process of human rights improvements in Colombia in recent years, can the same be said of organizations elsewhere? What explains the conditional success of organizations in Colombia, and, moreover, under what conditions can INGOs aid in human security advocacy worldwide?

This chapter moves the empirical focus of the book from the conditional impact of human security INGOs on "freedom from want" service provision to the conditional impact of human security INGOs on advocacy related to the "freedom from fear." Focusing specifically on human rights advocacy INGOs, as the subcategory of human security INGOs that concentrate mainly on outcomes related to the "freedom from fear," this chapter explores whether, when, and where INGOs will have an influence on a variety of human rights outcomes.

The hypotheses about whether and when human rights INGOs will have an influence on human security outcomes are based on the advocacy INGO game-theoretic model presented in Chapter 3. As shown below, the large-scale empirical results, using novel measures of human rights INGO activities and accepted measures of human rights performance within countries over a large time span, provide much support for the framework presented here. Advocacy INGOs can be powerful actors for human rights, but their impact can vary by issue, state level characteristics, and international support.

The results presented here show that human rights INGOs are more likely to have an effect on issues where the domestic population and the international community—the community that some organizations are biased in favor of—are more in agreement about the utility or benefits of the likely advocacy outcome. This reflects the book's central mantra that not all INGOs are motivated to give a domestic population what it wants but has not been able to achieve on its own. On issues that are divisive for the domestic and international communities—for example, where the domestic community may not in fact want the outcome that some INGOs are advocating for—I find that the whole human rights INGO sector is likely to have little impact on actual outcomes. In short, at least in the immediate time period, the international biases of some organizations can spoil the likelihood of advocacy success for all.

Additional findings presented in this chapter reiterate how state-level vulnerabilities, accessibility to global advocacy actors, and international community support can condition advocacy success. In line with the central theme of the book, the empirical results also support the idea that INGOs that send signals of their motivational orientations are more likely to get the support of other actors who are critical to their work. This can ultimately have an impact on INGO success on even issues where both the international and domestic communities are more in agreement about the utility of the advocated outcome. In short, the results here suggest that advocacy INGOs can be influential actors for some human security advocacy outcomes but that organizations differ in their underlying motivations, a difference that can be reflected in the desires of the domestic and international communities that often work with the organizations. Understanding these dynamics can help organizations and donors structure their work in ways that could ultimately improve their success record.

The chapter is organized as follows. First, I concisely review the basic logic of the advocacy INGO game-theoretic model presented in Chapter 3 and the hypotheses that flow from the solution to this model. Then, I outline the research strategy utilized in this chapter, focusing on the ways in which I measure the dependent and independent variables necessary for hypothesis testing. After doing so, I present the large-scale empirical evidence and discuss the findings, providing whenever possible anecdotal support for the large-scale results.

Like before, the quantitative methodology undertaken here is somewhat novel for the study of INGOs and adds to our empirical knowledge about this type of international actor. In no way, however, is this methodology presented as the only or best way to examine the impact of advocacy INGOs; the global, quantitative approach is simply one way of examining the effects of INGOs that is useful as far as it overcomes biases inherent with selecting only successful INGO movements (Risse 2002). Whenever possible, I leave the statistical "nuts and bolts" to the chapter's appendix and focus in the text only on substantive findings and graphical representations of the statistical results.

EXPECTATIONS FOR ADVOCACY INGO CONDITIONAL EFFECTIVENESS

As discussed in Chapter 3, the advocacy INGO theoretical model results provide many interesting and testable implications. To briefly restate, the model is based around the idea that not all advocacy INGOs are motivated primarily by "shared values" with the domestic population. Instead of the traditional connotation of advocacy INGOs as principled actors working selflessly to help a repressed domestic population with what that population wants but has been unable to get for itself, the model allows for the idea that some organizations are motivated mainly by a private desire to advocate only for what their international donors and stakeholders desire. These organizations have a personal desire to obtain the international community's support and, because of this motivational structure, are willing to advocate for the extreme outcomes desired by the international donor community, even if these outcomes fly in the face of what the domestic population in that state actually wants. Therefore, in the advocacy world, there are both organizations that have the canonical motivations to help the domestic population with what it wants and organizations that are motivated mainly for personalistic reasons, in line with what their international donor community desires.

In this world, where one type of organization reflects the desires of the domestic community and another type reflects its bias in favor of the international community, an organization can send a signal of its motivational structure to the communities it interacts with. These communities—both domestic and international—can be critical in getting advocated changes in human rights practices but do not know for certain the motivational structure of the organization they are interacting with unless the INGO sends a separating signal. At the end of the day, the INGO's effect depends on the support the organization receives, together with the vulnerability of the state to advocacy pressure.

This model structure provides many testable implications concerning whether and under what conditions advocacy INGOs will be successful at improving human security advocacy outcomes. Chapter 3 concluded with outlining six testable hypotheses that flow from the theoretical framework. First, issue area matters: as Advocacy INGO Hypothesis 1 contends, the problems of internationally biased organizations are exacerbated on issues where the domestic and the international communities desire different advocated outcomes. On these divisive issues, it is less likely that the advocacy INGO will get the support of both the domestic and international communities, limiting any overall outcome on the issue at hand. Conversely, on less divisive issues, where the domestic and international communities, although having a different preference order, still place sufficient value on the outcomes that all types of INGOs are advocating for, it is more likely that advocacy INGOs will get the necessary support for measurable effects, even if the advocacy is on an issue of strategic importance to the state, like its ability to control its population through torture or political killings.

Within even the most nondivisive of issues, however, the model still provides some implications about when measurable effects are more likely. As Advocacy INGO Hypothesis 2 contends, advocacy INGOs are more likely to have an impact on human security advocacy outcomes in states that are vulnerable to a combination of internal and external pressures. Largely consistent with the existing Keck and Sikkink (1998) framework, as regime vulnerability increases, we should expect advocacy INGOs to be more successful.

Further, when we focus on nondivisive issues, where both the international and domestic communities sufficiently value even the advocacy of the organizations not consistent with their preference structure, the signals that INGOs send can be useful at getting the support of the community that would not support it otherwise. As such, Advocacy INGO Hypothesis 3 suggests that INGOs that send signals should be especially successful at achieving these more moderate, nondivisive advocated outcomes, even after accounting for the self-selection factors that would make advocacy INGOs more likely to send these signals in certain cases.

The theoretical model also contends that the success of advocacy INGOs will be more likely when the domestic community faces lower costs of working with advocacy INGOs. Given that advocacy organizations are often global and can work completely outside the state where they are advocating for changes, these costs would be less when a domestic population has more information and personal connections to the outside world, as outlined in Advocacy INGO Hypothesis 4.

Additionally, Advocacy INGO Hypothesis 5 contends that the international community's support should condition the advocacy INGOs' impact; the international community is only willing to support advocacy INGOs in situations where the organization is more likely to get an outcome the community greatly desires. This logic also implies, however, that the international community may be unwilling to support advocacy INGOs in states with a vibrant domestically grown NGO sector. Given that it would rather support organizations that share its preference order for advocated outcomes, international donors may shy away from supporting the INGO sector in states where they think they are less likely to face organizations that share their bias. This logic, which counters some of underlying enthusiasm of donor support for civil society growth, forms the basis of the final hypothesis, Hypothesis 6.

HUMAN SECURITY ADVOCACY OUTCOMES: WHAT OUTCOME TO FOCUS ON

To test Hypotheses 1 to 5, the necessary dependent variables must focus on advocacy outcomes consistent with "freedom from fear." In other words, the dependent variables used here must capture a variety of human rights outcomes that INGOs are often advocating on. Further, these outcomes, at least to test Hypothesis 1, must vary in their divisiveness. Specifically, for Hypothesis 1, I need a measure that represents a human rights outcome that could reasonably be considered nondivisive for the international and domestic communities that work with INGOs: although these communities may want something slightly different, both communities sufficiently value the outcomes that both domestically consistent and internationally biased types of INGOs are advocating for. This measure will then be used as the dependent variable to test Hypotheses 2 to 5. Also for Hypothesis 1, however, I need an additional measure of a human rights outcome that could be considered divisive. This measure must capture a human rights outcome where the preferences for the domestic and international communities could be argued to be divergent: what one community desires may not be what the other community wants as a result of the INGOs' work.

Many different outcomes could meet this baseline requirement. Human rights INGOs focus on a variety of different human rights outcomes—everything from improving prison conditions to lessening bullying among youths (UIA 2008/2009). Some focus mainly on improving human rights outcomes in a very small issue set; for example, multiple organizations focus mainly on improving the right to leisure among children. Other organizations, alternatively, focus, at least in their mission, on improving all human rights listed in the Universal Declaration of Human Rights, the nonbinding UN document that underlies much of the world's human rights regime (Welch 2001). Given that much human rights scholarship sees various types of human rights mutually reinforcing and connected, many human rights INGOs have taken a very all-encompassing view of human rights in their advocacy. As Nelson and Dorsey (2008) contend, the end of the Cold War marked a shift in many INGOs' strategies and mission focus; some development INGOs began to adopt a "rights-based" approach to development at the same time that many human rights INGOs began to expand both to economic, social, and cultural rights (ESC) and to focus on advocacy related to "new" rights, like "campaigns for essential medicines, right to water, and women's reproductive health rights" (20).

Nonetheless, both in practice and in mission, some organizations have focused, at least historically, on only a small subset of the rights that are nonderogable—that is, cannot be taken away in times of emergencies—in the binding UN International Covenant on Civil and Political Rights. These rights, including the right to life, freedom from torture, and freedom from the retroactive use of penal laws, cannot be suspended in times of national emergency (Hafner-Burton et al. 2011). All other human rights, including all rights in the UN International Covenant on Economic, Social, and Cultural Rights, can be suspended in a national emergency. The focus on this very limited set of rights, according to Kenneth Roth (2004), executive director of Human Rights Watch, is mainly one of strategy:

> Human Rights Watch's experience has led me to believe that there are certain types of ESC issues for which our methodology works well and others for which it does not. In my view, understanding this distinction is key for an international human rights organization such as Human Rights Watch to address ESC rights effectively. Other approaches may work for other types of human rights

groups, but organizations such as Human Rights Watch that rely foremost on shaming and the generation of public pressure to defend rights should remain attentive to this distinction. (64)

In other words, at least some prominent INGOs are focusing only on advocacy related to human rights where "there is relative clarity about the nature of the violation, violator, and remedy" (Roth 2004, 72). Further, as Roth points out, the outcomes of interest for this project should probably reflect government actions related to human rights practices, as human rights organizations, according to Roth, "are at our most effective when we can hold governmental (or, in some cases, non-governmental) conduct up to a disapproving public" (67).

In line with this discussion of both the diversity of issue area focus and the concentration of many organizations on strategies that focus on improvements in government human rights practices, I choose to focus on two mainstream issues for human rights INGOs: women's rights and physical integrity rights. I restrict my focus to these areas not to negate the "new" advocacy of some organizations but to choose issues that a large segment of the human rights INGO sector would be actively working on. Even Human Rights Watch, which Roth's piece makes clear restricts its focus to only a very small subset of rights, has a very active strategy related to women's rights. The organization's women's rights division began in 1990, the date used as the starting point for much of the empirical analysis in this chapter. A large subsection of human rights organizations listed in the *Yearbook of International Organizations*, the go-to source book for all things INGO, have mission statements that include reference to women's rights (UIA 2008/2009).

Physical integrity rights, defined as the rights of freedom from torture, political imprisonment, extrajudicial killing, and disappearances, reflects the other set of core rights that Roth and other human rights INGOs often focus on. These are the rights typically thought of as nonderogable. They meld well with Risse and Sikkink's (1999) conceptual focus on "rights of the person" in their groundbreaking study of the process through which human rights improvements occur, as discussed in Chapters 2 and 3 (2).

Further, both sets of human rights—physical integrity rights on one hand and women's rights on the other—give me some leverage over the necessary concept of divisiveness to the domestic and international communities. Although these sets of rights make up the core agenda of many human rights INGOs, it is reasonable to conclude that physical integrity rights are much less divisive for the international and domestic communities than women's rights. This simply means that women's rights are issues for which the domestic and international communities that support INGOs want very different advocacy outcomes, while physical integrity rights, ceteris paribus, is a less divisive issue for these communities. Unlike women's rights, where domestic populations, even female populations, may stress cultural or religious justifications for a restraint on full equality between sexes, there is less of this international-domestic tension with physical integrity rights, where comparatively less has been said and written concerning, for example, cultural rights justifications for torture or political killing. As Brems (1997) remarked concerning a subsegment of women's rights advocacy:

> For instance, in a culture where female circumcision is practiced, the prohibition of torture and cruel, inhuman, or degrading treatment (prohibited under Article 5 of the Universal Declaration of Human Rights and Article 7 of the International Covenant on Civil and Political Rights) may be completely accepted, while the classification of female circumcision as such treatment is rejected. (144)

The remark is similar to Sundstrom's (2005, 2006) work concerning the limited domestic support that INGO advocacy related to the divisive issue of gender equality had in Russia in the 1990s in relation to less-divisive issues, like advocacy against conscription. Sundstrom's (2005) work also points out, however, that some women's rights issues were less controversial among the Russian domestic public than others, including work against domestic violence. Nonetheless, on the whole, physical integrity rights seems to be a broad advocacy issue where domestic-international divisiveness is not as present as in the broad issue of advocacy related to women's rights outcomes.

This logic, although perhaps controversial for advocates, comes straight from historic debates concerning the relative influence of cultural relativity and universality in the application of the Universal Declaration of Human Rights (Donnelly 1984; Baehr 2000). Mayer (1995) states, "There are two basic positions that one can take on women's human rights: the universality and the cultural relativist" (176). The international universality position contends that "the international community has the right to judge, by reference to international standards, the ways states treat their own citizens," while the cultural relativist position "argues that members of one society may not legitimately condemn the practices of societies with different traditions" (176).

Now, to note, many human rights INGOs take the position that advocacy for women's rights has to be culturally sensitive and in tune with the existing positions of the population it is trying to help (Abu-Lughod 2002; Ayotte and Husain 2005). Other INGOs, however—consistent with the underlying tension in this book—more squarely take the position that international norms and desires, if divergent from domestic preferences, should dominate their advocacy work (Clark et al. 2006). In line with Sundstrom (2005, 2006) and my Advocacy INGO Hypothesis 1, this approach could limit overall advocacy success. This is not to say that domestic preferences for women's rights cannot become more in line with international norms but that this process is a long-term endeavor and would require successful framing of an issue as one consistent with the desires of the domestic population that the INGO is working on behalf of.

Given this use of both government actions related to women's rights outcomes as an issue that is comparatively more divisive for the international and domestic communities writ large and government actions related to physical integrity rights outcomes as an issue that is comparatively less divisive, the question now is what types of outcomes related to this issue should we focus on? Here, I focus on human rights *de facto* instead of human rights *de jure*: I do not focus on treaty adherence but instead on actual practices within the state. Much has been written concerning the limitations of the UN treaty system (Hathaway 2002; Hafner-Burton and Tsutsui 2005; Vreeland 2008; Simmons 2009). Many countries sign treaties as mere "window dressing" (Hafner-Burton and Tsutsui 2005), and a large segment of treaty scholars contend that the system is not set up to be easily translated into changes in human rights practices. Although treaty ratification could be a step in a longer process that does in fact bring about changes in practices on the ground, for this project, I focus only on actual practices on the ground. This allows me to avoid capturing only "tactical concessions" made to advocates on paper that a regime does not implement in practice and provides a more difficult test of INGO effectiveness.

Therefore, I utilize as my dependent variables on human rights outcomes measures that come from the Cingranelli-Richards Human Rights Dataset. The nice thing about this data set for the purposes of this project is that it (a) focuses on government practices as opposed to just overall human rights conditions, (b) mainly captures de facto as opposed to de jure rights, and (c) includes measures for both physical integrity rights and women's rights. For physical integrity rights, I use the Cingranelli and Richards (2010) physical integrity index, which is a compilation of scores relating to "torture, extrajudicial killing, political imprisonment, and disappearance" (Cingranelli and Richards 2010, 3). The scores of this index range from 0 to 8, with 0 indicating no governmental respect of physical integrity and 8 indicating full governmental respect for these rights.

For women's rights, I use three separate indices for women's rights in the Cingranelli and Richards (2010) data set: women's political rights, women's social rights, and women's economic rights. All of these measures vary from 0 to 3; a higher score on these indices indicate that the rights were better protected. One thing to note here: for the women's rights variables in the data set, reflecting the idea that government protection of women's rights issues requires both government actions and legal protections, a top score on these indices reflect whether the rights are "guaranteed by law and the government fully and vigorously enforced these laws in practice" (Cingranelli and Richards 2010, 7). The measure of women's political rights captures "the rights to vote, run for political office, hold elected and appointed government positions, join political parties, and petition government officials" (7). The measure of women's social rights captures all of the following rights and the extent to which "systematic discrimination based on sex may have been built into law": equal inheritance, marriage and divorce equality, international travel, citizenship for children/ spouse, property rights in marriage, "participation in social, cultural, and community activities," education, property rights, freedom from "female genital mutilation of children and adults without their consent," and forced sterilization (8). This measure was removed in 2005. Finally, the women's economic rights measure includes performance on rights related to "equal pay, profession choice, employment, equality in hiring, job security, nondiscrimination, freedom from sexual harassment, and the ability to work at night, in the military, and in dangerous occupations" (7).

Given that this project focuses mainly on the post–Cold War time period, over 60 years since the creation of the Universal Declaration of Human Rights, are rights on the ground globally really not protected? In other words, in this era where we are "winning the war on war" (Goldstein 2011), are populations still repressed? Unfortunately, the answer is "yes." The modal category is not full respect for any of the rights. In fact, over time, the world average for these rights does not improve substantially. Worth noting, however, is that the world mean women's political rights variable has been increasing since 1991. And, in certain countries, movement over time is evident: for example, Nicaragua went from a 0 in 1982 to a 6 in 2007. The Ivory Coast, however, went from a perfect 8 in 1982 to a 2 in 2010.[1]

HUMAN RIGHTS INGOS: LARGE-SCALE DATA SOURCES

Although conceptually it is clear that human rights INGOs' activities, specifically their campaigns for human rights outcomes, should be examined, empirical proxies for human rights INGO campaigns or activities have been scant. There exists no international clearinghouse for the activities of human rights INGOs; no data set is available on all actions taken by human rights INGOs concerning a state.

Only very recently have a small number of scholars begun to identify quantitative proxies for the mobilization campaigns of human rights INGOs; most have then used these proxies as independent variables in studies of whether INGOs have an impact on human rights outcomes, as outlined in Chapter 2. Starting most prominently with Landman (2005), Hafner-Burton and Tsutsui (2005), and Neumayer (2005), the proxy for human rights INGO campaign mobilization was the number of all types of INGOs that have a membership base within a state. By membership base, these data are capturing whether or not an INGO reports having a citizen-member within the state (UIA 2008/2009). In other words, this is a count of the number of INGOs that report having a volunteer or member within a state in a specific year. I use "member" or "membership" data with reference to the data to be consistent with larger cross-disciplinary literature on INGOs (Boli and Thomas 1999; Tsutsui and Wotipka 2004; Smith and Wiest 2005). These studies all used data collected from the *Yearbook of International Organizations*, the data source compiled by the Union of International Associations (UIA), as discussed in Chapter 5.

Because Hafner-Burton and Tsutsui (2005), Landman (2005), and Neumayer (2005) use the *Yearbook* measure of the number of all types of INGOs that have members within a state, their studies focus more on the human rights impact of the level of overall civil society and not specifically on the impact of the activities of specifically human rights INGOs.

As a first cut, therefore, in looking for data that capture the activities of human rights INGOs, it seems important to use only data on INGOs with a human rights mission statement. For this, I use data collected from the *Yearbook* on human rights–specific INGOs; Smith and Wiest (2005, 2012) provided these data. Drawing on a procedure similar to the one Tsutsui and Wotipka used in their collection of data on the years 1978, 1988, and 1998, Smith and Wiest coded INGOs as human rights INGOs if their missions or aims reflected a human rights agenda and created a country-year variable for the number of human rights INGOs that report having volunteers or a membership base within a country in a given year. These data were collected from the hard copies of the *Yearbook* at 2- to 3-year intervals from 1953 to 2005; linear interpolation was utilized to fill in the years not coded. Given its time span and its issue area focus, these data represent a real advance in the study of human rights INGOs.

However, one potential problem with using *Yearbook* data that have not been adequately examined in the extant cross-disciplinary literature is the large number of INGOs that are included in the *Yearbook* but do not supply details of their operations. This is extremely problematic for advocacy INGOs, which, unlike service INGOs, often do not have permanent offices in the states where they are working. Therefore, unlike the case for service INGOs, data from the *Yearbook* on secretariat or office location cannot be substituted for human rights INGO membership data as a robustness check. For example, Human Rights Watch, by most accounts the second-largest human rights INGO in the world, does not report any membership data to the *Yearbook*, despite, according to their mission, the organization's global focus (UIA, 2008/2009). Therefore, existing studies, such as Landman (2005) and Neumayer (2005), that use UIA data as a proxy for INGO activities are missing the activities of arguably one of the most global INGOs. This issue would also be problematic in Smith and Wiest's (2005, 2012) issue-specific INGO data.

Perhaps a more serious problem than the use of INGO membership data as a proxy for human rights INGO activities is the idea that many existing qualitative and quantitative studies of the impact of human rights INGOs fail to address the potential endogeneity between the presence of human rights INGOs with members within a state and the human rights practices of a state. Existing research within sociology interested in human rights INGOs with members within a state as the dependent vàriable further highlights the potential endogeneity in this approach. As Tsutsui and Wotipka point out in their 2004 *Social Forces* article, in the years 1978, 1988, and 1998, human rights INGOs were more likely to have members/volunteers in a state where there was a high degree of political rights and civil liberties, which they measure using the Freedom House (2001) scales. Based on this finding, therefore, it is plausible that high levels of human rights performance could lead to a relaxation of restrictions of the activities of human rights INGOs with members within a state and, thus, to the proliferation of the organizations.

At the same time—as Hafner-Burton and Tsutsui, Landman, and Neumayer (2005) and the general transnational advocacy literature all stress—human rights INGOs' activities should lead to higher levels of human rights performance. These two strains of literature highlight the potential endogenous relationship between human rights INGOs with members within a state and the human rights practices of a state. Without explicitly accounting for this potential endogeneity, any observed effect of the *Yearbook*-based human rights INGO data on human rights practices could be spurious (Wooldridge 2006).

If an endogenous relationship was present between the UIA human rights INGO membership data and human rights performance and this relationship was unaccounted for, the statistical results would be biased and, in effect, useless at providing much-needed evidence for the impact of human rights INGOs (Wooldridge 2006). As I show below, the *Yearbook* human rights INGO membership data and the more general nonissue-specific *Yearbook* INGO membership data, such as that used by Hafner-Burton and Tsutsui, Landman, and Neumayer, are endogenous to human rights performance outcomes when measured in the same year. Therefore, in order to correctly examine the impact of human rights INGOs to human rights performance, I have to use statistical models that account for endogeneity when using human rights INGO membership data as my key independent variable.

Moreover, although the issue-specific *Yearbook*-based membership data are a useful first cut at capturing the activities of human rights INGOs, they do not adequately capture what human rights INGOs actually do in the struggle for human rights improvement—that is, they do not capture the strategic targeting of governments by human rights INGOs in the public arena. In other words, although the *Yearbook* data can be useful to gauge local mobilization by INGOs, they do not capture "shaming and blaming" or "naming and shaming" activities by INGOs.

Very recently, scholars have developed a few proxies for this shaming concept. First, Ron, Ramos, and Rodgers (2005) collected data on the number of Amnesty International background reports and press releases. Hafner-Burton (2008) used these data, and they were not linked to human rights performance; in fact, more Amnesty International reports are linked to an increase in the likelihood of torture in the next year. Other uses of similar Amnesty International data, however, have been linked to increases in human rights performance and decreases in the intensity of mass killings (DeMeritt 2012; Hendrix and Wong 2012; Krain 2012). Franklin (2008) collected data on a wider sample of shaming activities by both domestic and international NGOs in "Facts on File or Keesing's Record of World Events" in six Latin American countries and found that shaming is an effective strategy for lessening repression as external economic vulnerability increases in a state (193).

Although these novel measures all add much to our overall empirical knowledge of how shaming influences human rights practices, in both my solo and coauthored works, I wanted a measure of human rights INGO shaming that (a) captured the work of multiple human rights INGOs, (b) is available for a global sample, (c) restricts the focus to only negative government targeting, and (d) includes only events of shaming that actually make the public arena. In other words, although the Ron and colleagues (2005) measure and other measures of Amnesty International's work (Hendrix and Wong 2012; Meernik et al. 2012) give us much insight into the work and possible impact of that specific organization, Amnesty International is somewhat unique in the human rights community and is only one organization out of hundreds, or even thousands, with similar human rights–specific mission statements. To the extent that other organizations could possibly use a different strategy toward shaming states, these Amnesty International measures miss any possible effect of their work. Franklin's (2008) strategy of looking at a wider swath of organizations overcomes this issue but, at present, is only available for a very small sample of Latin American countries, a region that Hafner-Burton and Ron (2013) contend is unique in its human rights advocacy situation. Franklin's strategy of only looking at human rights criticism that appears in new archives also restricts the focus to only negative, shaming activities, as opposed to just informational pressure releases, which could be present in many of the Amnesty International–based measures. In short, Franklin's measure appears best suited for capturing the shaming activities of multiple human rights INGOs against governments but is only available for six countries.

To create a measure of human rights INGO shaming that addresses these dynamics and shortcomings of extant data sets, I began with a list of human rights INGOs from the *Yearbook*. I coded INGOs in the *Yearbook* as human rights–specific based on the mission statement the organization provided to the *Yearbook*. In my early work (Murdie and Bhasin 2011; Murdie and Davis 2012a; Bell, Clay, and Murdie 2012), the list I used had 432 human rights INGOs in it. In my later work (starting with Murdie and Peksen 2012), including for the variable used here, the list expanded to include 1166 organizations.

Using this list of human rights INGOs, Virtual Research Associates, the company that produced the original Integrated Data for Event Analysis (IDEA) data set, used a quantitative content analysis program to isolate all events in Reuters Global News Service concerning these INGOs daily from 1990 to 2009.[2] The IDEA data are organized in a "who" did "what" to "whom" manner for each particular event, over 10 million events in the complete data set (King and Lowe 2003). This procedure isolated 11,268 distinct events where a human rights INGO was cited and the event is directed at a specific country.

Given that these events include both positive and negative actions, I wanted to restrict my focus to only conflictual human rights targeting. Therefore, I first isolated only events that are not classified on the Goldstein (1992) scale of events as "cooperative." Then, given that I am only interested in events that are directed at governments, I restrict the "target" of the event to only government actors or agents. Further, because I am interested primarily in events where human rights INGOs are the source actor, I restrict the "source" of the event to only NGOs, the closest category of actors in the IDEA framework.

What do the remaining events look like? For example, on July 28, 1995, under the header "MEXICO: Rights group slams Mexican army on Chiapas abuses," Human Rights Watch called on the Mexican government to halt and investigate abuses perpetrated by the military in the state of Chiapas, in southern Mexico. In the event data I used, this event is listed as conflictual; it is a "criticize or denounce" event in the IDEA framework. The source of the action is the organization and the target of the action is the Mexican military. This type of event forms the basis for my measure of human rights INGO shaming.

Additionally, as the key independent variable in the analyses here, reflecting the central mechanism in the extant literature, I utilize yearly change in this count of human rights INGO shaming events. This is an improvement, I feel, from my extant work. Using change in this count allows me to capture the idea that a state's leadership reacts to increasing human rights INGO shaming campaigns by improving its human rights performance (Keck and Sikkink 1998; Risse, Ropp, and Sikkink 1999). Unlike the membership or secretariat data on service INGOs discussed in Chapter 5, which were used to capture the level of goods or services provided by service INGOs within a year, this data captured short-term campaigns by human rights INGOs. A campaign is typically thought of as a concentrated effort by human rights INGOs for a brief period of time on a specific issue or targeted state (Hopgood 2006). As such, the mechanism through which human rights INGOs work to impact policy and behavior outcomes is not a constant level of "shaming" or events but, instead, an increase in events or "shaming." This more precisely relates to the central mechanism discussed in the extant TAN literature (Keck and Sikkink 1998; Risse and Ropp 1999). As an illustration, it was not Amnesty's constant shaming of Latin American and Asian countries that won it the Nobel Prize in 1977; rather, it was Amnesty's increase in advocacy events, particularly its shaming of despotic regimes in Latin America and Asia, that won it the Nobel Prize specifically for its "campaign against torture" (Hopgood 2006).

Campaigns, or sudden increases in advocacy events, reflect how many advocacy INGOs work. Although, for example, Amnesty International, Human Rights Watch, and other INGOs often try to keep activities going in many areas of the world simultaneously, it is only during campaigns, when activities are concentrated and increased within a specific state or on a specific issue, that the organization's leadership expects a response in a state's human rights performance (DeMars 2005; Hopgood 2006). By utilizing change, my measure of human rights INGO shaming accounts for this dynamic.

Worth noting, unlike the *Yearbook*-based human rights INGO membership measure discussed above, this resulting measure, human rights INGO shaming mobilization, is not endogenous to human rights performance. This is determined by the Durbin-Wu-Hausman test, using the same instruments used in the human rights INGO membership models, as discussed below. Additionally, the correlation between this measure and the Smith and Wiest (2005) data on human rights INGO membership is less than 0.10, demonstrating that these measures are reflecting very different activities and involvement by human rights INGOs and, consequently, different pathways through which human rights INGOs work to improve human rights performance. For the human rights INGO shaming mobilization variable, this reflects the "naming and shaming" campaigns. For the human rights INGO membership variable, this reflects the domestic level of involvement in the "world society" of human rights organizations (Boli and Thomas 1999; Tsutsui and Wotipka 2004; Smith and Wiest 2005).

Figure 5.1 provides a graphical representation of the world mean level of human rights INGO shaming and the world mean amount of human rights INGO shaming mobilization (i.e., the measure as yearly change). In this figure, I weighted the variables by a measure of media coverage: this is the natural log

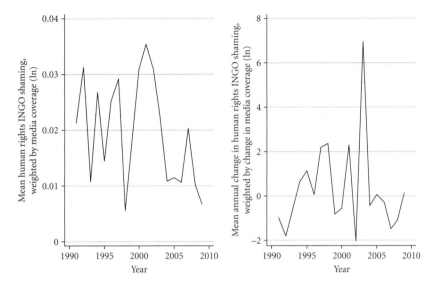

Figure 5.1 Human rights INGO activities within a country over time, 1990–2009

of the total number of reports about a country in Reuters Global News Service. In the statistical models, I include this media coverage variable as a control; it is useful in ensuring that any increased levels of shaming are not just due to an overabundance of Reuters reports about a particular country in a particular year. As this figure shows, there has not been an average increase in shaming/ shaming mobilization across the time period.

STATISTICAL MODELING DECISIONS

Previous research has shown a few key factors that influence human rights performance. These factors could have a confounding influence with human rights INGOs and thus need to be controlled for in all the statistical models in this chapter. First, developed states typically respect rights better (Mitchell and McCormick 1988; Henderson 1991; Poe and Tate 1994; Poe et al. 1999; Cingranelli and Richards 1999; Richards et al. 2001). The possibility of revolt due to economic scarcity decreases as development improves, perhaps lessening possible opportunities for repression by elites (Poe and Tate 1994). Likewise, citizens with more economic resources could be better able to work against repressive regimes (Poe and Tate 1994; Richards et al. 2001). Therefore, I include as a control the natural log of GDP per capita, in constant US dollars in all statistical models (WDI 2012).

Many other studies link consolidated democracy to increases in human rights realization (Henderson 1991; Poe and Tate 1994; Hofferbert and Cingranelli 1996; Cingranelli and Richards 1999; Poe et al. 1999; Davenport and Armstrong 2004). Democracy provides alternative outlets for the handling of conflict by governmental officials and, moreover, a voice to the domestic public in order to publicize and potentially oust human rights abusers (Henderson 1991; Poe and Tate 1994; Davenport and Armstrong 2004). Given this established relationship, I control for regime type by including the revised combined polity index, ranging from −10 (strongly autocratic) to +10 (strongly democratic) (Marshall and Jaggers 2010).

Having a domestic civil conflict occurring within a state opens up the possibility of lots of human rights abuses. I include a dichotomous control for the existence of any intrastate conflict within a state's borders from the UCDP/PRIO Armed Conflict Dataset (2010) Models with the addition of a control for interstate conflict, which was increasingly rare during the post-1990 time period (Goldstein 2011), did not change the results presented here. I also included a control for the natural log of population size, reflecting the idea that a large population could just create more opportunities for violence (WDI 2012). And, as mentioned, all models include a control for the media coverage.

Due to the time series, cross-sectional nature of the data set, except where noted, I use a general estimating equation modeling approach with an AR(1) correlation structure and robust standard errors. Additionally, because I am interested only in how human rights INGOs influence state improvement in human rights, I restrict my focus to only states without continual "perfect" human rights records. In other words, this decision helps ensure that my results are not driven by a few high-performing, mainly Western countries. I have taken a similar approach in earlier work (Murdie and Davis 2012a; Bell, Clay, and Murdie 2012). When the variable for human rights INGO shaming mobilization is used, and thus simultaneous equation methods to account for endogeneity are not used, I measure the dependent variable at one year after I measure the independent variables. In other words, the statistical models utilize lagged independent variables or can be thought of as measuring the impact of human rights INGO shaming mobilization on future human rights performance.

Given these basic modeling discussions, I now turn to discussing the individual statistical modeling decisions taken for each hypothesis and the results of the statistical tests. Of course, special attention is paid to understanding the substantive significance of these models.

1. The Impact of Human Rights INGO Depends
on the Issue at Hand

To test Advocacy Hypothesis 1, concerning the differing effects of advocacy mobilization across issue areas, I run separate models for each of the Cingranelli and Richards (2010) human rights variables discussed above: physical integrity rights, women's political rights, women's social rights, and women's economic rights. Again, the expectation is that there will be a positive effect of human rights INGO mobilization on physical integrity rights but that the effect on women's rights, as a more divisive human rights issue for the international and domestic community, will be more tenuous, if there is one at all.

This statistical strategy is very straightforward: the key independent variable of human rights INGO shaming mobilization is used for separate statistical models for each CIRI human rights variable; the control variables outlined above are also included. For the women's rights variables, given the small number of categories, I use an ordered probit model with robust standard errors clustered on country.[3] I run both models with and without a lagged dependent variable; results to the key independent variable remain consistent.

What do I find?[4] Results of these tests largely support my hypothesis: human rights INGO shaming mobilization has a positive and statistically significant effect on physical integrity rights but no discernible impact on any of the women's rights indicators. As expected, because women's rights are issues where the desires of the international and domestic community may be likely to diverge, it is less likely that the whole human rights INGO sector—including both those that are internationally biased and domestically consistent—will be able to get the constant support necessary to make a measurable impact for human rights. Conversely, for physical integrity rights, where the preferences of both the domestic and the international communities that work with INGOs are more likely to be in closer alignment, human rights INGO shaming mobilization is likely to have a positive influence on these rights.

For physical integrity rights, the effect of human rights INGO shaming mobilization is quite large. This is illustrated in Figure 5.2, which shows the substantive impact of the key theoretical variables on the change in CIRI physical integrity rights score. With all of the variables at their mean in the sample, as the human rights INGO shaming variable moves from its minimum to its maximum value in the data set, the expected increase in physical integrity rights is almost a whole point (0.815 with a 95% confidence interval of 0.124 to 1.483). As a reminder, the CIRI Physical Integrity Rights scale has a range

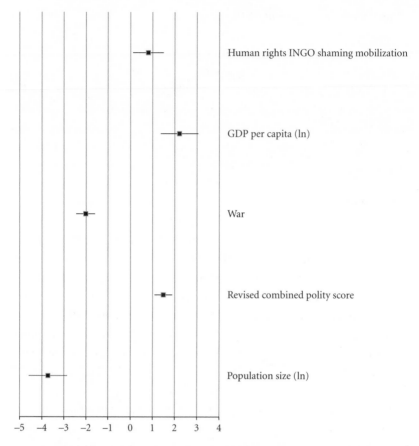

Figure 5.2 Substantive effect of human rights INGO shaming mobilization on physical integrity rights

NOTE: All results were calculated using CLARIFY with an OLS regression mode with robust standard errors clustered on country. The box indicates the mean expected change in CIRI physical integrity rights; the line indicates the 95% confidence interval.

from 0, indicating no governmental respect for physical integrity, to 8, indicating full governmental respect for physical integrity rights. This change from the minimum to the maximum score is quite substantial when we compare it to similar changes in the value of some of the variables capturing accepted explanations for human rights performance in the data set. Although not as large as the expected mean effect of changing a country from a consolidated authoritarian regime to a consolidated democracy, for example, as Figure 5.2 shows, the confidence intervals for these two variables do overlap. Given the very real difficulties in regime change, of course, the fact that merely increasing shaming has anywhere near the effect as a full democratization process on physical integrity rights is incredible.

In looking at the expected changes in human rights performance from smaller, incremental increases in human rights INGO shaming mobilization, although the size of the effect diminishes, the key insight—that shaming mobilization has a positive influence on physical rights performance on the ground—remains. Take, for example, the change in physical integrity rights that is expected to occur when human rights shaming mobilization goes from no shaming events in a year to four shaming events in a year. With all the other variables in the model at their mean levels, this change is expected to result in about a quarter of a point increase in a country's physical integrity rights score (0.232 with a 95% confidence interval of 0.034 to 0.426). A good example of this sort of increase in human rights INGO shaming mobilization occurred in Nigeria during the early 2000s—from 2000 to 2002. As would be expected by the model results, within Nigeria during this time period, physical integrity rights also increased, going from a score of 1 in 2000 to score of 3 in 2002. Nigeria during this time period did not drastically change its regime type; it was a middling democracy (revised combined polity score of 4) starting in 1999 and continuing through the end of the sample. Its population size and GDP per capita did not change substantively during this time period, and it did not have a civil conflict within its borders during these years.[5] In short, without focusing on the work of human rights INGOs, in particular their shaming mobilization, during this time period, it is difficult, given the other variables in the model, to explain this change in physical integrity rights within Nigeria.

Does this statistical result hold up to a "reality check"? Case study and anecdotal research about Nigeria also supports this role of human rights INGO shaming mobilization during this time period. For example, Jonathan Power (2001) chronicles his work with Amnesty International in Nigeria in 1999 and 2000 in his book *Like Water on Stone: The Story of Amnesty International*. In 1999, for example, Power interviewed a recent released political prisoner in Heathrow Airport in London. When Power asked directly whether the work of Amnesty International had any effect on his release, the man replied, "It's like constant drips of water on a stone. It seems to make little difference, but over time it does" (17). Beginning in July 2000, Power went to Lagos, Nigeria, with a team of investigators from the organization interested in reports of physical integrity rights, especially extrajudicial killings. The team met with local leaders and expanded their focus to civil liberties as well as physical integrity rights promotion. The recent *Legitimizing Human Rights NGOs: Lessons from Nigeria* by Obiora Chinedu Okafor (2006) would also support this increase in human rights INGO activity on physical integrity rights in Nigeria during this time period.

Despite the potential for increased realization of physical integrity rights that is associated with human rights INGO shaming mobilization, I find no statistically significant impact of this mobilization on women's rights, regardless of the measure I use (social, economic, or political) to capture women's rights. Tables of these statistical results are available in the chapter appendix.

This finding concerning the limited role of human rights INGO shaming mobilization on women's rights is in line with the implications of the game-theoretic advocacy INGO model: because women's rights is often an issue where the domestic population, as a whole, does not place sufficient value on the international community's policy or behavioral goals, advocacy INGOs are less likely to gain the support of the domestic community, leading to little or no impact from their advocacy efforts. Worth noting, of the standard Poe and Tate (1994) controls, GDP per capita (ln), and regime type are statistically significant in most models. More large-scale research into the causes of women's rights definitely seems necessary, especially given the very little existing published work that utilizes this measure (Cingranelli and Richards 2010).

This lack of human rights INGO mobilization success on women's rights across countries is certainly discouraging for hard-working advocates. It is, however, consistent with the qualitative and journalistic record, and, in most regards, the explanations given are consistent with my theoretical story. At the onset, it is just an issue where there appears to be more internationally biased organizations, perhaps signifying a greater distance between domestic preferences and international preferences in this issue area. Take, for example, the 1970s and 1980s work by INGOs for women's rights in Africa. As Welch (1995) points out, one of the early movers in the INGO community was an organization called the Women's Information Network (WIN): "In many respects, WIN was the mother of other NGOs that focus on the rights issues confronted by half of humanity" (92). WIN wanted "immediate action" from women "all around the world" "on behalf of their abused African sisters (92). However, this approach could be taken as "imposing galling Western norms on other settings" (92) During WIN's early days, however, as "UN bodies" and "Western-based spokespersons" discussed how to change women's rights, "notably absent were African women themselves" (93). Later efforts, however, specifically taken by the very domestic stakeholder-centric Inter-African Committee on Traditional Practices, were reflective of domestic preferences and incremental changes, typically resulting in better advocacy results. Similar sentiment is reflected in Kouzzi and Bordat's (2012) account in the appropriately named book *Self-Determination and Women's Rights in Muslim Societies* about the work of the organization Global Rights in Morocco in 2007:

> [The campaign] started with activities designed to engage women at the grassroots level in the development of the content of a violence against women law. Organizers felt that this approach was necessary to ensure that women's voices were heard and their experiences and opinions incorporated in the law. (44)

Because many women's rights issues are those where domestic preferences can vary from international desires, it is difficult to place the concentrated support of both these various actors behind INGOs. Without signals about the INGO's motivations, fear of supporting an internationally biased organization can limit domestic support to any INGO active on the issue, regardless of whether the organization is actually working in ways consistent with domestic preferences. As Mokhtari (2012) explained:

> [Internationally biased advocacy in the Middle East] decried women's rights and minority rights violations in highly sensationalist and decontextualized terms, implying a hierarchy of cultures and peoples, reminiscent of colonialist discourses. This made Middle Eastern populations uneasy about adopting the language of human rights. (195)

The mobilization of human rights INGOs in Nigeria during the time period discussed above reiterates this point; although there were successes by some individual INGOs (Welch 1995), overall the efforts of the entire community were not such to improve women's rights.

As a robustness check on the impact of human rights INGOs on both these nondivisive and divisive human rights issues, I also ran models where the natural log of the total number of human rights INGOs with a member/volunteer within a state, as coded by Smith and Wiest (2005) from the *Yearbook*, was substituted for the key independent variable. As mentioned, there are potential problems with endogeneity that must be dealt with when this independent variable is used. In other words, it seems likely that states with high respect for human rights could lead to more human rights INGOs having members within the state, contrary to my expectation that high numbers of human rights

INGOs with members within a state lead to higher state respect for human rights. This potential endogeneity, sometimes referred to as "reverse" causation, violates the classic ordinary least squares statistical assumption of recursivity, leading to biased and inconsistent estimates (Dhrymes 1994; Wooldridge 2006).

Therefore, for each independent variable, I run a time-series, cross-sectional data model two-stage least squares regression.[6] The first-stage dependent variable is Human Rights INGO Count, and the second-stage is the CIRI Physical Integrity Rights Index. In this approach, exogenous instruments are used in the first-stage regression to predict a new variable that does not violate the recursivity assumption. This new variable is substituted for the endogenous independent variable in the second-stage approach, leading to consistent estimates (Dhrymes 1994; Wooldridge 2006).

Like all two-stage approaches for dealing with endogeneity, it is necessary to find an instrument that has no direct causal path to the human rights variables but is still correlated, conditional to the covariates, to the human rights INGO. Drawing on the sociology literature, I use the natural log of tourism arrivals and the yearly percent increase in telephone mainlines (WDI 2012). Both of these instruments are utilized because they indicate connections to the outside world; they are crucial to the activities of human rights INGOs, but not expensive, not indicative of democracies, and, moreover, not linked to a state's human rights performance (Boli and Thomas 1999; Zinnes and Bell 2002; Tsutsui and Wotipka 2004).

The results of the two-stage least squares model concerning the impact of Human Rights INGO count on physical integrity rights reiterates the potential that human rights INGOs have, even after accounting for the endogeneity suspected in the key independent variable. As shown in the table in the chapter appendix, the instrumented human rights INGO membership count variable has a positive and statistically significant impact on physical integrity rights.[7] After accounting for endogeneity, the substantive effects of an increase from the minimum to the mean value of Human Rights INGO Count, holding everything else at its mean and/or median, is over a 1-point increase in CIRI physical integrity rights (1.534 with a 95% confidence interval from 1.027 to 2.016). Further, the model allows me to reject the null of no endogeneity in human rights INGO model, indicating that the two-stage approach was necessary.[8] Additionally, the instruments are valid predictors of human rights INGO membership/volunteer levels.[9]

Using a two-stage approach also reiterates the lack of findings for the women's rights models, with one exception: I do find evidence that the number of human rights INGOs with members/volunteers has a positive and statistically significant impact on women's political rights. This follows from the framework here for two reasons. First, of the three indicators used here— women's political rights, social rights, and economic rights—political rights are likely to be the least-divisive issue during this time period; it is also the right most protected worldwide, as indicated in Figure 5.2. Second, this new indicator, the number of human rights INGO levels with a member or volunteer in the state, would be more indicative of some domestic buy-in than the measure for shaming mobilization. At the very least, having a member or volunteer within a country provides more opportunities for incorporating the desires of the domestic population than simply "naming and shaming" the state from anywhere in the world.

As a whole, these statistical tests provide overwhelming support for Advocacy INGO Hypothesis 1: human rights INGOs' activities have a great impact on nondivisive issues but, as a whole sector, have an insignificant impact on those issues that divide the international and domestic populations. This finding stresses the need for organizations, even if biased in favor of the international community, to work mainly on outcomes that reflect the desires of the population they are trying to help. If short-term changes are required, extreme advocacy in favor of international donor biases may not be effective and may undermine the success of the entire sector on that human rights issue.

2. The Impact of Human Rights INGO Depends on the Internal and External Vulnerability

Advocacy INGO Hypothesis 2 examines how a state's vulnerability conditions the impact of advocacy INGOs, even on nondivisive issues. This hypothesis, although derived from the formal model, is consistent with earlier, nonformal discussions of the state's vulnerability from Keck and Sikkink (1998) and Risse, Ropp, and Sikkink (1999). For a statistical model to test this hypothesis, I again use Cingranelli and Richards's (2010) physical integrity rights index as the dependent variable and create a key independent variable by interacting human rights INGO shaming mobilization with (1) measures that capture the state's vulnerability in internal pressure and (2) measures used to capture vulnerability of external pressure. To capture a state's level of vulnerability to internal pressure, I use a measure of democracy, a scale from 0 (least democratic) to 10 (most democratic) in the Polity IV project (Marshall and Jaggers 2010).[10] The expectation is that a more democratic country is more vulnerable to internal pressure, leading to a greater effect of advocacy INGOs on human security advocacy outcomes. When a country's leadership faces competitive elections at regular intervals, a leader that wants to stay in power will have to be responsive to the desires of the state's citizens. Human rights INGO shaming mobilization heightens the awareness of the human rights situation to the domestic population within the state (Davis, Murdie, and Steinmetz 2012). Theoretically, as clearly presented by both Keck and Sikkink (1998) and Risse, Ropp, and Sikkink (1999), this process can start a domestic mobilization effort aimed at getting a government to stop its abusive practices. As a country becomes more democratic, it is more likely that this heightened domestic advocacy would be successful due to the vulnerability that a democratically elected leader would face at the ballot box.

To capture state vulnerability to external pressure, I run three different models, each with a different measure of external vulnerability: the amount of net development assistance and aid in constant US dollars, trade, and exports (Gleditsch 2002; WDI 2012).[11] Each of these measures, which are weighted by the size of the country's gross domestic product, captures a different aspect of a state's vulnerability to external pressure. If third-party states and multilateral donors, for example, are motivated by human rights INGO shaming mobilization to increase their own pressure on a state from abroad, they could attach conditionality human rights requirements on aid. Therefore, countries with higher aid levels should be more responsive to increases in human rights INGO activity, leading to a greater human rights outcome. When looking at shaming by the UN Commission on Human Rights, Lebovic and Voeten (2009), however, do not find evidence that bilateral donors actually condition aid in response to shaming; only multilateral donors, like the World Bank, actually reduce aid following sanctioning. Given that most countries tend to receive more aid from a small set of bilateral donors instead of multilateral agencies, then, the findings of Lebovic and Voeten (2009) may suggest that overall levels of aid will not be a likely source of external vulnerability for human rights INGO shaming mobilization.

The same general idea of external vulnerability, however, applies to trade and exports; when a state is dependent on foreign trade, particularly exports, for economic survival, it should be more responsive to international community pressure facilitated by human rights INGO shaming mobilization. The international community writ large, including individual consumers of products from the targeted country, can retaliate by boycotting the targeted state's products. Therefore, as countries become more vulnerable, through trade and export dependency, to external pressure caused by increases in human rights INGO mobilization, there should be a greater impact on human rights performance. Following Brambor and colleagues (2006), I include all constitutive terms in the model and include all the standard controls discussed above.

As expected, the results support the general idea that the effect of human rights INGO shaming mobilization will be conditioned by both the internal and external vulnerability of the state. However, this hypothesis is only supported when external vulnerability is measured in terms of trade or exports; I find no evidence that aid, as a measure of external vulnerability, combines with internal vulnerability to condition the effectiveness of shaming mobilization.[12]

The conditional effectiveness of shaming mobilization when external vulnerability is measured by exports is illustrated in Figure 5.3. This figure graphs the marginal effect of human rights INGO shaming mobilization at different

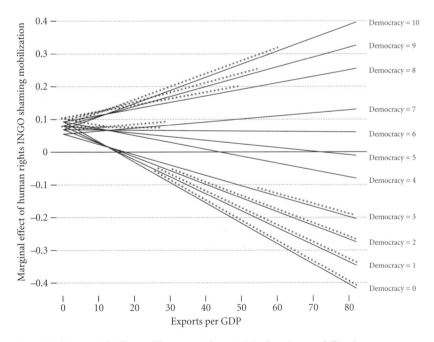

Figure 5.3 Marginal effects of human rights INGO shaming mobilization on physical integrity rights as international (export/GDP) and domestic (democracy) vulnerability increases

levels of democracy as exports increase. The y axis of the graph shows the marginal effect of human rights INGO shaming mobilization on physical integrity rights. The x axis represents the range of the variable used to capture external vulnerability, exports weighted by GDP, in the sample. The various lines represent the different values of democracy in the sample; again, this variable goes from 0, indicating a state is not democratic, to 10, indicating a state is a consolidated democracy. The stars above the lines indicate significance at the 95% level of the marginal effects concerning that particular democracy score. In short, as this figure shows, when human rights INGO shaming mobilization occurs in states that are vulnerable to both internal and external pressure, increased activism is more likely to produce outcomes consistent with the goals of the organization. Importantly, this graph shows that human rights INGO shaming will have a positive and statistically different effect on physical integrity rights as the level of democracy increases for most of the range of exports. Past a certain level of exports, although the point predictions given on the graph do show that the effect on physical integrity rights is different at different levels of democracy, the findings do not reach conventional levels of statistical significance. This can be explained, at least in part, by the fact that the countries that are past this very high level of export dependence (i.e., China, Liberia) are not democracies. At these very top ends of external vulnerability, however, as shown in the lower half of the figure, nondemocratic countries are not likely to have a positive influence on physical integrity rights as a result of human rights INGO shaming mobilization. In short, external vulnerability alone is not sufficient for the success of human rights INGO shaming mobilization on physical integrity rights.[13]

These findings support Advocacy INGO Hypothesis 2, as a state's vulnerability to internal and external pressure increases, the impact of human rights INGO shaming mobilization increases. This is largely in line with Keck and Sikkink (1998). When a country is highly democratic, and thus vulnerable to domestic pressure, and more dependent on trade or exports, and thus vulnerable to international pressure, human rights INGOs are able to have a greater influence on physical integrity rights. This research shows perhaps an unintended consequence of economic globalization (Russett, Oneal, and Davis 1998; Reuveny and Li 2003; Pevehouse 2005). As a democracy becomes more dependent on trade or exports, its ability to be effectively "shamed" by human rights INGO shaming activities improves. This shaming could come not only from third-party states but from individuals boycotting goods from the targeted state.

Does this statistical result hold up to a qualitative "reality check"? Anecdotes from quite a few cases support this general phenomenon. First, take the case of China in the late 1990s. The country, a constant low performer on physical integrity rights, especially the rights of freedom from torture, political killing, and political imprisonment, was constantly shamed at increasing levels by human rights INGOs in the late 1990s. Based on the quite large export-centric trade-dependent economy in China during this time period, many would assume that China was vulnerable to external pressure. Spurred on by human rights INGO shaming mobilization, many citizen groups organized protests of Chinese products for human rights reasons during this time period, including many products made by American multinational companies in China, like Levi Strauss and Nike (Shaw 1999; Isik-Vanelli 2004). Although some of these boycotts were concerning labor rights, other boycotts were for general physical rights conditions in China, especially its use of the death penalty and torture on political dissidents. For example, the organization Tibet Truth (2012) asks US supporters not to buy Chinese products, displaying on its website the following message:

When we buy goods manufactured in Communist China, we are innocently contributing to a system that imprisons any who speak out and uses torture and the death penalty to suppress any dissent of democratic expression. To buy anything made in China is to take trade away from countries that value democratic principles civil, political, and labour rights. In fact, through our purchase we are sponsoring a form of fascism where oppression and tyranny are mixed with capitalism. Yet, as consumers we have a tremendous potential to influence and send a forceful message to the Chinese Regime by choosing to boycott all goods made in Communist China.

Multinational companies are worried about the possibility of human rights boycotts when deciding to do business in China. For example, as Isik-Vanelli (2004) wrote in *Doing Business in China*:

Customers worldwide have enough power to boycott products of a firm aligning its [Human Resources] practices in China with Chinese standards, as opposed to international or home country standards. The firm needs to be aware of their customers' bargaining and boycotting power when deciding the applicable policies. (18–19)

In short, because of the plethora of "Made in China" products throughout the world, human rights INGOs often shame with the idea that the government is vulnerable to outside pressure, making any effect shaming mobilization would have on physical integrity rights that much more likely.

Despite this potential for external vulnerability to heighten any effect of human rights INGO shaming mobilization, China does lack almost all internal vulnerability. For the time period of this study, China was definitely not a democracy; it scored the lowest score, a zero, on the democracy scale every year from 1949. As such, the Chinese government was not vulnerable to internal pressure facilitated by human rights INGO shaming, something vividly displayed to the world in the Tiananmen Square protests of 1989. Without this ability, there is unlikely to be a positive effect on physical integrity rights in the short term as a result of human rights INGO shaming mobilization.

Why would human rights INGOs continue to shame a country like China, given its invulnerability to internal pressure? I would argue that shaming may still be the likely strategy of advocates for many different reasons. First, shaming may be part of a strategy that extends beyond influencing before in the targeted state; perhaps shaming can help individuals in neighboring states cross borders and assist in increasing pressure from below. This was part of the logic underpinning my work with Sam Bell and K. Chad Clay (2012): volunteers from neighboring states may be able to heighten pressure for human rights improvement. Second, shaming may produce long-term increases in internal vulnerability that would not be captured in this more short-term analysis. As such, shaming taken regarding China now may have residual effects on the amount of internal vulnerability the state has 20 or 30 years in the future. And, finally, shaming may just be undertaken for solidarity reasons in invulnerable states; even if improvement is unlikely in the short run, the organization may be motivated to shame even the most intractable cases.

On the flip side, anecdotes abound concerning the positive side of Figures 5.3 as well. When a country is vulnerable to both internal and external pressure, the effect of human rights INGO shaming mobilization is heightened. Take, for example, the case of Mexico in the early and mid-1990s. In 1990, physical integrity rights in Mexico were among the worst in the world; torture and political killings, in particular, were so widespread that Human Rights Watch (1990) reported that "an array of abuses" had "become an institutionalized part of Mexican society" (1). Human rights INGO shaming mobilization was occurring, spearheaded in great part by Human Rights Watch, bringing attention of the horrendous practices in Mexico to the world community (HRW 1992).

This time period also corresponds to increases in both internal and external vulnerability for the Mexican state. First, in 1989, there was a split in the long-running ruling party, increasing space for the domestic population to advocate for human rights in an increasingly open political system. By 1994, the country was a "4" on the democracy scale; by 1997, it was a "6," increasing to a high of "8" by 2000.

Additionally, external vulnerability was increasing during this time period for Mexico. Mexico was negotiating for a free trade agreement with Canada and the United States in the early 1990s, the North American Free Trade Agreement (NAFTA). In the run-up to the agreement coming into force in 1994, exports were already increasing from Mexico; they continued to increase drastically for the whole decade. This focus on trade with Mexico made the state vulnerable to external human rights pressure. For example, even though the US administration was against it, in September 1990, the US House had hearings on the human rights conditions in Mexico (US House of Representatives 1990; HRW 2001). Many representatives from human rights INGOs spoke at these talks, resulting in the human rights conditions of Mexican citizens being listed as a concern in the yearly NAFTA Accountability Acts in the United States.[14] As Hafner-Burton's (2005) work shows, human rights language in trade agreements can have its own independent effect on human rights. As such, the work of human rights INGOs, in facilitating this human rights language, may also work through this mechanism. Spilker and Böhmelt (2012), however, question Hafner-Burton's findings, arguing that states self-select as to when to include human rights language in trade agreements, limiting any independent effect.

Nonetheless, as a result of this increase in both international and domestic pressure that was facilitated by INGOs, human rights performance in Mexico did increase during the 1990s; although there was some oscillation, it never returned to the levels of 1990. In short, based both on large-scale statistical analyses and anecdotal cases, Hypothesis 2 is supported. External and internal vulnerability heighten the work of human rights INGOs on nondivisive human rights. Although this idea has long been touted in human rights theory, it has not received much empirical attention. Human rights INGO shaming mobilization works to produce short-term benefits when states are vulnerable to the pressure that the shaming mobilization can bring. Without this vulnerability, although not impossible, the success of human rights INGOs in the short term is much less likely.

3. The Impact of Human Rights INGOs on Nondivisive Issues Will Be Greater When More INGOs Send Signals

The third hypothesis in this chapter concerns advocacy INGOs' signals about their underlying motivations and the effect these signals can have on nondivisive human rights. As mentioned, one thing that is interesting in the advocacy INGO game-theoretic model is that these signals never influence the behavior of both communities. Regardless of the type of organization that is sending the signal (internationally biased or domestically consistent), only one of the communities is reacting to the signal when it offers its support; the other community is either never going to support advocacy INGOs or is always going to support advocacy INGOs. In fact, internationally biased INGOs that signal only garner the support of one community, making it, somewhat counterintuitively, more likely to get the more moderate outcome that would be preferred by the domestic community. Conversely, domestically consistent INGOs often signal to get the support of one community when it already has the support of the other community, leading to a more likely moderate outcome as well.

Taken together, this logic implies that INGOs that signal—because they are able to get the support of a community that would otherwise not support them—should be better able to achieve human rights improvement on issues that would be domestically consistent, or more in line with the moderate advocacy outcomes that the domestic community prefers. Like the focus on signals in the previous chapter, I do have to be concerned with self-selection here: human rights INGOs would be more willing to signal in situations where they expect, ex ante, to receive a greater benefit.

To test this hypothesis, I focus again on the nondivisive issue that has been used to test the previous hypotheses: Cingranelli and Richards's (2010) physical integrity rights index. I again use a two-stage least squares approach to account for any self-selection.[15] The key independent variable here is the number of human rights INGOs that are founded within the country and have signaled to the international and domestic communities through gaining consultative status with the United Nations Economic and Social Council (ECOSOC). As mentioned in previous chapters, this signal has resonance with both the international and domestic communities an INGO often interacts with and is often proudly displayed on INGO documents and websites. The signal requires that the organization has a mission that is consistent with the work of the United Nations; given that we are interested here in physical integrity rights, an issue where the international and domestic communities are both likely to have preferences more in line with each other and with the United Nations, the signal represents a proxy that fits well for our purposes. Using the *Yearbook*'s CD-ROM edition, I recorded the founding year and location for all human rights INGOs in the data set. I also recorded whether the INGO had consultative status with ECOSOC.[16] I include all control variables from the previous models, as well as the general human rights INGO shaming mobilization variable. I use the same instruments for human rights INGO presence as when I focused on the human rights INGO membership/volunteer data, discussed above.

What does this model show? The statistical table of results, in the chapter's appendix, shows that this hypothesis is supported in the analysis.[17] Human rights INGOs that signal through registration with UN ECOSOC are especially successful at getting improvements in physical integrity rights because this signal is a way to get the support of a community that would not support it otherwise. However, this effect only works on issues that are nondivisive: statistical results where women's rights variables were used as the dependent variable do not show statistical significance. This effect on physical integrity rights is illustrated in Figure 5.4. When all variables are at their mean in the sample, as the instrumented signaling human rights INGO variable goes from its minimum to its maximum in the sample, there is expected to be over a 2-point increase in a country's physical integrity rights index (2.582 with a 95% confidence interval of 1.741 to 3.410). This is similar in effect to changes in canonical factors of human rights performance, like regime type and GDP per capita.

This result highlights, especially for domestically consistent human rights INGOs, that signaling may be a necessary component to get the support of the international community, which aids in their overall success on the ground. In a situation, like found in the advocacy INGO game-theoretic results for the *Domestic Leader Equilibrium*, where the domestic community is going to support their efforts anyway, this signal may aid in getting the international community support necessary for improvements on nondivisive human rights issues. Although the focus here is on UN ECOSOC, there are many other possible ways that an INGO can send this signal, including attending international conferences and linking with other INGOs in the world community (Clark, Friedman, and Hochstetler 1998; Murdie 2014; Murdie and Davis 2012b). However, these signals are not costless; for struggling INGOs in the Global South,

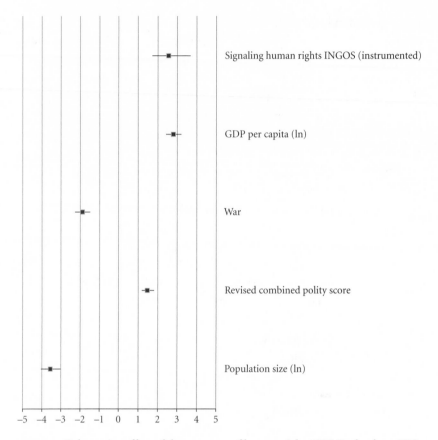

Figure 5.4 Substantive effect of the presence of human rights INGOs that have UN ECOSOC status on physical integrity rights

NOTE: All results were calculated using CLARIFY with an OLS regression mode with robust standard errors clustered on country. The box indicates the mean expected change in CIRI physical integrity rights; the line indicates the 95% confidence interval.

signaling may be too costly (Murdie 2014; Murdie and Davis 2012b). The results presented here, however, would encourage the world community to be aware of the importance of these signals for even domestically oriented INGOs; they aid in getting the concentrated support of both the domestic and international community, ultimately having an influence on the physical integrity rights.

For internationally biased INGOs, these signals may also aid in the achievement of more moderate, nondivisive human rights goals. Even though this signal may only garner the support of the international community for this type of INGO, this support may be enough to get the more moderate outcomes that the domestic community prefers. As such, even if the signal is undertaken for personalistic reasons for the internationally biased INGO, the end result may be an improvement in physical integrity rights that the domestic community actually prefers.

4. The Impact of Human Rights INGO Depends on Costs of Information and Social Contact for the Domestic Population

Advocacy Hypothesis 4 is based on the idea that the domestic community will be more willing to support advocacy INGOs when the costs this community faces for its support are lower. If the domestic community can offer its support to an advocacy INGO at lower costs, it is more likely to support the INGO it is interacting with, even if that INGO does not share its same preference order. Because the support an INGO gets from the domestic community aids in pressuring the state from below, as these costs of INGO support decrease for the domestic community, it is more likely that the work of the INGO will translate into improvement in human security advocacy outcomes.

To test this hypothesis, I must look for a statistically significant positive effect on physical integrity rights from an interaction between human rights INGO shaming mobilization and indicators for the diminishing costs a domestic population could face for interacting with advocacy INGOs. Many different possibility variables could capture these costs. First, I could utilize a measure of domestic association rights, reflecting the idea that the domestic community may be dissuaded from working with human rights INGOs when domestic restrictions on association are high. For example, if there are restrictions on the ability of citizens to associate in political parties or trade unions within a state, these same restrictions could make the costs for the domestic community of working with human rights INGOs higher. To test this idea of domestic costs, I utilize a measure from Cingranelli and Richards (2010) of a state's performance related to freedom of association. This measure, which varies from 0 to 2, with greater scores indicative of more respect, captures a state's performance on the "right of citizens to assemble freely and to associate with other persons in political parties, trade unions, cultural organizations, or other special-interest groups" (4).

Importantly, however, support provided to human rights INGOs from the domestic community is not always thwarted by restrictions on association. Human rights INGOs often still send volunteers into a state even when freedom of association is restricted; anecdotal evidence presented in Bell, Clay, and Murdie

(2012) highlights how organizations often want to be in a state and work a domestic population undetected if domestic association costs are sufficiently high. Further, because human rights INGO shaming mobilization can occur outside of the state, a domestic population that has restrictions on association may still be able to work with advocacy INGOs if the ability to interact and work with these transnational organizations is unencumbered. In other words, if there are still avenues through which contact with the outside world could occur, a domestic population may still be able to readily support an advocacy INGO, even if domestic restrictions of association are high.

This conceptualization of the costs of domestic citizens for support to the INGO is unlike the situation with development INGOs or service organizations more generally. Because service INGOs typically require a presence within the state in order to carry out their work, restrictions on domestic association rights harms the ability of service INGOs to deliver basic human security services, as shown in Chapter 4. Here, however, since advocacy INGOs can work to "shame and blame" from outside a state's borders, restrictions on association rights do not necessarily equate to an impossible working relationship between domestic citizens and the advocacy INGO. If there are still ways for information and contact to occur beyond the country's borders, the cost of supporting an advocacy INGO may still be relatively low for a domestic population, leading to a more likely human security advocacy outcome.

Take, for example, the situation in Myanmar (Burma). Even though the domestic population's rights to association, as measured by the Cingranelli and Richards (2010) freedom of association measure, has not improved since 1981 and is at the lowest level in the world, the population's access to international information flows, like television, newspapers, and Internet access, has drastically increased during this time period. This increase may have made it less costly for domestic citizens to take part in the growing "Free Burma" human rights INGO mobilization efforts in the late 1990s and early 2000s (AI New Zealand 2012). A similar dynamic has occurred in Bahrain, for example, where domestic advocates, forbidden from associating or traveling outside their state, were still able to phone in their presentation to an international advocacy event at the UN Human Rights Council (Bahrain Center for Human Rights 2010). If domestic citizens are able to leave their state to interact with international advocates abroad or if they are able to communicate with advocates outside of their state via phone, this would also imply a lower cost for supporting INGOs for the domestic population. This dynamic has recently been taking place concerning Saudi Arabia; although there are severe restrictions on advocacy by human rights INGOs internally within the state and drastic restrictions on domestic freedom of association, domestic advocates have still managed to work with human rights INGOs via telephone interviews and international travel presentations (AI 2008a; Wilcke 2008).

In order to capture this dynamic, I utilize two measures from the KOF Index of Globalization (Dreher 2006; Dreher, Gaston, and Martens 2008). First, I use a measure of personal, internationalized contact. This measure is an index based on a country's international telephone traffic, transfers (percent of GDP), international tourism, foreign population as a percent of total population, and international letters per capita. The index ranges from almost 0, indicative of very little personal contact, to almost 100, indicating a very large degree of personal, internationalized contact for that particular country in that particular year. Second, I use the KOF Index of Globalization's measure of information flow; this measure captures a country's level of Internet users, televisions, and trade in newspapers (Dreher 2006; Dreher, Gaston, and Martens 2008). It, too, ranges from almost 0 to almost 100.

These three indicators of domestic costs for supporting advocacy INGO efforts (domestic association, personal contact, and information flows) are each interacted with human rights INGO shaming mobilization and used as the key independent variable in separate models where the dependent variable, like before, is physical integrity rights. I utilize the same statistical modeling decisions and standard control variables as in previous hypotheses. Worth noting, these variables that capture domestic costs, even the two indicators that are both from the KOF Index of Globalization, are capturing distinct conceptualizations of domestic costs of support to INGOs. The raw correlation between the KOF variables in the sample used in this chapter is 0.69. The raw correlation between the KOF Index of Globalization personal contact measure and Cingranelli and Richards's freedom of association measure is 0.18, and the raw correlation between the KOF Index of Globalization information flows measure and freedom of association is 0.29.

What do the results of the statistical models imply here? Although there is no conditional influence of freedom of association on the relationship between human rights INGO shaming mobilization and physical integrity rights, the impact of human rights INGO shaming mobilization on a country's physical integrity rights does increase as a country's costs for domestic support to INGOs decreases, as measured as either improved personal contact or increased

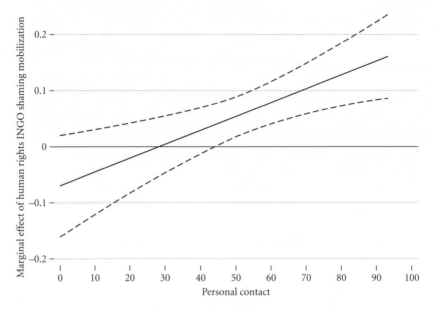

Figure 5.5 Marginal effects of human rights INGO shaming mobilization on physical integrity rights as personal contact with global world increases

information flows.[18] The marginal effect of human rights INGO shaming mobilization as the KOF Index of Globalization personal social contact variable increases is shown in Figure 5.5. As expected, when this variable increases, indicative of lower costs for the domestic population to work with advocacy INGOs, the likely effect on physical integrity rights is heightened. This makes much intuitive sense: when it becomes easier for a population to connect, even internationally, with advocacy INGOs, the population is more likely to support advocacy INGOs, leading to a greater impact on nondivisive advocacy issues.

Robustness checks also reiterate that it is domestic conditions that provide international connections, not particular domestic political structures that are the key driving force here in conditioning the influence of human rights INGOs.[19] When the variable capturing information flows or personal contact was replaced with World Bank measures of political stability and voice and accountability, the same conditional relationship with human rights INGO shaming mobilization was not found (Kaufmann et al. 2009). In other words, completely nonpolitical connections to outsiders can influence the costs the domestic population faces for supporting INGO efforts. Although internal vulnerability from domestic political structures can be important for the effect of human rights INGOs, as described above, the costs the domestic population faces for interacting with human rights INGOs are not completely determined by domestic political structures. In fact, the results found here concerning personal contact and information flows continue to hold when the sample is restricted to only nondemocracies on Cheibub, Gandhi, and Vreeland's (2010) scale.

These findings highlight how some information technology—namely, telecommunication and Internet technologies—can aid advocacy in repressive regimes. Simply because a regime has restricted association rights within a country does not mean that the work of human rights INGOs will be thwarted. If information flows or personal contact to the rest of the world remains high, human rights INGO shaming mobilization can still translate into measurable results in human rights practices. This type of scenario, where domestic association rights are nonexistent but the KOF Globalization Index variables of information flows and personal contact are high—70 or greater—include such diverse countries as Latvia, Greece, Kuwait, Bahrain, and Singapore. In other words, even though the population is restricted from associating at home, it still may be able to connect and support human rights INGOs through social media, telephone, and international travel.

Do these findings hold up to a nonstatistical "reality check"? One particular type of international information flow, the Internet, received much attention during and immediately after the Arab Spring of 2011 as a way to connect repressive populations to the larger advocacy network, including human rights INGOs. As UN Human Rights Council Special Rapporteur Frank La Rue (2011) reported immediately following the Arab Spring:

> The Internet is one of the most powerful instruments of the twenty-first century for increasing transparency in the conduct of the powerful, access to information, and for facilitating active citizen participation in building democratic societies. Indeed, the recent wave of demonstrations in countries across the Middle East and North African region has shown the key role that the Internet can play in mobilizing the population to call for justice, equality, accountability and better respect for human rights. (4)

La Rue's report does address potential problems with universal Internet access, including criminal activities, but concludes that "the Internet has become an indispensable tool for realizing a range of human rights" and "ensuring universal access to the Internet should be a priority for all states" (22). As in the analysis presented here, La Rue sees the Internet as an "'enabler' of other human rights" (19).

One thing that would restrict the ability of human rights INGOs to function in this way, of course, would be censorship of websites or social media applications where a domestic population would work with human rights INGOs. This has occurred in China, for example where human rights INGOs have frequently been blocked by the regime. Amnesty International's website was blocked prior to the 2008 Beijing Olympic Games and then briefly unblocked immediately before the games. Since the games, the website has again been blocked by authorities (AI 2008b, 2009a). China is not the only country to try to selectively block Internet access to human rights INGOs. During the height of the Arab Spring, Saudi Arabia blocked Amnesty International after it obtained information related to further restrictions on expression in the regime (Flock 2011). Many advocates try to work through creative means around Internet censorship, but such restrictions would be likely to impede the success of human rights INGO shaming mobilization by increasing the costs the domestic population would face for supporting human rights INGOs.

These findings, although rather intuitive, are novel in the human rights and INGO literature. In general, we are just beginning to see how NGOs use the Internet in their work. Most of this work has focused on the ways in which organizations use the Internet to connect to one another or connect to outside advocates (Warkentin 2001; Welch 2001). Here, however, the focus has been shifted to the ways in which NGOs can use the Internet to connect to domestic citizens, something that anecdotal evidence suggests does occur, even when domestic association rights are restricted. The conditional relationship supported here would imply that INGOs should see the Internet as a tool to increase domestic mobilization, even mobilization in very repressive states.

5. The Impact of Advocacy INGOs Is Greater When International Community Support Increases

Like the increased effect of advocacy INGOs when domestic support is present, the effect of advocacy INGOs should be conditional on the international community's support. When this support has increased, the overall effect on human security advocacy outcomes should be heightened. To test this logic presented in Advocacy INGO Hypothesis 5, the impact of human rights INGO shaming mobilization on nondivisive human rights outcomes must be conditional on the support the INGOs receive from the international community.

How should this international community support be captured empirically? In Chapter 4, remember that I measured international community as support to NGOs in the form of financial assistance from donor countries. This made a lot of sense in the context of development INGOs working in developing countries: because service INGOs work to provide goods and services, one of the key pathways through which the international community aids service INGOs is just by increasing their ability to purchase goods and services. In other words, for the service INGO sector, international community support can be summarized nicely as international financial support. By giving funds to service INGOs, the international community is aiding the ability of principled service INGOs to carry out their mission. Although the international community can do other things to aid service INGOs, like volunteering their time and manpower, financial assistance to INGOs is often at the heart of what service INGOs desire from the international community. Contrast this, however, with advocacy INGOs, like human rights INGOs. Instead of needing funds from the international community, advocacy INGOs often need the international community to join in their advocacy pressure of a targeted state. Organizations want their shaming mobilization to be joined by pressure from third-party states, intergovernmental organizations, and even multinational corporations. This is the central idea in Keck and Sikkink's (1998) boomerang theory: INGO mobilization works best when combined with pressure from above the targeted state.

Given this idea of what international support consists of for advocacy INGOs, I use a country-year measure of the number of events in Reuters Global News Service where an international actor of any type—intergovernmental organizations, public figures, multinational corporations, and third-party states, for example—shames a targeted state and cites a human rights INGO in the report. An earlier version of this measure was used and explained in depth in my *International Studies Quarterly* piece with David R. Davis (2012a). This international community shaming measure captures events like what happened on August 1, 1997, when Reuters reported that a "UN rights representative criticizes Burundi," and the UN representative highlighted a recent Amnesty International report in his criticism; the UN's criticism can be classified as international community support to Amnesty International shaming mobilization efforts. In line with my theory, this support should heighten the effect of human rights INGOs on the country.

Although third-party states and intergovernmental organizations make up the majority of the reports, it is worth noting that public figures and just general international group support also are found in this measure. A good example of this from the data set would be the group of international "scholars" that join Amnesty International in shaming China for the arrest of a domestic blogger on November 4, 2003. This variable ranges from 0 events in a given country-year to 37 events concerning the United States in 2003. Other states where much international community support is given to human rights INGOs include Russia in 2003, Israel in 2002, and China in 1996.

Based on this conceptualization of international community support, to test Hypothesis 5, the key independent variable is an interaction term between this measure and human rights INGO shaming mobilization, as outlined above. I use Cingranelli and Richards's measure of physical integrity rights as the dependent variable and include the same control measures used in the rest of the chapter. I also follow the same statistical modeling decisions.

As shown in Figure 5.6, the empirical results support Hypothesis 5.[20] When international community support to human rights INGOs increases, the marginal effect of human rights INGO shaming mobilization increases. In fact, it

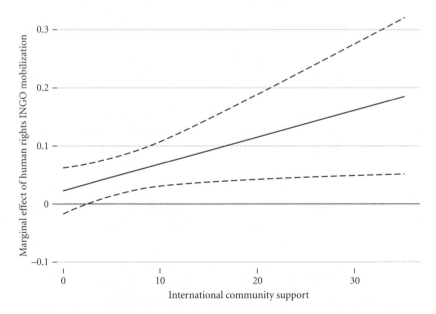

Figure 5.6 Marginal effects of human rights INGO shaming mobilization on physical integrity rights as international community support increases

does not take a lot of international community support, only 1 or 2 events, for the expected marginal effect of human rights INGOs to be positive. In other words, although the results of Hypothesis 1 show that, on average, human rights INGO shaming mobilization can work to improve physical integrity rights on its own, when coupled with international community support, this effect is amplified.

Although these results are consistent with the nonformal theoretical framework of Keck and Sikkink, empirical support of this idea prior to this work has been very scant. The results illustrate how human rights INGOs, an actor that specializes almost exclusively in "soft" power, can be aided by support from international actors that have more "hard" power, like third-party states. However, my measure of international community support makes no distinction about where the support comes from; not all actors classified as the international community specialized in hard power. As such, the result also illustrates how the soft power of INGOs can be aided by other actors with soft power, like public figures or relatively minor intergovernmental organizations. As the canonical work of Keck and Sikkink points out, when like-minded actors join in and pressure a state from above, improvements in basic human rights are likely.

For advocates, the results stress the importance of getting international community support for "forgotten" cases. When the international community joins in its pressure, improvements are more likely. Further, the results presented here, although intuitive, call into question some of the negative implications of Bob's (2005) *The Marketing of Rebellion*. If international support aids the work of human rights INGOs, any strategic selection of cases that are better for "marketing" human rights to the international community may actually be a way to get more bang for the buck in advocacy. If the international community is not going to join in and support shaming mobilization, although improvements can still happen, as shown, for example, by the positive range on the 95% confidence interval, a positive influence of human rights INGO mobilization is not assured. Some selection of cases that are of preexisting interest to the international community may be necessary to start a process by which other cases can get international community support. This is, of course, a fine line for INGOs. Consistent with the results presented concerning Hypothesis 1, if the process of gaining international community support moves advocates away from issues that are of any intensive value to the domestic community, this marketing strategy can backfire for actual success on the ground. Nonetheless, these results stress how, if focusing on an issue that is nondivisive for the international and domestic community, getting powerful international actors on board with the shaming mobilization effort will aid overall advocacy success.

6. The International Community Is More Likely to Support Advocacy INGOs When There Are Fewer Domestically Oriented INGOs

Advocacy INGO Hypothesis 6 states that the international community would rather support advocacy INGOs that share its same preference order. When the international community believes they are more likely to be interacting with an organization that is in favor of the same extreme advocacy outcomes that it is, it will be more likely to offer support, even if that support is increasing in its cost. Conversely, when the international community believes it is more likely to be supporting organizations that are not internationally biased but instead share preferences with the domestic community, the international community is less likely to offer their support.

Although this hypothesis may seem straightforward at first blush, it does suggest a powerful limitation to any idea of international support to local civil society. Instead of supporting organizations that are "home grown," the international community is likely supporting organizations that are nonprincipled in the sense that they will go against the preferences of the population they are supposedly trying to help. Taken to the extreme, this may encourage the proliferation of more organizations that are internationally biased, limiting the ability of INGOs to be successful on more divisive human rights issues because the domestic community does not share the preferences of these internationally biased—and internationally supported—organizations.

How can I evaluate this hypothesis? For the independent variable, I need a proxy for the underlying proportion of organizations in a country that are not internationally biased. Further complicating matters, this measure has to be exogenous to international support, which is the dependent variable in the analysis. For this proxy, I turn to the *Yearbook of International Organizations* again, this time relying on its data concerning the founding location of all human rights INGOs in the data set and their ECOSOC status. Because consultative status with ECOSOC can be indicative of international bias, at least on divisive human rights issues where the preferences of the UN do not reflect the preferences of the domestic community, I created a country-year variable of the number of human rights INGOs that had been founded within the state but do not have consultative status with ECOSOC. Again, this variable is only a proxy of the proportion of domestically oriented human rights INGOs within a state, but it does reflect the idea of whether organizations are "home grown" but not sending signals that that they have a mission consistent with UN work. Although the UN mission may be domestically consistent for nondivisive human rights, for divisive human rights issues, like women's rights or cultural rights, for example, the UN mission could be argued to be more in line with international preferences. I use the natural log of this measure in the statistical models.

For the dependent variable, which must capture the amount of support the international community gives to INGOs, I first use the international community shaming measure used for Hypothesis 4. Again, this is the number of events in Reuters Global News Service where an international actor shames a targeted state. When using this indicator, I have to account for the specific count nature of this dependent variable. First, to account for the overdispersion in the data set, I must run a negative binomial model. Second, I run a zero-inflated version of this model, which allows me to account for two types of countries in the sample: those that are likely to always be without international support (i.e., those that are never subjected to international community shaming) and those that may be without international support but could receive this support (i.e., those that could be shamed by the international community). The approach first runs a binary logit model to account for whether a country is "never shamed" and then runs a count model to predict the number of international community shaming reports in those countries that could be shamed. I use the total number of Reuters reports (natural log) as the inflation factor here. I include controls for the regime type of a country, its physical integrity rights, and the number of total reports in Reuters (natural log). Additionally, I run a model with yearly fixed effects and robust standard errors, lagging all independent variables in the analysis.[21]

Of course, international community support via shaming is not the only way that the international community could offer their support to INGOs. As Sundstrom (2006) points out in the case of Russia, the donor community often offers financial support to organizations that share its preferences, not wanting to support organizations that are domestically consistent. To test this idea, consistent with Hypothesis 6, in a larger cross-national sample, I use Official Development Assistance (ODA) from states that are in the Organization for Economic Cooperation and Development (OECD) for the purpose of supporting government and civil society, in millions of constant US dollars, as the dependent variable. My key independent variable remains the same: the number of human rights INGOs founded in a state that do not have ECOSOC status, which serves as a proxy again for the number of domestically consistent human rights INGOs. I restrict my focus to only aid recipient states and include physical integrity rights, regime type, GDP per capita (natural log), total aid (natural log), and population size (natural log) as control variables. I run an ordinary least squares regression with yearly fixed effects and robust standard errors and lag all of the independent variables one year in the statistical models.

One final thing is worth mentioning for both of these statistical models on international community support and domestically consistent INGOs: what should we do about internationally biased INGOs? For both dependent variables—international shaming support and financial support—I run models where I include as an additional control variable the natural log of the number of locally founded human rights INGOs that do have consultative status with ECOSOC. Again, the expectation is the exact opposite of the domestically consistent INGO proxy: as this variable increases, I should expect more international community support.[22]

What do the statistical results imply?[23] Regardless of whether I measure international community support as shaming events or as financial support, I find that the number of domestically consistent INGOs has the negative and statistically significant impact on the amount of international support provided in the next year. However, I find a positive and statistically significant relationship between the proxy for internationally biased organizations and international community support. In short, as homegrown domestically consistent advocacy INGOs increase, the international community is less likely to offer their support to the total INGO sector. This community would rather support internationally biased organizations that reflect their preference order.

Figure 5.7 illustrates this effect when the dependent variable is ODA aid for government/civil society support. When all variables are at their means in the sample, as the indicator for the number of human rights INGOs with domestic preferences goes from its minimum to its maximum in the sample, there is expected to be over a $17 million drop in support to government/civil society (90 percent confidence interval between −34.974 and −1.837). Conversely, as the indicator for the number of human rights INGOs with internationally biased preferences increases in the sample, there is expected to be an increase of over $32 million in aid for governance/civil society purposes (90 percent confidence interval between 12.066 and 52.077). Although these changes are substantively smaller than similar changes in other variables in the model, as shown in this figure, these results do indicate that the international community is more likely

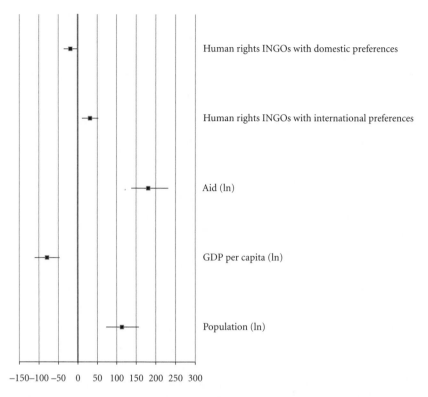

Figure 5.7 Substantive impact of domestically oriented INGOs on international community support (ODA aid to government / civil society, in millions)

NOTE: All results were calculated using CLARIFY with an OLS regression mode with robust standard errors clustered on country. The box indicates the mean expected change in CIRI physical integrity rights; the line indicates the 95% confidence interval.

to only support growth in civil society when it is clear that this growth is reflective of the international community's preferences. In other words, unlike conventional wisdom, the international community does not look at all growth in civil society equally and as a positive thing; it only wants to support cases where it is clear that the civil society growth reflects its preference order.

Does this result hold up to a nonquantitative "reality check"? A recent case study on Israeli-based domestic NGOs highlights that this dynamic is also occurring internally within countries, with NGOs that operate in line with the wishes of donors receiving the most international or governmental donations (Berkovitch and Gordon 2008). As Berkovitch and Gordon (2008) contend, this could have powerful repercussions on the nature of advocacy work:

NGOs that appropriate interests which coincide with the donors' "directives" have a higher probability of receiving funds. Thus, the dependency of NGOs on external funding helps shape almost every aspect of human rights work, including the agenda of rights NGOs, their modes of operation, and the victims of violations with which they deal. (896).

In other words, by only supporting organizations that share their preferences, to the extent that international community support aids in advocacy success, as shown above, the biases of the international community likely shape many aspects of advocacy work, perhaps in ways that could overall limit the potential of INGOs to influence human security outcomes. As Clark and colleagues (2006) point out, this donor dominance in North Africa made many internationally aligned human rights INGOs jump on the bandwagon for the full eradication of female genital cutting; there was simply little money for any other form of human rights advocacy in the region during the 1990s.

This result illustrates Sundstrom's (2006) point that not all international support to INGOs should be viewed as supporting domestic civil society growth; to the extent that domestic and international preferences vary on an issue, international community support to INGOs will likely support groups that do not share the domestic community's preferences, perhaps limiting the overall long-term success of the advocacy movement on divisive advocacy issues in particular. This is definitely a constraint on the international community's likelihood of supporting truly bottom-up civil society growth.

While I would caution any conclusions that demonize international community support, the results presented here would suggest that domestically oriented INGOs have a difficult road to travel. Support from the international community aids their work but, if they are working on issues which are divisive for the international and domestic communities, this support may be hard to come by. In general, this result reiterates the necessity of long-term advocacy work to influence preferences and, hopefully, change divisive human rights issues into those issues where both the international and domestic communities can finds a middle-ground on which to focus their advocacy efforts.

CONCLUSION

Do advocacy INGOs matter for "freedom from fear" human security outcomes? Focusing specifically on human rights INGOs, the results of this chapter give a resounding "yes" to the potential human rights INGOs have on stopping human rights abuses and improving human rights performance within states.

However, consistent with the empirical implications of the advocacy INGO game-theoretic model, this chapter also highlights many factors that condition the extent of the impact these INGOs have on human security advocacy outcomes. Some of these implications from the formal model are consistent with long-held ideas and discussions from nonformal work, including Keck and Sikkink (1998) and Risse, Ropp, and Sikkink (1999). The results in this chapter are based on a somewhat novel quantitative approach; however, as discussed above, the results do hold up to qualitative and practitioner-based "reality checks."

First, these results highlight the utility of relaxing the assumption that all INGOs are principled and share the preference order of the domestic population of the state where the INGO, by its very mission statement, is working to help. Instead of reflective of the domestic community's preferences, some INGOs have preferences that are biased in favor of their international donors, as feared by Gordenker and Weiss (1995). When the focus is on human security advocacy outcomes where the preferences of the domestic community and the international community are somewhat congruent, as is the case with basic physical integrity rights protection, complications from these various motivational types of advocacy INGOs do not limit the overall success of the sector. However, when the focus is on human security advocacy outcomes where the preferences of the domestic and international communities are more divergent, like women's rights, the existence of both internationally biased and domestically consistent advocacy INGOs limits the success of the whole movement. Perhaps this is why Amnesty International took so long to adopt a focus on economic, social, and cultural rights; it knew that these more divisive issues, such as women's social rights, would be less successful advocacy attempts due to the variation in community preferences, reflected in diversity of INGO goals on these issues (Hopgood 2006). Because of the variation in community preferences, only on nondivisive issues can the use of signaling aid in the achievement of human security advocacy outcomes. This research thus extends Gordenker and Weiss's (1995) discussion of donor-dominance in INGO work and provides evidence for how variation in advocacy INGO motivations can influence on-the-ground advocacy outcomes.

Further, the results presented here show that not all states are ripe for human rights INGO advocacy success. States that are vulnerable to international and domestic pressure, where costs for the domestic community are low, and those where the international community is likely to join in advocacy attempts are those where success is most likely. These results are consistent with earlier non-formal ideas of where INGOs are likely to work best; however, they have largely not been qualitatively or quantitatively empirically examined (Keck and Sikkink 1998). To the extent that INGOs can work to lower barriers for domestic community support or coincide their advocacy campaigns with times of international vulnerability, their overall success on basic physical integrity rights protection will be heightened.

However, the results also support a cautionary footnote into the behavior of the international community toward advocacy INGOs: because INGOs can be dependent on financing from international donors, some human rights INGOs can be easily swayed by their donors' preferences, often at the expense of the desires of the domestic population. The results in this chapter would support ongoing efforts by human rights INGOs to set up permanent locations and long-term relationships with local groups, to work to ease the costs the domestic population faces for interacting with INGOs, and, moreover, to structure their advocacy to reflect the desires of the domestic population.

Table 5.1 Impact of human rights INGO shaming mobilization on human rights performance

Variable	(1) Physical integrity rights	(2) Women's social rights	(3) Women's economic rights	(4) Women's political rights
Human rights INGO shaming mobilization	0.04219** (0.020)	0.00088 (0.017)	−0.00887 (0.017)	−0.00693 (0.019)
Population (ln)	−0.54998*** (0.062)	−0.06746 (0.054)	−0.09921** (0.048)	0.06027 (0.044)
War	−0.52851*** (0.164)	−0.30873** (0.157)	−0.24303** (0.123)	−0.19337 (0.130)
Media coverage (differenced)	−0.14258*** (0.043)	−0.02344 (0.033)	0.01637 (0.033)	−0.12854*** (0.040)
GDP per capita (ln)	0.46065*** (0.078)	0.19455** (0.076)	0.33886*** (0.071)	−0.06037 (0.068)
Revised combined polity index	0.06831*** (0.011)	0.06883*** (0.014)	0.04788*** (0.013)	0.07350*** (0.013)
Constant / cut 1	9.41513*** (1.202)	−0.50155 (1.039)	−0.36941 (0.991)	−1.53954* (0.866)
Cut 2	— —	1.44135 (1.048)	1.94772* (1.046)	−0.33201 (0.898)
Cut 3	— —	2.57427** (1.032)	3.65551*** (1.068)	2.35947*** (0.897)
Observations	2267	1686	2248	2369

NOTE: Robust standard errors in parentheses.
$^*p < 0.1$, $^{**}p < 0.05$, $^{***}p < 0.01$.

Table 5.2 Impact of human rights INGO presence (instrumented) on human rights performance

Variable	(1) Physical integrity rights	(2) Women's social rights	(3) Women's economic rights	(4) Women's political rights
Human rights INGO (ln) (instrumented)	2.64914* (1.493)	−0.04946 (0.589)	0.12490 (0.412)	1.16291** (0.563)
Population (ln)	−1.00559*** (0.309)	−0.02151 (0.119)	−0.06629 (0.086)	−0.18337 (0.117)
GDP per capita (ln)	0.07907 (0.193)	0.15788** (0.076)	0.13358** (0.054)	−0.16386** (0.073)
War	−4.34049*** (0.800)	−0.33917 (0.319)	−0.08369 (0.224)	−0.12348 (0.302)
Revised combined polity index	−0.02118 (0.060)	0.05210** (0.024)	0.01978 (0.017)	0.00198 (0.023)
Constant	11.32336*** (1.892)	0.36503 (0.724)	0.85314 (0.531)	1.91854*** (0.715)
Observations	836	814	822	835

NOTE: Second stage results; standard errors in parentheses.
$^*p < 0.1$, $^{**}p < 0.05$, $^{***}p < 0.01$.

Table 5.3 Impact of human rights INGO shaming mobilization, conditional on internal and external (export) vulnerability

Variable	(1) Physical integrity rights
Human rights INGO shaming mobilization * export * democracy	0.00102** (0.000)
Human rights INGO shaming mobilization * export	−0.00622*** (0.002)
Human rights INGO shaming mobilization * democracy	−0.01297 (0.010)
Export * democracy	0.00668** (0.003)
Human rights INGO shaming mobilization	0.09297 (0.063)
Export (percent of GDP)	−0.00451 (0.012)
Democracy	0.09485*** (0.025)
Population (ln)	−0.54024*** (0.091)
War	−0.93280*** (0.227)
Media coverage (differenced)	−0.07434 (0.071)
GDP per capita (ln)	0.32399*** (0.104)
Constant	10.15783*** (1.855)
Observations	1185

NOTE: Robust standard errors in parentheses.
$^{*}p < 0.1$, $^{**}p < 0.05$, $^{***}p < 0.01$.

Table 5.4 Impact of signaling human rights INGOs (instrumented) on human rights performance

Variable	(1) Physical integrity rights	(2) Women's social rights	(3) Women's economic rights	(4) Women's political rights
ECOSOC signaling human rights INGOs (instrumented)	0.81271** (0.324)	0.13694 (0.112)	0.09497 (0.070)	0.09687 (0.087)
Population (ln)	−0.84953*** (0.121)	−0.10870** (0.042)	−0.00286 (0.026)	−0.08929*** (0.034)
GDP per capita (ln)	0.07072 (0.150)	0.11796** (0.055)	−0.06419 (0.041)	0.11316*** (0.039)
War	−2.49749*** (0.230)	−0.15041* (0.080)	0.01339 (0.077)	−0.01573 (0.064)
Revised combined polity index	0.04799*** (0.013)	0.04379*** (0.006)	0.03711*** (0.006)	0.02473*** (0.005)
Human rights INGO shaming mobilization	0.04940 (0.094)	0.00473 (0.023)	−0.01144 (0.020)	−0.01325 (0.013)
Constant	17.42698*** (2.857)	1.81504* (0.992)	2.18462*** (0.630)	1.73737** (0.774)
Observations	769	744	769	756
R^2	0.313	0.369	0.127	0.331

NOTE: Second stage results; robust standard errors in parentheses.
*$p < 0.1$, **$p < 0.05$, ***$p < 0.01$.

Table 5.5 Impact of human rights INGO shaming mobilization, conditional on domestic support costs (personal contact)

Variable	*(1)* *Physical integrity rights*
Human rights INGO shaming mobilization * personal contact	0.00248*** (0.001)
Personal contact	0.02269*** (0.008)
Human rights INGO shaming mobilization	−0.06973 (0.046)
Population (ln)	−0.43359*** (0.071)
War	−0.51357*** (0.162)
Media coverage (differenced)	−0.13185*** (0.043)
GDP per capita (ln)	0.19552* (0.119)
Revised combined polity index	0.06630*** (0.010)
Constant	8.75472*** (1.202)
Observations	2241

NOTE: Robust standard errors in parentheses.
$^*p < 0.1$, $^{**}p < 0.05$, $^{***}p < 0.01$.

Table 5.6 Impact of human rights INGO shaming mobilization, conditional on international community support

Variable	(1) Physical integrity rights
Human rights INGO shaming mobilization * international community support	0.00462* (0.003)
International community support	−0.02386 (0.019)
Human rights INGO shaming mobilization	0.02347 (0.024)
Revised combined polity index	0.06797*** (0.011)
Population (ln)	−0.54120*** (0.064)
War	−0.53715*** (0.163)
Media coverage (differenced)	−0.14416*** (0.043)
GDP per capita (ln)	0.46457*** (0.077)
Constant	9.25551*** (1.233)
Observations	2267

NOTE: Robust standard errors in parentheses.
$^*p < 0.1$, $^{**}p < 0.05$, $^{***}p < 0.01$.

Table 5.7 Determinants of international community support (shaming)

Variable	*(1)* *International community support (shaming)*
Human rights INGOs with domestic preferences	−0.25976*** (0.083)
Human rights INGOs with international preferences	0.09484 (0.078)
Revised combined polity score	−0.01636* (0.010)
Physical integrity rights	−0.23715*** (0.030)
Media coverage	0.23766** (0.111)
Constant	−1.90883** (0.820)
Media coverage (inflation)	−1.12067* (0.616) 5.90839
Constant (inflation)	(3.665) −0.45479**
Ln alpha	(0.189)
Observations	681

NOTE: Robust standard errors in parentheses.
*$p < 0.1$, **$p < 0.05$, ***$p < 0.01$.

Table 5.8 Determinants of international community support (aid)

Variable	(1) International community support (aid)
Human rights INGOs with domestic preferences	−16.01635* (9.108)
Human rights INGOs with international preferences	9.17474*** (3.385)
Physical integrity rights	0.92725 (1.524)
Revised combined polity score	2.67628*** (0.651)
Aid (ln)	21.95314*** (3.188)
GDP per capita (ln)	−17.59571*** (4.275)
Population (ln)	15.61753*** (3.452)
Constant	−518.68628*** (72.035)
Observations	377
R^2	0.469

NOTE: Robust standard errors in parentheses.
*$p < 0.1$, **$p < 0.05$, ***$p < 0.01$.

6 INGOS—POSSIBLE ANGELS FOR HUMAN SECURITY?

AT THE TIME of this book's writing, human security—freedom from want and fear—was simply not a reality for a large proportion of the world's inhabitants. Concerning freedom from want, although there are far fewer people living on less than $1.25 a day than five or ten years ago (Chandy and Gertz 2011), there are still more people hungry today than in 1990 (IFPRI 2012). And despite much worldwide economic growth, almost 40 percent of the world's population still lacks basic sanitation (UNICEF and WHO 2012). Most of the world is also not free from fear. In 2010, over 85 percent of countries had some evidence of government abuse of basic physical integrity rights. Over 83 percent of countries had evidence of governmental use of torture on its citizens, and 82 percent of countries had less than perfect protection of women's economic rights (Cingranelli and Richards 2010).

Given this sad reality, what tools exist to combat human *in*security? For freedom from want, the world has tried many options, including everything from bilateral foreign aid to all-out military intervention. None of these options, of course, are without their drawbacks and many scholars have questioned whether they actually deliver measurable human security service outcomes the majority of the time (Collier and Hoeffler 2004; Easterly 2006; Bellamy 2008; Lake and Fariss 2012). For issues concerning freedom from fear, there also exists a broad "toolbox" of state and intergovernmental options to improve human rights, including international treaties, sanctions, and military actions. Many of these options, however, are either just not successful most of the time (Hathaway 2002; Hafner-Burton and Tsutsui 2005; Murdie and Davis 2010) or, even more troubling, have the potential to actually backfire and further harm an already precarious human security situation (Wood 2008; Peksen 2009, 2012; Peksen and Drury 2009).

At the end of the Cold War, one set of actors stood out as a possible savior of the world's insecure: international non-governmental organizations (INGOs). These groups, like Doctors Without Borders, Oxfam, Amnesty International, and Human Rights Watch, were seen as the world's best option for human security, drastically changing state-society relations. As McGann and Johnstone (2005) remarked:

> World politics has undergone a radical and often-overlooked transformation in the last 15 years, resulting neither from the collapse of the Soviet Union nor the rising tide of fundamentalism, but from the unprecedented growth of non-governmental organizations around the globe. NGOs or Civil Society Organizations (CSOs) have moved from backstage to center stage in world politics and are exerting their power and influence in every aspect of international relations and policy making. NGOs have been a positive force in domestic and international affairs, working to alleviate poverty, protect human rights, preserve the environment, and provide relief worldwide. (65)

Like many others, these authors take the success of NGOs as almost a given, continuing to say that the positives of NGOs are so great that "few, therefore, have felt the need to take a critical look at the effectiveness and accountability of these organizations" (65).

This millennial view of NGOs, focusing mainly on organizations that are international in their scope and focus, was reflected in much of the constructivist literature in international relations at the time. Most of the academic literature saw the potential of INGOs as unique, something linked to the organizations' "principled" motivational composition and position in a larger network of concerned advocates (Keck and Sikkink 1998; Risse, Ropp, and Sikkink 1999; Kelly 2005; Risse 2010).[1] This was in stark contrast to the conventional, state-centric realist view of nonstate actors, which gave little credence to the potential of any nonstate actor, including INGOs, to matter in a state-centric world of realpolitik (Waltz 1979; Geeraerts 1995). And, yet, according to the dominant theoretical literature concerning INGOs at the time, these organizations were supposed to be constricting even the most basic ways a government controlled its own population through force.

As time continued, however, whispers—and then shouts—of on-the-ground problems with INGOs drew their potential role as protectors and providers of human security into question. Story upon story of organizations pocketing money meant for food relief or sanitation began to circulate around the human security community (Huggler 2005; Mojumdar 2006; Birrell 2012). Even INGOs with missions for providing things as idealistic as child welfare and refugee relief were going into countries not out of a desire to help the vulnerable domestic population but to get donations for their own private use. As Kumar (2012) remarked, there were many tales of organizations being formed solely because "opening an NGO is one of the easiest ways of minting money." With little formal oversight, running an NGO allowed the heads of the organization to fund a "lavish lifestyle" with "houses, property, foreign trips, and expenses on children educations," all of which "contradicts their claims of social service." For organizations promoting human rights, stories of groups adopting their whole advocacy agenda in order to attract funding from a couple of international donors also circulated (Khidr 2006; Roelofs 2006; Wenzel 2006). Some advocacy organizations were accused, by both governments and local citizens, of being nothing but an arm to a larger imperial power, advocating for things unwanted by the repressed population they were supposed to be helping (Wallace 2004; Harvey 2006).

In short, despite their early praise as human security providers, it became clear to many that INGOs were "part of the problem," just another actor or pathway that would not work (Schuller 2007). A revisionist strand of international relations literature reflected these on-the-ground problems, often throwing out any hope that INGOs could actually improve human security (Petras 1997; Cooley and Ron 2002; Bob 2005; Goonatilake 2006; Sundstrom 2006; Ferris 2011). Despite all of this theoretical attention, however, very few extant studies have actually evaluated the potential effects of INGOs on any large scale. So at the end of the day, who is right? Are INGOs really the "angels" of the early accounts and academic literature, drastically improving human security (Tvedt 1998)? Or are INGOs, because of their personalistic motivations and rent-seeking behavior, really doing nothing for the world's insecure?

This book stands separate from much of the extant work on INGOs in international relations. In my framework of INGO effectiveness, I do not categorize INGOs as a coherent group of either "angels" or "devils." I relax—but do not altogether abandon—the assumption from the canonical literature that INGOs are "principled" actors motivated by "shared values" with the community they are supposedly trying to help (Keck and Sikkink 1998; Risse, Ropp, and Sikkink 1999; Risse 2010). Instead, there also exists INGOs motivated in mainly "nonprincipled" ways, like a service INGO taking money for private rents or an advocacy INGO working only for the policies that an international donor wants. This motivational information is private; a domestic or international actor interacting with an INGO does not know the organization's motivational structure ex ante. Only the INGO itself knows whether it is primarily motivated for private gain or whether it is motivated to help improve human security in ways desired by the local community.

Even when I relax this principled assumption—and acknowledge the ways in which nonprincipled organizations can complicate both domestic and international interactions in the human security community—this book empirically finds that, in many instances, the whole INGO sector does live up to the early hype and improves human security. The INGO sector is still important for human security even when we do not assume that the sector is composed solely of angels. In short, even when some organizations are "devils," INGOs can still—under many conditions—be a positive force for ensuring that people are free from want and fear.

OVERVIEW OF FINDINGS

Given this framework, this book offers many answers to questions of when and where INGOs are likely be effective actors for human security. To begin, in states and on issues where INGOs with nonprincipled motivations are less likely to flourish, we are more likely to see measurable results. In the realm of human security service provision, this very basic statement underlies the novel finding that INGO success is conditioned by government control of corruption within a country. When corruption is not controlled, it can be assumed that there is a greater proportion of rent-seeking service INGOs active in the country. The presence of these rent-seeking organizations can limit the support the whole INGO sector receives from both domestic and international actors, leading to a diminished sector-wide effect on the ground. Likewise, in the realm of human security advocacy, this basic idea implies that organizations will be less successful on issues where there is expected to be many internationally biased organizations with preferences for outcomes that are of little immediate value to the domestic community. In practice, this means that issues of women's rights protection are less successful, on the large scale, for the INGO sector, than issues of basic physical integrity rights protection.

Further, in acknowledging that not all INGOs have principled motivations, this book addresses a real problem for those interacting with INGOs on the ground: without additional information about the organization they are interacting with, actors critical to INGO success do not know ex ante whether they are facing an organization with preferences that are of little to no value for them. They could be facing a development organization, for example, that is just going to "take the money and run" (Pitner 2000)! Because of this variation in INGO motivational structures, organizations have to send signals of their motivational "type" to these actors. For the service INGO realm, where all actors, both domestic and international, would like to avoid supporting a rent-seeker, this book finds that INGOs which signal their non-rent-seeking motivations through the UN Economic, Social, and Cultural (ECOSOC) system are more likely to gain the support necessary to actually deliver services on the ground. For the advocacy INGO realm, where motivational differences in INGOs are reflected in differences in the preferences of the international and domestic communities, the results presented here highlight the role of the UN ECOSOC signal on advocacy success, but only on issues where preferences for advocacy outcomes do not greatly diverge for the international and domestic communities.

Finally, this book offers many state and structural conditions which make INGO success more likely. In general, if it is less costly for the domestic community to interact with INGOs, the human security impact of these organizations increases. For service INGOs, this means that urban countries are more likely to be positively affected by INGOs. Likewise, when a country's government does not restrict empowerment rights, it is more likely that domestic citizens will work with service INGOs in ways that ultimately influence human security. In general, a domestic population is more willing to support service INGOs, even given high costs, if the population values the service more; this implies that certain service provision activities, like contraceptive clinics, will be more successful based on whether the domestic community supports the effort at the onset. Similarly, for human rights advocacy INGOs, globalization makes working with advocacy INGOs, who are often active outside of the repressive country, easier and states where the domestic population can more readily interact with advocacy INGOs via the Internet or even international mail are more likely to have improvements in physical integrity rights attributable to INGOs. Additionally, when the international community provides more support to the work of INGOs, human security is more likely to improve. This result holds both in the service realm and in the advocacy realm. Advocacy INGO success is also dependent, as could be expected from the extant literature, on the internal and external vulnerability of the targeted state.

IMPLICATIONS FOR SCHOLARSHIP

The central argument underlying this broad set of findings challenges the extant academic literature in many ways. First, for grand or meta-theory in international relations, unlike realism would predict, this book shows that nonstate actors do matter, even on issues as crucial to regime survival as use of force against civilians. Although this idea of realism presents almost a strawman argument against the potential of INGOs, it is critical to acknowledge that this conclusion does not rest on any idealistic notion of INGO motivations. The principled assumption from the constructivist literature is not required for us to conclude that INGOs matter in world politics.

For constructivism, this book reiterates the potential of INGOs made clear in the canonical Keck and Sikkink (1998) and Risse, Ropp, and Sikkink (1999), albeit with some very important caveats. Like constructivism, where the focus has predominantly been on advocacy INGOs and rights promotion, the argument and results presented here highlight the role of international advocates in norm transmission and behavior change (Finnemore and Sikkink 1998). In particular, the results here stress the central role of INGOs in contributing to improvement in human rights through the causal process outlined in this larger literature: INGOs work with the domestic community from "below" the targeted state and with the international community "above" the targeted state to increase pressure for human rights improvement (Brysk 1993; Keck and Sikkink 1998). The theoretical argument presented here follows a similar causal pathway and the empirical results show that the support the INGO receives from these communities can be critical to the overall success of the organization.

Unlike the canonical literature, however, I do not take this support as a given: like Bob's (2005) revisionist work, I allow INGOs to be involved in an area not because they have been called to the domestic community at the onset but because of other motivational goals. Taking a step back in the causal chain and allowing for the theoretical process of advocacy to include the decision of the domestic community to support the INGO or not allows my framework to examine the factors that make support "from below" likely, including both issue resonance and domestic community costs of support. Although issue resonance is a topic that has been given some attention in the larger constructivist literature (Checkel 1997; Cortell and Davis 2000; Keck and Sikkink 1998; Risse

2002), this book provides concrete empirical tests for how the preexisting resonance of an advocacy issue within the domestic population can influence INGOs' success in that specific locale. Of course, like Risse (2010) makes clear, INGOs are not "stupid," and the results presented here concerning the role of issue resonance in conditioning the influence of INGOs on human security outcomes provide an alternative strategic explanation for issue nonemergence (Bob 2005; Carpenter 2007, 2010). The argument and findings of this book would suggest that issues of little resonance with one community—domestic or international—and of little value to the other community—are likely to be issues "non grata" by INGOs, whose on-the-ground success depends on getting at least one of these communities to support their work. Further, much of the existing constructivist literature concerns, at least theoretically, the process of long-term preference change (Checkel 1997; Finnemore and Sikkink 1998). Here, I show that, although long-term preference change may still be possible on issues with little domestic resonance, short-term measureable results are not. To the extent that a lack of short-term results limits the ability of INGOs to stay within the locale or creates a backlash against the organization, this book would suggest that long-term preference change in a domestic population as a result of INGO efforts may be unlikely without considerable reframing of an issue to make it appear more consistent with domestic preferences.

Moreover, unlike the dominant constructivist literature on INGOs, I do not see INGOs as a homogeneous lot that all have motivations for "shared values" (Keck and Sikkink 1998; Risse 2010). INGOs, as highlighted above, can have nonprincipled motivations. And, not to belabor the point too much, my framework is also different from much of the constructivist, revisionist literature on INGOs in international relations in that I do not assume the nonprincipled motivations of some INGOs implies nonprincipled motivations for all INGOs (Cooley and Ron 2002; Bob 2005). Understanding how the proportion of nonprincipled organizations can vary by issue focus and by location is critical, as outlined above, for developing a comprehensive framework of the conditional effects of INGOs on human security outcomes.

Relaxing the assumption that all INGOs are principled also allows this book to bring service organizations into the international relations theoretical literature on INGOs, which has tended to overwhelmingly focus on advocacy INGOs and often attributes the same patterns of behavior and motivational issues to both advocacy and service organizations. I argue that a fundamental difference exists between nonprincipled INGOs that focus primarily on service provision and those that focus primarily on advocacy. As outlined in detail in Chapters 2 and 3, for service INGOs, a nonprincipled organization is a rent-seeker, but for advocacy INGOs, a nonprincipled organization is one that has motivations for what its international donors want but not what the domestic community actually desires. Attention to these dynamics highlights how the domestic and international communities fundamentally react differently to nonprincipled organizations across these realms. When faced with a nonprincipled service INGO, both the international donor community and the domestic community are in agreement that they get little value from this rent-seeker. Conversely, if the nonprincipled INGO is advocacy in orientation, the international community has preferences that are more in line with it than with the principled organization. As such, the tension in the advocacy INGO realm, once we relax the principled assumption, is that not all actors share the same ordering of preferences. This leads to a more complex signaling environment for advocacy INGOs and a more complex environment for domestic-international interactions in the realm of advocacy. These differences between advocacy and service INGOs have been all but ignored in the larger international relations literature.

Beyond meta-theory and INGO-specific studies, this book speaks to the role of information—and the lack thereof—in driving the nature of interactions in international relations (Jervis 1970; Downs and Rocke 1995; Fearon 1997; Sartori 2003). At the onset of their interaction, the actors that can support INGOs are uninformed of the exact motivational structure of the INGO they are facing. Instead of knowing whether INGO X is principled or not, the domestic and interactional communities only know the general proportion of principled organizations to nonprincipled organizations in the location. Their lack of precise information—and subsequent dependence on only coarser information—factors quite strikingly into other actors' decision of whether or not to support any INGO they come across. As this proportion increases in favor of the INGO with a motivational type that is of value for the actor, in most situations, it is more likely to support any organization it comes across. In other words, in a situation where most INGOs are principled, there can be a few "bad apples" that slip through the cracks and get supported. These situations can create a lot of international buzz—as occasionally happens in the United States and France—but the information environment is such that these mistakes are likely to happen.

There are many other situations in international relations where scholars have categorized the information environment in similar terms, including the interactions of states where resolve for war-fighting is unknown (Fearon 1997; Huth 1999; Weeks 2008) and situations where information about regime commitment to political economic policy changes are unknown (Rodrik 1989; Haggard and Maxfield 1996; Kerner 2009). In broader terms, the situation with INGOs and the communities they are interacting with is simply a principal-agent situation, where the principal, the communities, lack certain information about the agent, here the INGO and its motivational structure (Miller 2005; Hawkins et al. 2006). The theoretical framework in this book pushes the envelope, however, and examines these informational dynamics where there are multiple principals—the domestic and international communities—and, at least in the realm of advocacy, these principals have differing preferences for the type of organization they would like to support. This idea flows quite nicely from the nonformal discussion of the NGO world in Cooley and Ron (2002) and Prakash and Gugerty (2010). More generally, however, informational issues that have to do with multiple principals and a single agent have received less attention in the broad international relations literature, but the multiple principal informational dynamics of this book appear to readily apply to other situations, like when multiple states are simultaneously choosing alliance partners or when a foreign policy leader is deciding on a course of action when the preferences of the domestic and international communities differ.

Further, this book stresses how the informational environment can be influenced by the INGOs themselves; they can send costly signals of their motivational type to the domestic and international communities. This relates to the larger signaling literature in international relations, which has typically focused on signals sent by states actors (Jervis 1970; Weeks 2008; Fang 2008; Chapman 2011). Again, in the advocacy world, because of variation in the preferences of the domestic and the international communities, these actors can react quite differently to the signals INGOs send. Unlike conventional signaling models, therefore, the audiences do not all respond similarly to the signal sent and signals are sent by the informed player with this dynamic at play. This signaling situation rarely appears in the larger international relations literature, which tends to identify a unified response to the signaling behavior (Jervis 1970; Fearon 1997; Kerner 2009).

Likewise, the use of the signaling framework speaks to the larger literature in public policy and American politics on signals through voluntary accountability programs among nonprofits (Gugerty 2009; Tschirhart 2010; Gugerty and Prakash 2010). This book pushes this framework to examine how an organization's signal will be observed, and can be interpreted differently, by multiple audiences. The empirical focus in this book is on the signal sent by INGOs through registration with UN ECOSOC; again, this adds to the larger literature on nonprofits by focusing on a signal that has not received attention in extant scholarship. The focus on this signal illustrates how INGOs can utilize intergovernmental organizations as a way to provide information to other actors that are necessary for their work.

Like any academic endeavor, this book makes many simplifications that deserve further unpacking. By no means is it intended to cover the entire nuance of INGOs on the ground. As a result, the contributions of this book could be extended in future scholarship in many ways. First, this book is novel in its use of the signal of ECOSOC. As mentioned in Chapter 2, ECOSOC consultative status is the major way INGOs have access to the UN arena. However, other possible intergovernmental organizations exist through which INGOs can signal their motivations, including the International Labour Organization, the Organization of American States, and the European Commission. Many of these intergovernmental organizations, especially regional organizations, may be viewed differently by domestic populations in the region in question. This could be especially interesting in the world of advocacy, where signals often reiterate internationally biased motivations, especially on very divisive advocacy issues.

Theoretically, this work divides organizations into two realms: advocacy and service. However, with the rise of "rights-based" approaches, there are more organizations that can be classified as "hybrids," with both a service delivery and an advocacy mission (Jordan and Van Tuijl 2000; Kelly 2005; Nelson and Dorsey 2008; Murdie and Davis 2012b). In line with this book, we can easily assume that these hybrids could have the nonprincipled problems of both advocacy and service organizations: they could be internationally biased and rent-seekers. This could complicate the preferences of the international community, which might be willing to support the organization because of its advocacy preferences but not willing to support it because of its rent-seeking status.

Many of the assumptions in the theoretical model could be further relaxed to provide additional hypotheses that would be of interest to INGO scholars. First, the model allows for two communities, domestic and international, and assumes uniform preferences within these communities. There are situations, however, where these actor groupings may be bifurcated to the extent that including more communities would be useful. For example, on a particular advocacy issue like the elimination of drone strikes, the international community may be divided into those with extreme preferences and those with more moderate advocacy preferences.

Moreover, the game-theoretic model on service INGOs presented here makes a very strong assumption when it comes to nonprincipled rent-seekers: they are assumed not to deliver any services at all. Although anecdotal evidence definitely supports the idea that many service INGOs supply no services whatsoever, as discussed in Chapter 2, there are other organizations, of course, where rent-seeking, although present, is minimal. Future work could divide the nonprincipled category into multiple groups, including a full rent-seeking organization where no services are provided and a partial rent-seeking organization that still provides some services. As the proportion of this middle category increases, the domestic and international community may be more willing to support all INGOs they come across, regardless of signal sent.

The theoretical framework in this book focuses on international NGOs; the same dynamics extend, however, to organizations that are completely domestic. For example, Brass (2012) found both self-interested and "saintly" motivations in the decision making of Kenyan NGOs (393). Likewise, as Dupuy, Ron, and Prakash (2012) recently wrote, the issue of international bias in advocacy NGOs has been seen in many domestic contexts in the Global South. Extensions to this book's framework could incorporate these ideas and examine how international funding and motivational issues influence domestic civil society success on human security outcomes. This would also be a useful way to incorporate the ideas of this book with the ideas of Sundstrom (2006) concerning domestic NGOs and foreign funding.

Likewise, I examine two specific areas of human security: development and human rights. Further empirical work would be useful to expand the focus to other areas of human security, including health and environment. For health INGOs in particular, the issues of "hybrids," discussed above, could be especially apparent.

IMPLICATIONS FOR HUMAN SECURITY

Underlying all the game theory and statistics of this book is a very simple question: how can concerned citizens ensure that human security is protected? More specifically, how best can INGOs contribute to human security protection? The argument and empirical results of this book imply several concrete recommendations—for the donor community, for domestic citizens and advocates, and for INGOs themselves—that would improve the potential of INGOs to advance human security. I now conclude with these precepts.

First, the international actors—including IGOs, states, and even third-party citizens—are in a potentially important spot for aiding INGOs. Their assistance, in terms of money or just advocacy attention, can help the human security success of INGOs. However, there is one important qualification here: if international actors focus only on supporting human security "fads," on issues that might be of value to them but where there is little domestic interest, their support of INGOs may be for naught. This finding extends both to service and advocacy. This implication is hardly novel; many have touted that INGOs must take local stakeholder interests into account for success (Calnan 2008; Neba 2009; CMEF 2011). What is novel, however, is that this book shows exactly how important this idea is; if a domestic population does not value what the organizations is doing, the success of the effort can be severely curtailed, at least in the short term. What is even more troubling, at least in the case of advocacy, is that being in a sector where there are likely to be INGOs that are motivated by international donations to fads can limit the achievements of the whole sector, as was shown in the case of women's rights.

What does this imply for the international community? First, if the fad is important for human security, pains must be taken to ensure domestic community buy-in. This could entail reframing the issue to make it more appealing to local populations; it could mean that the donor community must moderate or change its goals entirely. Second, dealing with these issues may require more international donor coordination. As shown in the case of advocacy, when issues are sufficiently divisive, having some INGOs work for the extreme desires of their donors limits the success of the whole group. To the extent that the international donor community can work to quell the extreme preferences of others in their community, this could eliminate the distance between the internationally biased INGO's preferences and the domestically consistent INGO's preferences, increasing the likelihood, in many instances, of human rights advocacy success.

Second, for the international donor community, this book questions the practice of directing aid to the general INGO community in corrupt countries as a way to bypass corruption and supply government services. By acknowledging that INGOs do not all have principled motivations, it is easy to see that that some INGOs are likely to be as corrupt as the governments that donors are trying to bypass. In corrupt countries, these organizations do not fear prosecution for their rent-seeking and may actually think they could be likely to receive more international donations in an environment where donors feel hesitant to fund a corrupt government. As a result, the whole INGO sector can actually have a negative influence on human security service provision in corrupt countries, as shown in Chapter 4. This book still argues that international donations greatly aid INGO success, even in corrupt countries, however, this result only holds because the international donor community is relying on signals about INGO motivations when they are deciding which INGOs to fund. If, even in corrupt countries, donations are directed mainly to INGOs that have signaled their underlying non rent-seeking motivations, donations will aid human security outcomes. For the donor community, this book thus reinforces a powerful constraint on existing ideas that INGOs can serve as an alternative to corrupt states in providing services. Rent-seeking by INGOs is not controlled in corrupt states and, unless donors are paying attention to the signaling behavior of the organizations they are supporting, their funds will not improve service provision.

Relatedly, this book would support international donor community efforts to build and support signaling mechanisms for INGOs. The mechanism addressed in this book comes from the IGO community—the UN ECOSOC process—and ECOSOC has tried to eliminate barriers for INGOs from the Global South to participate in the process. The results here would support such efforts because, as long as the signal is still "costly" enough to make it too expensive for rent-seeking INGOs to want to mimic it, lowering the barrier for less historically well-funded organizations to participate in the process will help organizational funding and will ultimately help the success of the organizations on basic service provision and protection of basic physical integrity rights, as shown in Chapters 4 and 5. I would caution, however, against the utility of donors creating too many signals with overlapping requirements. In other words, my recommendation is that the donor community looks at existing signals and helps support efforts to eliminate unnecessary barriers for signaling across geographic or developmental divides. However, my recommendation would not be, of course, that each donor creates its own duplicate signaling mechanism, which could create such high costs of signaling for INGOs as to eliminate their use of the mechanism.

Finally, for the international donor community, this books highlights that not all areas where INGOs are working are "ripe" for success. International donors, when trying to evaluate INGOs and program success, need to keep this in mind. For service delivery, countries with rural populations and where domestic empowerment rights are restricted are more difficult. For advocacy, countries without many global communication connections or with invulnerable regimes are also less likely to see advocated changes as a result of INGO activities. Although this does not imply that the donor community should avoid supporting INGOs in these areas, it does imply that the donor community needs to be aware of these conditions and, perhaps, allow for programs to have differential success metrics in different locales. As another strategy, international donor funds to improve empowerment rights and increase globalized communication may be useful first steps for latter success at service provision and physical integrity rights advocacy, respectively.

In general, the implications of this book for domestic advocates themselves are far less bleak than in Bob (2005) and other works that acknowledge that INGO motivations may not all be for principles or shared values with the domestic population. For a domestic group interested in improving its human security through INGOs, the results highlight that domestic groups hold considerable power over actual outcomes. For INGOs to be successful, in most instances, they need the support of the domestic community. This is an alternative view to Bob, for example, which focuses on how advocacy INGOs can cherry-pick which domestic groups to help. Here, I highlight that the process through which we actually see human security results on the ground also involves some cherry-picking of INGOs by the domestic advocates themselves. If an organization that is motivated by some sort of international or donor bias is working on an issue that is of little value to the domestic population, this population can withhold all support or can utilize the organization in invulnerable states to achieve its own goals. This logic was outlined in Chapter 3. Of course, the logic here does not contradict the issue raised in Bob concerning the existence of organizations in certain locales for personalistic reasons but does stress that even internationally biased organizations can aid in the achievement of human security goals, something Bob doubts is possible in the conclusion of his work (181–186).

Further, domestic populations do not have to be passive participants in the process by which INGOs determine their service provision or advocacy goals. To the extent that domestic groups can actively press INGOs to alter their service delivery patterns or change their advocacy goals to be more reflective of the domestic populations they are working with, this book's results show that everyone—both INGOs and domestic populations—may stand to benefit. Some advocacy organizations with internationally biased preferences may be willing to reframe their goals slightly if a domestic population would support a slightly altered set of advocacy outcomes. This could be argued to have occurred with the issue of female genital cutting, for example, where current work by INGOs on women's rights tend to downplay any immediate goal of the full eradication of this practice in favor of goals that are of more value to the domestic population where the INGO is working (Kouzzi and Bordat 2012).

Much more importantly, this work stresses that INGOs are not all equal in their motivations and that domestic advocates must be careful to not throw out the whole sector because of problems with a few "bad apples." Relying on the signals INGOs send can be a useful way of ensuring that support is not given to organizations with motivational goals that are not going to be useful for the domestic population. Domestic advocates can help in spreading this information through their state, ensuring that organizations with something of value to the domestic population get the support that is necessary to aid human security on the ground.

For INGOs, this book also offers much food for thought. First, like highlighted before, organizations can aid their own success through working only on issues that have domestic resonance. If an advocacy INGO, for example, has motivations that are more in line with international preferences on an issue, it would still be advised to focus first on some sort of common ground issue that would be seen as more valuable to domestic stakeholders.

Likewise, for both service and advocacy organizations, INGOs can work to eliminate unnecessary costs that serve as barriers to domestic support. Providing transportation to domestic clinics, for example, or setting up mobile rural service stations helps overall outcomes. This idea is not revolutionary but the results here are novel in showing how detrimental high domestic costs can be for the human security success of the whole INGO sector.

And, finally, principled INGOs should remember that they hold the key in separating themselves from their nonprincipled counterparts. Although their motivations are private knowledge, they can send signals of their motivational type that are observed by the international and domestic community and do aid in their success for human security. INGOs' collective actions to "shame" those not living up to their mission statements may actually aid in the sector's success by serving as an alternative signal of underlying motivations.

INGOS: NEITHER ANGELS NOR DEVILS, BUT HUMAN SECURITY PROVIDERS

INGOs are a growing part of the world politics landscape. Many have heralded the organizations as potentially important players for human security because of their "pure" motivations (Ahmed and Potter 2006, 253). Others, however, have stressed how a system of little oversight and much cash has created an INGO sector dominated by those with very individualistic—and often perverse—motivations (Cooley and Ron 2002; Bob 2005). This book has argued that neither approach reflects reality. As such, neither view provides much insight into where and when INGOs will actually deliver on their promises to help human security.

Instead of either extant approach, the INGO sector is made up simultaneously of those with principled and those with nonprincipled motivations. Both of these types of organizations exist concurrently in an environment where others that work with INGOs—both domestic groups and international donors—do not know these motivational details. The existence of both of these types of organizations in an environment where others do not know this information ex ante complicates the interactions INGOs have in world politics. It can require INGOs to send signals of their motivational structure to the larger community and can ultimately condition the overall human security outcomes that can be attributed to INGO efforts.

Nonetheless, acknowledging that INGOs are not all "pure" does not negate the potential of the whole sector to matter for human security. The results of this book stress that INGOs can be powerful actors for improvement freedom from want and fear. Although there have obviously been some "bad apples" in the bunch, on a whole, the overall growth of the INGO sector bodes well for all of us interested in eradicating poverty and improving human well-being.

NOTES

Chapter 1

1. Another way to think of "freedom from want" is as the promotion of economic, social, and cultural rights in the Universal Declaration of Human Rights. "Freedom from fear" melds quite nicely with ideas of the political and civil rights. See Howard-Hassman (2012).

2. Where this issue of motivations has been acknowledged, it has not been theoretically or empirically extended to our understanding of the NGO sector's impact on the outcomes within the sectors the INGOs are working (Gordenker and Weiss 1997; Vakil 1997; Reinhardt 2009; Gugerty and Prakash 2010).

3. Both the introductory chapter and Thomas Risse's response chapter in Prakash and Gugerty (2010) are excellent examples of this debate.

Chapter 2

1. See also http://www.uia.be/2-conventional-categories.

2. Of the distinctions that do exist in many of the cross-disciplinary typologies, like Vakil (1997), the majority of these typologies appear to be easily adapted to the principled/nonprincipled distinction I make in the next chapter, especially when combined with the separate frameworks for understanding these dynamics for advocacy as opposed to service INGOs. I avoid unnecessary distinctions whenever possible so the discussion of NGOs does not turn into "alphabet soup" (Vakil 1997).

3. These examples are also humorously used in Murdie and Bhasin (2011).

4. To note, however, some of the TAN literature does mention that advocacy actors cannot be representative and are often not accountable (Sikkink 2002). The implications of this idea, however, have been undertheorized.

5. The extant literature does not have systematic theories or empirical accounts of differences between advocacy tactics by issue areas. This appears to be a fruitful area for future research.

6. I thank Carrie Wickham for numerous discussions about these mechanisms.

7. This state is often referred to in the practitioner literature as the "host" state; this is somewhat distinct from the common reference to states where advocacy organizations are working as "target" states and reflects the idea that service organizations, unlike advocacy organizations, are likely to be in a more cooperative and collaborative relationship with the regime where they are working (USAID 2012).

8. Recently, Engineers Without Borders Canada spearheaded a campaign designed to spread messages of service delivery failures in the INGO community. The organization has set up a website, www.admittingfailure.com, for the transmission of stories of NGO failure with an eye toward improving service delivery outcomes in the future.

9. To my knowledge, the nonprofit literature has not addressed the ECOSOC consultative status in this way.

Chapter 3

1. This is outlined by Bob (2005); see also Kelly (2005).

2. It is also consistent with much of the current international relations signaling literature (Fearon 1994, 1997; Weeks 2008).

Chapter 4

1. Visualizations of the distribution of this variable and its median level over time are provided in the online appendix: http://www.amandamurdie.org/help-or-harm .html.

2. The variable is stationary over time; conventional Fisher tests do not show the presence of a unit root, which might complicate our statistical interpretation. Results also hold with the addition of yearly fixed effects.

3. Visualizations of this variable are provided in the online appendix. Because the Fisher test for panel unit roots indicated variance nonstationarity in this series, I use the natural log of this raw data (ln) in all models (Maddala and Wu 1999). Unlike the relationship between human rights performance and similar data on human rights INGOs from the UIA, as discussed in Chapter 5, this variable is not endogenous to development outcomes, as determined by both the Wu-Hausman F test and the Durbin-Wu-Hausman chi-squared test (Wooldridge 2006).

4. Additionally, Jakub Kakietek and I recoded the Smith and Wiest (2005) data for the years 1998 and 2001. The correlation between our data and the Smith and Wiest (2005) data was over 0.97.

5. Additional controls were examined, such as annual rainfall amounts in the largest city within each state. Statistical and substantive findings were consistent. I follow Achen's (2005) "rule of three" and do not run a "garbage can" regression.

6. Following Brambor and colleagues (2006), all constitutive terms are included in the models using interaction terms in this chapter.

7. This result is presented in Table 4.1 in the chapter appendix.

8. All results also are consistent here when we eliminate India, which has a very large number of development INGOs, as shown in Figure 4.2. Results of t-tests also are consistent, of course, when using the natural log of development INGOs.

9. These results will all be available in the online appendix.

10. These results are also available in the online appendix.

11. These results are all provided in Table 4.2 in the chapter appendix.

12. The Durbin-Wu-Hausman test shows that a two-stage approach was necessary. Additionally, the instruments are validated both by being statistically significant in the first stage and by the above 10 Cragg-Donald F-Statistic (Baum et al. 2003; Wooldridge 2006). Worth noting, however, tourism is only marginally statistically significant in the first state. However, Baum and colleagues (2003) point out that the Cragg-Donald F-Statistic would be enough to validate the instruments. The insignificant Hansen's J Statistic also shows that the instruments are properly exogenous (Baum et al. 2003; Wooldridge 2006).

13. These results are presented in Table 4.3 in the chapter appendix.

14. I run an ordinary least squares regression here, because the results of Wooldridge (2002) tests for autocorrelation in panel data did not indicate that first-order autocorrelation was an issue. I did include yearly fixed effects.

15. These results are presented in Table 4.4 in the chapter appendix.

16. This result is presented in Table 4.5 in the chapter appendix.

17. Worth mentioning, this index is only correlated with the development INGO measure at 0.14 in the sample and is correlated with access to an improved water source at −0.14

18. These results are presented in Table 4.6 in the chapter appendix.

19. Results are also consistent with the inclusion of yearly fixed effects.

20. I remain cognizant, of course, of the idea that access to birth control could improve the role of women in the labor force in the future; however, for this model, I am interested in how the female population's previous activity in the workforce could condition the effect development INGOs on contraceptive fertility rates in the future. Because of this, I lag my measure of the percent of females in the labor force one year in this model. As such, the model specification does not allow for any simultaneity bias

21. These results are presented in Table 4.7 in the chapter appendix.

Chapter 5

1. Visualizations of this variable are provided in the online appendix.

2. The earlier data project (Murdie and Bhasin 2011, for example) was more restricted in temporal coverage.

3. Results are also consistent if an additional control for Islamic heritage is added to the statistical models.

4. Results presented in Table 5.1 in the chapter appendix.

5. It did, however, have a brief conflict in 2004 with a slight decrease in physical integrity rights, as the literature would expect (Poe and Tate 1994).

6. Because I am interested in how the effect of varying levels of human rights INGOs between units influences human rights, I run a between effects two stage model. Results are consistent if random effects are used instead (Wooldridge 2006). Given that panel data two-stage models for ordered variables do not exist, I run all the models as panel regressions.

7. This result is presented in Table 5.2 in the chapter appendix.

8. As determined by the Durbin-Wu-Hausman test (Baum et al. 2007).

9. This is determined by a Cragg-Donald F-Statistic of above 10, in addition to being shown to be properly exogenous by an insignificant Hansen's J Statistic (Baum et al. 2003; Wooldridge 2006).

10. A robustness test with Cheibub, Gandhi, and Vreeland's (2009) political regime measure is available in the online appendix. This result is similar in sign but is not significant, perhaps indicating that a fully functioning democracy is necessary for internal vulnerability to be sufficient enough for human rights INGO shaming mobilization to work.

11. I rely on Gleditsch's (2002) trade and exports data. Though it is available only until 2000, the coverage and reliability are much better, as discussed in Gleditsch.

12. These statistical results for exports are presented in Table 5.3. The online appendix includes tables of the results for the models where trade and aid are used to measure external vulnerability.

13. This general dynamic is very similar to the dynamic shown in the online appendix, where trade is the measure shown to signify external vulnerability.

14. See, for example, the text of US Senate Bill 1417, November 16, 1995.

15. I use autocorrelation- and heteroscedastic-consistent standard errors here. I chose to use the autocorrelation-consistent standard errors due to the amount of autocorrelation in the key independent variable.

16. The foundational data do not suffer from the same extent of missing data that the membership data do, as discussed above.

17. These results are presented in Table 5.4 of the chapter appendix.

18. The results for personal contact are provided in Tables 5.5 in the chapter appendix. The results for information flows and domestic association rights are provided in the online appendix.

19. These results are available in the online appendix to accompany this manuscript.

20. A table of these statistical results is provided in Table 5.6 in the chapter appendix.

21. I do restrict the sample to not include the United States, United Kingdom, and France. I do this for both theoretical and empirical reasons. Because these three countries are often those in the international community that are offering their support to INGOs, it does not make sense to include them when looking at how the international community responds to domestically oriented organizations; to include these three states could inadvertently include domestic support for domestically oriented organizations in the model. Further, these three states are statistical outliers in the data set, as identified by common conventional statistical tests (Barnett and Lewis 1994; Wooldridge 2006).

22. In the sample, this variable is correlated with the proxy for domestically consistent INGOs at less than the 0.3 level. The mean variance inflation factor (VIF) is still under 2, indicating that multicollinearity is not a problem in the analyses.

23. These results are provided in Tables 5.7 and 5.8.

Chapter 6

1. There were notable exceptions to this positive view of INGOs in the literature, however, some of which even predated Keck and Sikkink (1998). See, for example, Brett (1993).

REFERENCES

Abu·Lughod, Lila. 2002. "Do Muslim Women Really Need Saving? Anthropological Reflections on Cultural Relativism and Its Others." *American Anthropologist* 104(3): 783–790.

ACCU. 2000. "Literacy Watch Bulletin." No. 15. April 20. http://www.accu.or.jp/litdbase/literacy/nrc_nfe/eng_bul/BUL15.pdf.

Acemoglu, Daron, and Simon Johnson. 2007. "Disease and Development: The Effect of Life Expectancy on Economic Growth." *Journal of Political Economy* 115(6): 925–985.

Achen, Christopher H. 2005. "Let's Put Garbage-Can Regressions and Garbage-Can Probits Where They Belong." *Conflict Management and Peace Science* 22(4): 327–339.

Adhikari, Prakash. 2010. "Dailekh NGOs Giving Rural Areas a Miss." *Kathmandu Post*, November 11.

Adler, Emanuel, and Peter M. Haas. 1992. "Conclusion: Epistemic Communities, World Order, and the Creation of a Reflective Research Program." *International Organization* 46(1): 367–390.

AEGIS Trust. 2012. Twitter Post on July 9. https://twitter.com/Aegis_Trust.

Africa Research Bulletin. 2012. "Burkina Faso: Fighting Corruption." *Africa Research Bulletin: Economic, Financial and Technical Series* 48(12): 19369A–19369C.

Afrobarometer. 2008. Online Analysis. http://www.afrobarometer-online-analysis.com/aj/AJBrowserAB.jsp.

Ahmed, Shamima, and David M. Potter. 2006. *NGOs in International Politics*. Bloomfield, CT: Kumarian Press.

AKDN. 2012. "Aga Khan Development Network: Revitalising Zanzibar's Stone Town." http://www.akdn.org/Content/1000.

Akhtar, Aasim Sajjad. 2006. "The Professionalization of Political Culture." *Capitalism Nature Socialism* 17(3): 88–99.

Aldashev, Gani, and Thierry Verdier. 2010. "Goodwill Bazaar: NGO Competition and Giving to Development." *Journal of Development Economics* 91(1): 48–63.

Alesina, Alberto, and Beatrice Weder. 1999. *Do Corrupt Governments Receive Less Foreign Aid?* National Bureau of Economic Research. No. w7108.

Alger, Chadwick. 2002. "The Emerging Roles of the NGOs in the UN System: From Article 71 to a People's Millennium Assembly." *Global Governance* 8(1): 93–117.

Alonso, Alvaro, and Ruairí Brugha. 2006. "Rehabilitating the Health System After Conflict in East Timor: A Shift from NGO to Government Leadership." *Health Policy and Planning* 21(3): 206–216.

Amin, Ruhul, Stan Becker, and Abdul Bayes. 1998. "NGO-Promoted Microcredit Programs and Women's Empowerment in Rural Bangladesh: Quantitative and Qualitative Evidence." *Journal of Developing Areas* 32(2): 221–236.

Amin, Ruhul, and Yiping Li. 1997. "NGO-Promoted Women's Credit Program, Immunization Coverage, and Child Mortality in Rural Bangladesh." *Women and Health* 25(1): 71–87.

Amnesty International (AI). 2000. "United Nations Commission on Human Rights 56th Session (March 20 to April 28, 2000) Colombia." AI Index No.: IOR 41/05/00.

———. 2008a. "Amnesty International Annual Report on Saudi Arabia." Amnesty International Country Report.

———. 2008b. "Chinese Authorities' Broken Promises Threaten Olympic Legacy." July 28. http://www.amnesty.org/en/news-and-updates/report/chinese-authorities -broken-promises-threaten-olympic-legacy-20080728.

———. 2008c. "USA: CIA 'Waterboarding': Admission of a Crime, Now There Must Be a Criminal Investigation." AI Index: AMR 51/011/2008.

———. 2009a. "Amnesty International Report 2009—China." http://report2009 .amnesty.org/en/regions/asia-pacific/china.

———. 2009b. *Giving Life, Risking Death: Maternal Mortality in Burkina Faso.* London: Amnesty International Secretariat.

———. 2012. "Colombia: Annual Report 2012." http://www.amnesty.org/en/region/ colombia/report-2012.

Amnesty International (AI) New Zealand. 2012. "Timeline: Aung San Suu Kyi and Amnesty International." June 18. http://www.amnesty.org.nz/news/timeline-aung-san -suu-kyi-and-amnesty-international.

Anderson Association. 2012. http://www.andersonassociation.com/.

Andrews, Kenneth T., and Michael Biggs. 2006. "The Dynamics of Protest Diffusion: Movement Organizations, Social Networks, and News Media in the 1960 Sit-ins." *American Sociological Review* 71(October): 752–777.

Apodaca, Clair, and Michael Stohl. 1999. "United States, Human Rights Policy, and Foreign Assistance." *International Studies Quarterly* 43(1): 185–198.

Asal, Victor, Brian Nussbaum, and D. William Harrington. 2007. "Terrorism as Transnational Advocacy: An Organizational and Tactical Examination." *Studies in Conflict and Terrorism* 30(1): 15–39.

Auffhammer, Maximilian, and Ralf Steinhauser. 2007. "The Future Trajectory of US CO_2 Emissions: The Role of State vs. Aggregate Information." *Journal of Regional Science* 47(1): 47–61.

Austen-Smith, David. 1997. "Interest Groups: Money, Information, and Influence." In *Perspectives of Public Choice*, edited by Dennis C. Mueller, 296–321. Cambridge: Cambridge University Press.

Ayotte, Kevin J., and Mary E. Husain. 2005. "Securing Afghan Women: Neocolonialism, Epistemic Violence, and the Rhetoric of the Veil." *NWSA Journal* 17(3): 112–133.

Baehr, Peter R. 2000. "Controversies in the Current International Human Rights Debate." *Human Rights Review* 2(1): 7–32.

Bahrain Center for Human Rights. 2010. "Human Rights Defenders Expose Bahraini Government Violations at UN Side Event." http://www.bahrainrights.org/en/node/3389.

Baig, Adnan Sattar Rabia. 2001. "Civil Society in Pakistan: A Preliminary Report on the CIVICUS Index on Civil Society Project in Pakistan." CIVICUS Index on Civil Society Occasional Paper Series, Vol. 1, No. 11.

Bankole, Akinrinola, and Susheela Singh. 1998. "Couples' Fertility and Contraceptive Decision-Making in Developing Countries: Hearing the Man's Voice." *International Family Planning Perspective* 24(1): 15–24.

Banks, Nicola, and David Hulme. 2012. "The Role of NGOs and Civil Society in Development and Poverty Reduction." Working Paper 171, Brooks World Poverty Institute, University of Manchester, Manchester. http://www.bwpi.manchester.ac.uk/resources/Working-Papers/bwpi-wp-17112.pdf.

Barnett, Vic, and Toby Lewis. 1994. *Outliers in Statistical Data*. 3rd ed. Wiley Series in Probability and Statistics. Chichester, UK: Wiley.

Barro, Robert, and Jong-Wha Lee. 1993. "International Comparisons of Educational Attainment." *Journal of Monetary Economics* 32(3): 363–394.

Barry, Colin M., K. Chad Clay, and Michael E. Flynn. 2013. "Avoiding the Spotlight: Human Rights Shaming and Foreign Direct Investment." *International Studies Quarterly* 57(3): 532–544.

Baum, Christopher F., Mark E. Schaffer, and Steven Stillman. 2003. "Instrumental Variables and GMM: Estimation and Testing." *Stata Journal* 3(1): 1–31.

———. 2007. "IVENDOG: Stata Module to Calculate Durbin-Wu-Hausman Endogeneity Test After Ivreg." Statistical Software Components No. S494401, Department of Economics, Boston College.

Baum, Matthew, and David D. Lake. 2003. "The Political Economy of Growth: Democracy and Human Capital." *American Journal of Political Science* 47(2): 333–347.

Baur, Dorothea, and Hans Peter Schmitz. 2012. "Corporations and NGOs: When Accountability Leads to Co-Optation." *Journal of Business Ethics* 106(1): 1–13.

Bawah, Ayaga, James Phillips, and George Wak. 2005. "Does Women's Relative Income Predict Contraceptive Use in Ghana? An Assessment Using Bargaining Theory." International Union for the Scientific Study of Population, XXV International Population Conference, Tours, France.

BBC News. 2004. "NGOs: Achievers or Deceivers?" February 20. http://news.bbc.co.uk/2/hi/africa/3502733.stm.

———. 2012. "Russian Parliament Adopts NGO 'Foreign Agents' Bill." July 13. http://www.bbc.co.uk/news/world-europe-18826661.

Bearce, David H. 2003. "Societal Preferences, Partisan Agents, and Monetary Policy Outcomes." *International Organization* 57(2): 373–410.

Beardsley, K. 2008. "Agreement Without Peace? International Mediation and Time Inconsistency Problems." *American Journal of Political Science* 52(4): 723–740.

Bekkers, René. 2007. "The Benefits of Accreditation for Fundraising Nonprofits." Sixth Workshop of the Challenges of Managing the Third Sector, Venice.

Bell, Sam, K. Chad Clay, and Amanda Murdie. 2012. "Neighborhood Watch: Spatial Effects of Human Rights INGOs." *Journal of Politics* 74(2): 354–368.

Bellamy, Alex J. 2008. "The Responsibility to Protect and the Problem of Military Intervention." *International Affairs* 84(4): 615–639.

Ben Attia, Isolda Agazzi. 2004. "NGOs and GONGOs in the Context of the UN-CHR." In 57th Submission of the NGO-CHR.

Bengali, Shashank. 2009. "Bush Birth Control Policies Helped Fuel Africa's Baby Boom." *McClatchy Newspapers*, December 13.

Berhan, Sereke. 2002. "The NGO Conundrum." http://chora.virtualave.net/serekengo.ht.

Berkovitch, Nitza, and Neva Gordon. 2008. "The Political Economy of Transnational Regimes: The Case of Human Rights." *International Studies Quarterly* 52(4): 881–904.

Berthoud, Olivier. 2001. "NGOs: Somewhere Between Compassion, Profitability, and Solidarity." *Envio* (241).

Betsill, Michele M. 2008. "Environmental NGOs and the Kyoto Protocol Negotiations: 1995 to 1997." In *NGO Diplomacy: The Influence of Nongovernmental Organizations in International Environmental Negotiations*, edited by Michele M. Betsill and Elisabeth Corell, 43–66. Cambridge, MA: MIT Press.

Bhasin, Tavishi, and R. Mascarenhas. 2008. "The Effects of Foreign Aid on Recipient Use of Repressive Policies." Paper presented at the Annual Meeting of the MPSA National Conference, Chicago.

Bhatt, Nitin, and Shui-Yan Tang. 2001. "Delivering Microfinance in Developing Countries: Controversies and Policy Perspectives." *Policy Studies Journal* 29(2): 319–333.

Birrell, Ian. 2012. "Haiti and the Shaming of the Aid Zealots: How Donated Billions Have INCREASED Poverty and Corruption." http://www.dailymail.co.uk/news/article-2092425/Haiti-earthquake-How-donated-billions-INCREASED-poverty-corruption.html#ixzz2F2bT7m3m.

Black, David. 1999. "The Long and Winding Road: International Norms and Domestic Political Change in South Africa." In *The Power of Human Rights International Norms and Domestic Change*, edited by Thomas Risse, Stephen C. Ropp, and Kathryn Sikkink, 78–109. Cambridge: Cambridge University Press.

Bloodgood, Elizabeth. 2008. "Epistemic Communities, Norms, and Knowledge." Paper presented at the Annual Meeting of the International Studies Association Conference, San Francisco, March 26–29.

———. 2011. "The Interest Group Analogy: International Non-Governmental Advocacy Organisations in International Politics." *Review of International Studies* 37(1): 93–120.

Bloodgood, Elizabeth A., and Joannie Tremblay-Boire. 2011. "International NGOs and National Regulation in an Age of Terrorism." *Voluntas* 22(1): 142–173.

Bob, Clifford. 2005. *The Marketing of Rebellion: Insurgents, Media, and International Activism*. Cambridge: Cambridge University Press.

Boli, John, and David V. Brewington. 2007. "Religious Organizations." In *Religion, Globalization, and Culture*, edited by Peter Beyer and Lori G. Beaman, 203–231. Leiden: Brill.

Boli, John, and George M. Thomas. 1999. INGOs and the Organization of World Culture. In *Constructing World Culture International Non-Governmental Organization. Since 1875*, edited by John Boli and George M. Thomas, 13–49. Stanford, CA: Stanford University Press.

Bosman, Marieke. 2012. "The NGO Sector in Syria—An Overview." International NGO Training and Resource Centre. http://www.intrac.org/data/files/resources/746/Briefing-Paper-30-The-NGO-sector-in-Syria.pdf.

Boulding, Carew E. 2010. "NGOs and Political Participation in Weak Democracies: Subnational Evidence on Protest and Voter Turnout from Bolivia." *Journal of Politics* 72(2): 456–468.

Boulware-Miller, Kay. 1985. Female Circumcision: Challengers to the Practice as a Human Rights Violation. *Harvard Women's Law Journal* 8: 155–177.

Bowman, Woods. 2010. "Trends and Patterns in Third-Party Accountability Clubs." In *Voluntary Regulation of NGOs and Nonprofits: An Accountability Club Framework*, edited by Mary Kay Gugerty and Aseem Prakash, 64–84. Cambridge: Cambridge University Press.

Boyle, Elizabeth Heger. 2005. *Female Genital Cutting: Cultural Conflict in the Global Community*. Baltimore: Johns Hopkins University Press. Paperback edition.

Boyle, Elizabeth Heger, F. Songora, and G. Foss. 2001. "International Discourse and Local Politics: Anti-Female-Genital Cutting Laws in Egypt, Tanzania, and the United States." *Social Problems* 48(4): 524–544.

Brambor, T., W. R. Clark, and M. Golder. 2006. "Understanding Interaction Models: Improving Empirical Analyses." *Political Analysis* 14(1): 63–82.

Brass, Jennifer N. 2012. "Why Do NGOs Go Where They Go? Evidence from Kenya." *World Development* 40(2): 387–401.

Bratton, Michael. 1990. "NGOs in Africa: Can They Influence Public Policy?" *Development and Change* 21(1): 87–118.

Brems, Eva. 1997. "Enemies or Allies? Feminism and Cultural Relativism as Dissident Voices in Human Rights Discourse." *Human Rights Quarterly* 19(1): 136–164.

Brenton, Tony. 1994. *The Greening of Machiavelli: The Evolution of International Environmental Politics*. London: Earthscan.

Brett, Edward A. 1993. "Voluntary Agencies as Development Organizations: Theorizing the Problem of Efficiency and Accountability." *Development and Change* 24(2): 269–304.

Brown, David S., J. Christopher Brown, and Scott W. Desposato. 2008. "Who Gives, Who Receives, and Who Wins? Transforming Capital into Political Change Through Nongovernmental Organizations." *Comparative Political Studies* 41(1): 24–27.

Brown, L. David, and Mark H. Moore. 2001. "Accountability, Strategy, and International Nongovernmental Organizations." *Nonprofit and Voluntary Sector Quarterly* 30(3): 569–587.

Brysk, Alison. 1993. "From Above and Below Social Movements, the International System, and Human Rights in Argentina." *Comparative Political Studies* 26(3): 259–285.

Buckley, Robert. 2009. "Slumdogs Can Help Themselves Out of the Mire." *Financial Times*, February 23.

Bueno de Mesquita, Bruce, and George W. Downs. 2005. "Development and Democracy." *Foreign Affairs* 84(1): 77–86.

Buergenthal, T. 2000. "International Human Rights in an Historical Perspective." In *Human Rights: Concept and Standards*, edited by Janusz Symonides, chap. 1. Burlington, VT: Ashgate; Paris: UNESCO.

Bunce, Valerie, and Sharon L. Wolchik. 2006. "Favorable Conditions and Electoral Revolutions." *Journal of Democracy* 17(4): 5–18.

Busby, Joshua W. 2010. *Moral Movements and Foreign Policy*. Cambridge, MA: Cambridge University Press.

Buse, K., and G. Walt. 2000. "Global Public-Private Partnerships: Part I—A New Development in Health?" *Bulletin of the World Health Organization* 78(4): 549–561.

Büthe, Tim, Solomon Major, and André de Mello e Souza. 2012. "The Politics of Private Foreign Aid: Humanitarian Principles, Economic Development Objectives, and Organizational Interests in NGO Private Aid Allocation." *International Organization* 66(4): 571–607.

Calnan, Scott. 2008. *The Effectiveness of Domestic Human Rights NGOs: A Comparative Study*. Leiden: Martinus Nijhoff.

Cameron, John. 2000. "Development Economics, the New Institutional Economics and NGOs." *Third World Quarterly* 21(4): 627–635.

Campos, Nauro, Feisal Khan, and Jennifer Tessendorf. 2004. "From Substitution to Complementarity: Some Econometric Evidence on the Evolving NGO-State Relationship in Pakistan." *Journal of Developing Areas* 37(2): 49–72.

CAN. 2007. "Joint NGO EU Climate and Energy Policy Statement." Climate Action Network. http://www.climnet.org.

Carapico, Sheila. 2000. "NGOs, INGOs, GO-NGOs and DO-NGOs: Making Sense of Non-Governmental Organizations." *Middle East Report* 30(1): 12–15.

Cardenas, Sonia. 2007. *Conflict and Compliance: Responses to International Human Rights Pressure*. Philadelphia: University of Pennsylvania Press.

CARE International. 2003. "Security of Livelihoods for Afghan Returnees Project SoLAR II." Final Evaluation. www.careevaluations.org/.

Carpenter, R. Charli. 2007. "Setting the Advocacy Agenda: Theorizing Issue Emergence and Nonemergence in Transnational Advocacy Networks." *International Studies Quarterly* 51: 99–120.

———. 2010. *Forgetting Children Born of War: Setting the Human Rights Agenda in Bosnia and Beyond*. New York: Columbia University Press.

Carrillo, Arturo J. 2009. "Truth, Justice, and Reparations in Colombia: The Path to Peace and Reconciliation." In *Colombia: Building Peace in a Time of War*, edited by Virginia M. Bourvier, 133–158. Washington, DC: United States Institute of Peace.

Carrubba, Clifford J., Amy Yuen, and Christopher Zorn. 2007. "In Defense of Comparative Statics: Specifying Empirical Tests of Models of Strategic Interaction." *Political Analysis* 15(4): 465–482.

Ccocllo, Marcia. 1989. "Birth Control Doesn't Solve Peru's Problems." *New York Times*, February 4.

Chandy, Laurence, and Geoffrey Gertz. 2011. "Poverty in Numbers: The Changing State of Global Poverty from 2005 to 2015." Policy Brief 2011-01, Brookings Institution.

Chang, Eric, and Miriam A. Golden. 2010. "Sources of Corruption in Authoritarian Regimes." *Social Science Quarterly* 91(1): 1–20.

Chapman, Terrence. 2007. "International Security Institutions, Domestic Politics, and Institutional Legitimacy." *Journal of Conflict Resolution* 31(1): 134–166.

———. 2009. "Audience Beliefs and International Organization Legitimacy." *International Organization* 63(4): 733–764.

———. 2011. *Securing Approval: Domestic Politics and Multilateral Authorization for War*. Chicago: University of Chicago Press.

Chartier, Denis, and Jean·Paul Deléage. 1998. "The International Environmental NGOs: From the Revolutionary Alternative to the Pragmatism of Reform." *Environmental Politics* 7(3): 26–41.

Checkel, Jeffrey T. 1997. "International Norms and Domestic Politics: Bridging the Rationalist-Constructivist Divide." *European Journal of International Relations* 3(4): 473.

———. 2003. "Why Comply? Social Learning and European Identity Change." *International Organization* 55(3): 553–588.

———. 2005. "International Institutions and Socialization in Europe: Introduction and Framework." *International Organization* 59(4): 801–826.

Cheibub, José Antonio, Jennifer Gandhi, and James Raymond Vreeland. 2010. "Democracy and Dictatorship Revisited." *Public Choice* 143(1–2): 67–101.

Chiang, Pei-heng. 1981. *Non-Governmental Organizations and the United Nations: Identity, Role, and Function.* Westport, CT: Praeger.

Cingranelli, David L., and David L. Richards. 1999. "Respect for Human Rights After the End of the Cold War." *Journal of Peace Research* 36(5): 551–534.

———. 2001. "Measuring the Impact of Human Rights Organizations." In *NGOs and Human Rights: Promise and Performance*, edited by Claude E. Welch, 225–238. Philadelphia: University of Pennsylvania Press.

———. 2007. "CIRI Variables List and Short Description." http://ciri.binghamton.edu/documentation.

———. 2010. "Short Variable Descriptions for Indicators in the Cingranelli-Richards (CIRI) Human Rights Dataset." Document Version November 22. http://ciri.binghamton.edu/documentation/ciri_variables_short_descriptions.pdf.

Clark, Ann Marie. 2001. *Diplomacy of Conscience: Amnesty International and Changing Human Rights Norms.* Princeton, NJ: Princeton University Press.

Clark, Ann Marie, Elisabeth J. Friedman, and Kathryn Hochstetler. 1998. "The Sovereign Limits of Global Civil Society: A Comparison of NGO Participation in UN World Conferences on the Environment, Human Rights, and Women." *World Politics* 51(1): 1–35.

Clark, Cindy, Ellen Sprenger, and Lisa VeneKlasen. 2006. *Where Is the Money for Women's Rights.* Toronto: Association for Women's Rights in Development.

Clarke, Gerald. 1998. "Non-Governmental Organizations (NGOs) and Politics in the Developing World." *Political Studies* 46(1): 36–52.

Cohen, Michael A., Maria Figueroa Kupcu, and Parag Khanna. 2008. "The New Colonialists." *Foreign Policy* 16: 74–76.

Collier, Paul. 2000. *Economic Causes of Civil Conflict and Their Implications for Policy.* Washington, DC: World Bank.

Collier, Paul, and Anke Hoeffler. 2004. "Greed and Grievance in Civil War." *Oxford Economic Papers* 56(4): 563–595.

———. 2005. "Resource Rents, Governance, and Conflict." *Journal of Conflict Resolution* 49(4): 625.

Cooley, Alexander, and James Ron. 2002. "The NGO Scramble: Organizational Insecurity and the Political Economy of Transnational Action." *International Security* 27(1): 3–39.

Cortell, Andrew P., and James W. Davis Jr. 2000. "Understanding the Domestic Impact of International Norms: A Research Agenda." *International Studies Review* 2(1): 65–87.

Council of Microfinance Equity Funds (CMEF). 2011. "Aligning Stakeholder Interest in NGO Transformations: Emerging Good Practices." http://centerforfinancialinclu sionblog.files.wordpress.com/2011/05/cmef-aligning-stakeholder-interests-in-ngo-trans formations-emerging-good-practices-2011-5-24-final-sd.pdf.

Crabtree, Steve. 2012. "Almost All Nigerians Say Gov't Is Corrupt." http://www.gallup .com/poll/152057/almost-nigerians-say-gov-corrupt.aspx.

CSD. 2005. "NGO Policy Statement for CSD 15." http://www.cures-network.org.

Darnall, Nicole, and JoAnn Carmin. 2005. "Greener and Cleaner? The Signaling Accuracy of US Voluntary Environmental Programs." *Policy Sciences* 38(2–3): 71–90.

Davenport, Christian, and David A. Armstrong. 2004. "Democracy and the Violation of Human Rights: A Statistical Analysis from 1976 to 1996." *American Journal of Political Science* 48(3): 538–554.

Davis, David R., Amanda Murdie, and Coty Garnett Steinmetz. 2012. "'Makers and Shapers': Human Rights INGOs and Public Opinion." *Human Rights Quarterly* 34(1): 199–224.

De la Fuente, Angel, and Rafael Doménech. 2006. "Human Capital in Growth Regressions: How Much Difference Does Data Quality Make?" *Journal of the European Economic Association* 4(1): 1–36.

DeMars, William E. 2005. *NGOs and Transnational Networks: Wild Cards in World Politics.* London: Pluto Press.

DeMeritt, Jacqueline H. R. 2012. "International Organizations and Government Killing: Does Naming and Shaming Save Lives?" *International Interactions* 38(5): 597–621.

DePalma, Anthony. 2005. "9 States in Plan to Cut Emissions by Power Plants." *New York Times*, August 24.

Dhrymes, Phoebus J. 1994. *Topics in Advanced Econometrics: Linear and Nonlinear Simultaneous Equations.* New York: Springer.

Dhunpath, Rubby. 2003. "It's All Businesslike Now: The Corporatisation and Professionalisation of NGO in South Africa." *International Journal of Knowledge, Culture, and Change Management* 3: 1109–1124.

Dichter, Thomas W. 1996. "Questioning the Future of NGOs in Microfinance." *Journal of International Development* 8(2): 259–269.

Dieng, Adama. 2001. "The Contribution of NGOs to the Prevention of Human Rights Violations." In *The Prevention of Human Rights Violations*, edited by Linos-Alexander Sicilanos, 259–268. The Hague: Kluwer Law International.

Dietrich, Simone. 2013. "Bypass or Engage? Explaining Donor Delivery Tactics in Aid Allocation." *International Studies Quarterly* 57(4): 698–712.

Dixit, Avinash, Gene M. Grossman, and Elhanan Helpman. 1997. "Common Agency and Coordination: General Theory and Application to Government Policy Making." *Journal of Political Economy* 105(4): 752–769.

Dixon, Hayley. 2013. "Britain Second in World for Aid Spending." *The Telegraph*, April 4.

Dolhinow, Rebecca. 2005. "Caught in the Middle: The State, NGOs, and the Limits to Grassroots Organizing Along the US-Mexico Border." In *Working the Spaces of Neoliberalism*, edited by Nina Laurie and Liz Bondi, 164–185. Malden, MA: Blackwell.

Donnelly, Jack. 1984. "Cultural Relativism and Universal Human Rights." *Human Rights Quarterly* 6(4): 400–419.

———. 1998. *International Human Rights*. Boulder, CO: Westview Press.

———. 2003. *Universal Human Rights in Theory and Practice*. Ithaca, NY: Cornell University Press.

Downs, George W., and David M. Rocke. 1995. *Optimal Imperfection? Domestic Uncertainty and Institutions in International Relations*. Princeton, NJ: Princeton University Press.

Downs, George, David M. Rocke, and Peter N. Barsoom. 1996. "Is the Good News About Compliance Good News About Cooperation?" *International Organization* 50(3): 379–406.

Dreher, Axel. 2006. "Does Globalization Affect Growth? Evidence from a New Index of Globalization." *Applied Economics* 38(10): 1091–1110.

Dreher, Axel, Noel Gaston, and Pim Martens. 2008. *Measuring Globalisation: Gauging Its Consequences*. New York: Springer.

Dupuy, Kendra, James Ron, and Aseem Prakash. 2012. "Foreign Aid to Local NGOs: Good Intentions, Bad Policy." http://www.opendemocracy.net/kendra-dupuy-james-ron-aseem-prakash/foreign-aid-to-local-ngos-good-intentions-bad-policy.

E.O. 012598. 2005. "Subject: U/S Grossman Meets with Human Rights NGOS." http://www.cablegatesearch.net/cable.php?id=04BOGOTA4507.

EANNASO. 2003. "UNAIDS-AFRICASO Human Rights and HIV/AIDS Project in Tanzania." http://data.unaids.org/Topics/Human-Rights/tanzania_needs_assessment_en.pdf.

Easterly, William. 2006. *The White Man's Burden: Why the West's Efforts to Aid the Rest Have Done So Much Ill and So Little Good*. New York: Penguin Press.

Edwards, Michael, and David Hulme. 1995. *Non-Governmental Organisations: Performance and Accountability Beyond the Magic Bullet*. London: Earthscan / James & James.

———. 1996. eds. *Beyond the Magic Bullet: NGO Performance and Accountability in the Post–Cold War World*. West Hartford, CT: Kumarian Press.

Elbayar, Kareem. 2012. "Egypt's Restrictions on NGOs Violate International Law." *Washington Post*, March 13.

Ell, Darren. 2008. Haiti's Catch-22. *Dominion*, February 27.

Elman, Colin, and Miriam Fendius Elman, eds. 2003. *Progress in International Relations Theory*. Cambridge, MA: MIT Press.

Engender Health. 2012. "In Action." http://www.engenderhealth.org/files/factsheets/EngenderHealth-Factsheet-In-Action-English.pdf.

Evangelista, Matthew. 1999. *Unarmed Forces: The Transnational Movement to End the Cold War*. Ithaca, NY: Cornell University Press.

Evans, Sally. 2009. "Charities Feel Financial Squeeze." *Times* (South Africa), January 26.

Falola, Toyin, and Matthew M. Heaton. 2008. *A History of Nigeria*. Cambridge: Cambridge University Press.

Fang, Songying. 2008. "The Informational Role of International Institutions and Domestic Politics." *American Journal of Political Science* 52(2): 304–321.

Fearon, James. 1994. "Signaling Versus the Balance of Power and Interests: An Empirical Test of a Crisis Bargaining Model." *Journal of Conflict Resolution* 38(2): 236–269.

———. 1995. "Rationalist Explanations of War." *International Organization* 49(3): 379–414.

———. 1997. "Signaling Foreign Policy Interests: Tying Hands Versus Sinking Costs." *Journal of Conflict Resolution* 41(1): 68–90.

Fearon, James, and Alexander Wendt. 2002. "Rationalism v. Constructivism: A Skeptical View." In *Handbook of International Relations*, edited by Walter Carlsnaes, Thomas Risse, and Beth A. Simmons, 52–72. London: Sage.

Feldman, Shelly. 1997. "NGOs and Civil Society: (Un)stated Contradictions." *Annals of the American Academy of Political and Social Science* 554(1): 46–65.

Ferguson, James. 1990. *The Anti-Politics Machine: "Development," Depoliticization and Bureaucratic Power in Lesotho*. Cambridge: Cambridge University Press.

Ferris, Elizabeth. 2011. *The Politics of Protection: The Limits of Humanitarian Action*. Washington, DC: Brookings Institution Press.

Finnemore, Martha, and Kathryn Sikkink. 1998. "International Norm Dynamics and Political Change." *International Organization* 52(4): 887–917.

———. 2001. "Taking Stock: The Constructivist Research Program in International Relations and Comparative Politics." *Annual Review of Political Science* 4(1): 391–416.

Flock, Elizabeth. 2011. "Saudi Arabia Blocks Amnesty International Web Site After Anti-Terror Law Leak." *Washington Post*, July 25.

Florini, Ann. 2004. "Is Global Civil Society a Good Thing?" *New Perspectives Quarterly* 21(2): 72–76.

FORUSA. 2010. *Military Assistance and Human Rights*. Fellowship of Reconsolidation. http://forusa.org/sites/default/files/uploads/militaryaid100729web.pdf.

Fowler, Alan. 2002. Assessing NGO Performance: Difficulties, Dilemmas and a Way Ahead. In *NGO Management*. London: Earthscan.

Francie. 2011. "A Critique of NGOism." http://www.rebelpress.org.nz/files/imminentre-bellion9.pdf.

Franklin, James C. 2008. "Shame on You: The Impact of Human Rights Criticism on Political Repression in Latin America." *International Studies Quarterly* 52(1): 187–211.

Freedom House. 2001. Annual Survey of Freedom Country Scores.

———. 2011. "Countries at the Crossroads 2011—Burkina Faso." November 10. http://www.unhcr.org/refworld/docid/4ecba651c.html.

Freeman, Marsha A. 2008. "Women's Human Rights in the Twenty-First Century: Crisis, Challenge, and Opportunity." In *Human Rights in Crisis*, edited by Alice Bullard, 67–83. Aldershot, UK: Ashgate.

French, Howard W. 1995. "The Leader of Nigeria Is Elusive." *New York Times*, October 20. http://www.nytimes.com/1995/10/20/world/the-leader-of-nigeria-is-elusive.html.

Frieden, Jeffrey A., David Lake, and Kenneth A. Schultz. 2013. *World Politics: Interests, Interactions, Institutions*. New York: Norton.

Frumkin, Peter. 2002. *On Being Nonprofit: A Conceptual and Policy Primer*. Cambridge, MA: Harvard University Press.

Fyvie, C., and A. Ager. 1999. "NGOs and Innovation: Organizational Characteristics and Constraints in Development Assistance Work in the Gambia." *World Development* 27(8): 1383–1395.

Gayle, Helene D. 2007. "A Message from Our President: Welcome to CARE's Recruitment Website." http://www.care.org/career.

Geeraerts, Gustaaf. 1995. "Analyzing Non-State Actors in World Politics." *Centrum voor Polemologie, Vrije Universiteit, Brussel, Pole-Papers* 1(4).

Gibelman, Margaret, and Sheldon R. Gelman. 2001. "Very Public Scandals: Nongovernmental Organizations in Trouble." *Voluntas* 12(1): 49–66.

Gilboa, Eytan. 2005. "The CNN effect: The Search for a Communication Theory of International Relations." *Political Communication* 22(1): 27–44.

Gleditsch, Kristian. 2002. "Expanded Trade and GDP Data." *Journal of Conflict Resolution* 46(5): 712.

Gleditsch, Kirstian Skrede, and Michael D. Ward. 2006. "Diffusion and the International Context of Democratization." *International Organization* 60(3): 911–933.

Gleick, Peter H. 1996. "Basic Water Requirements for Human Activities: Meeting Basic Needs." *Water International* 21: 83–92.

———. 2000. "The Changing Water Paradigm: A Look at Twenty-First Century Water Resources Development." *Water International* 25(1): 127–138.

Glickman, Harvey. 2005. "The Nigerian '419' Advance Fee Scams: Prank or Peril?" *Canadian Journal of African Studies* 39(3): 460–489.

Godoy, Angelina Snodgrass. 2002. "Lynchings and the Democratization of Terror in Postwar Guatemala: Implications for Human Rights." *Human Rights Quarterly* 24(3): 640–661.

Goldstein, Joshua. 1992. "A Conflict-Cooperation Scale for WEIS Data." *Journal of Conflict Resolution* 36(2): 369–385.

———. 2011. *Winning the War on War: The Decline of Armed Conflict Worldwide.* New York: Plume.

Goonatilake, Susantha. 2006. *Recolonisation: Foreign Funded NGOs in Sri Lanka.* London: Sage.

Gordenker, Leon, and Thomas G. Weiss. 1995. "Pluralizing Global Governance: Analytical Approaches and Dimensions." *Third World Quarterly* 16(3): 357–387.

———. 1997. "Devolving Responsibilities: A Framework for Analysing NGOs and Services." *Third World Quarterly* 18(3): 443–456.

Gourevitch, Peter A., and David A. Lake. 2012. "Beyond Virtue: Evaluating and Enhancing the Credibility of Non-Governmental Organizations." In *The Credibility of Transnational NGOs: When Virtue Is Not Enough,* edited by Peter A. Gourevitch, David A. Lake, and Janice Gross Stein, 3–34. Cambridge: Cambridge University Press.

Gourevitch, Peter A., David A. Lake, and Janice Gross Stein, eds. 2012. *The Credibility of Transnational NGOs: When Virtue Is Not Enough.* Cambridge: Cambridge University Press.

Grande, Elisabetta. 2004. "Hegemonic Human Rights and African Resistance: Female Circumcision in a Broader Comparative Perspective." *Global Jurist Frontiers* 4(2): 1–21.

Grant, Ruth, and Robert O. Keohane. 2005. "Accountability and Abuses in World Politics." *American Political Science Review* 99(1): 29–43.

Granzer, Sieglinde. 1999. "Changing Discourse: Transnational Advocacy Networks in Tunisia and Morocco." In *The Power of Human Rights: International Norms and Domestic Change,* edited by Thomas Risse, Stephen Ropp, and Kathryn Sikkink, 109–133. Cambridge: Cambridge University Press.

Gruenbaum, Ellen. 2001. *The Female Circumcision Controversy: An Anthropological Perspective.* Philadelphia: University of Pennsylvania Press.

Gugerty, Mary Kay. 2008. "The Effectiveness of NGO Self-Regulation: Theory and Evidence from Africa." *Public Administration and Development* 28(2): 105–118.

———. 2009. "Signaling Virtue: Voluntary Accountability Programs Among Nonprofit Organizations." *Policy Sciences* 42(3): 243–273.

———. 2010. "The Emergence and Design of NGO Clubs in Africa." In *Voluntary Regulation of NGOs and Nonprofits: An Accountability Club Framework,* edited by Mary Kay Gugerty and Aseem Prakash, 228–252. Cambridge: Cambridge University Press.

Gugerty, Mary Kay, and Aseem Prakash, eds. 2010. *Voluntary Regulation of NGOs and Nonprofits: An Accountability Club Framework*. Cambridge: Cambridge University Press.

Gurr, Ted. 1970. *Why Men Rebel*. Princeton, NJ: Princeton University Press.

Hafner-Burton, Emilie M. 2005. "Trading Human Rights: How Preferential Trade Agreements Influence Government Repression." *International Organization* 59(3): 593–629.

———. 2008. "Sticks and Stones: Naming and Shaming the Human Rights Enforcement Problem." *International Organization* 62(4): 689–716.

Hafner-Burton, Emilie, Laurence Helfer, and Christopher Fariss. 2011. "Emergency and Escape: Explaining Derogation from Human Rights Treaties." *International Organization* 65(4): 673–707.

Hafner·Burton, Emilie M., and Kiyoteru Tsutsui. 2005. "Human Rights in a Globalizing World: The Paradox of Empty Promises." *American Journal of Sociology* 110(5): 1373–1411.

Haggard, Stephan, and Sylvia Maxfield. 1996. "The Political Economy of Financial Internationalization in the Developing World." *International Organization* 50(1): 35–68.

Hagher, Iyorwuese. 2011. *Nigeria: After the Nightmare*. Lanham, MD: University Press of America.

Hahn, Kristina, and Anna Holzscheiter. 2005. "The Ambivalence of Advocacy." Global International Studies Conference Istanbul, Bilgi University, August.

HAI. 2008. "NGO Code of Conduct for Heath Systems Strengthening Initiative." Heath Alliance International. http://www.ngocodeofconduct.org/pdf/ngocodeofconduct .pdf.

Haines, Herbert H. 1984. "Black Radicalization and the Funding of Civil Rights: 1957–1970." *Social Problems* 32(1): 31–43.

Hall, Rodney Bruce. 1999. *National Collective Identity: Social Constructs and International Systems*. New York: Columbia University Press.

Harvey, David. 2006. *Spaces of Global Capitalism*. New York: Verso Books.

Hathaway, Oona. 2002. "Do Human Rights Treaties Make a Difference?" *Yale Law Journal* 111: 1935–2042.

Haugaard, Lisa. 2012. "Testimony Before the United States Congress Tom Lantos Human Rights Commission." May 17. http://tlhrc.house.gov/docs/transcripts/2012_5_17 _Threats%20to%20Civil%20Society/Lisa%20Haugaard%20Testimony.pdf.

Hawkins, Darren G. 2002. *International Human Rights and Authoritarian Rule in Chile*. Lincoln: University of Nebraska Press.

Heinrich, Volkhart Finn. 2001. "The Role of NGOs in Strengthening the Foundations of South African Democracy." *Voluntas* 12(1): 1–15.

Henderson, Conway W. 1991. "Conditions Affecting the Use of Political Repression." *Journal of Conflict Resolution* 35(1): 120.

Hendrix, Cullen S., and Wendy H. Wong. 2012. "When Is the Pen Truly Mighty? Regime Type and the Efficacy of Naming and Shaming in Curbing Human Rights Abuses." *British Journal of Political Science.* Available Online First.

Hestres, Luis E. 2007. "Peace for Vieques: The Role of Transnational Activist Networks in International Negotiations." Paper presented at the Annual Meeting of the International Studies Association 48th Annual Convention, Chicago.

Hiel, Betsy. 2007. "Saudi Activists Face Long Fight for Human Rights." *Pittsburgh Tribune-Review,* May 27.

Hillhorst, Dorothea. 2002. "Being Good at Doing Good? Quality and Accountability of Humanitarian NGOs." *Disasters* 26(3): 193–212.

Hocking, Brian, and Michael Smith. 1990. *World Politics: An Introduction to International Relations.* Upper Saddle River, NJ: Prentice Hall / Harvester Wheatsheaf.

Hofferbert, Richard I., and David L. Cingranelli. 1996. Democratic Institutions and Respect for Human Rights. In *Human Rights and Developing Countries,* edited by David L. Cingranelli, 145–162. Greenwich, CT: JAI Press.

Hojnacki, Marie, David C. Kimball, Frank R. Baumgartner, Jeffrey M. Berry, and Beth L. Leech. 2012. "Studying Organizational Advocacy and Influence: Reexamining Interest Group Research." *Annual Review of Political Science* 15: 379–399.

Hopf, Ted. 1998. "The Promise of Constructivism in International Relations Theory." *International Security* 23(1): 171–200.

Hopgood, Stephen. 2006. *Keepers of the Flame: Understanding Amnesty International.* Ithaca, NY: Cornell University Press.

Hotez, Peter J. 2001. "Vaccine Diplomacy." *Foreign Policy,* May 1. http://www.foreignpolicy.com/articles/2001/05/01/vaccine_diplomacy.

Howard-Hassmann, Rhoda. 2012. "Human Security: Undermining Human Rights?" *Human Rights Quarterly* 34(1): 88–112.

H.R.F.S. 2008. "Human Rights First Society Take Action Statements."

Huggler, Justin. 2005. "Afghan Candidate Calls for Expulsion for 'Corrupt' NGOs." *The Independent,* September 13.

Hulme, David, and Michael Edwards. 1997. *NGOs, States and Donors: Too Close for Comfort?* London: Palgrave Macmillan.

Human Rights First (HRF). 2005. "Human Rights First's Concerns Regarding Human Rights Defenders and Justice and Accountability in the Americas." http://www.humanrightsfirst.org/wp-content/uploads/pdf/05114-hrd-hrf-sum-ameri-stat.pdf.

Human Rights Watch (HRW). 2001. "Trading Away Rights: The Unfulfilled Promise of NAFTA's Labor Side Agreement." 13(2B). http://www.hrw.org/reports/2001/nafta/.

Hundley, Kris, and Kendall Taggart. 2013. "Above the Law: America's Worst Charities." CNN News. http://www.cnn.com/2013/06/13/us/worst-charities.

Huth, Paul K. 1999. "Deterrence and International Conflict: Empirical Findings and Theoretical Debates." *Annual Review of Political Science* 2: 25–48.

ICNL. 2009. "Letter from the Editor." *Global Trends in NGO Law* 1(1). http://www.icnl .org/research/trends/trends1-1.html.

International Food Policy Research Index (IFPRI). 2012. "Global Hunger Index: The Challenge of Hunger: Ensuring Sustainable Food Security Under Land, Water, and Energy Stresses." http://www.ifpri.org/sites/default/files/publications/ghi12.pdf.

IRIN. 2008a. "Cambodia: Arsenic in Mekong Putting 1.7 Million at Risk." http://www .irinnews.org/printreport.aspx?reportid=81493.

———. 2008b. "Global: NGOs Pare Down in Face of Financial Crisis." IRIN News: A Service of the UN Office for the Coordination of Humanitarian Affairs. October 27.

Isik-Vanelli, Hakime. 2004. *Doing Business in China*. Munich: GRIN Verlag.

Jabine, Thomas B., and Richard P. Claude, eds. 1992. *Human Rights and Statistics: Getting the Record Straight*. Philadelphia: University of Pennsylvania Press.

Jakobsen, Susanne. 1999. "International Relations and Global Environmental Change: Review of the Burgeoning Literature on the Environment." *Cooperation and Conflict* 34: 205–236.

———. 2000. "Transnational Environmental Group, Media, Science, and Public Sentiments(s) in Domestic Policy-Making on Climate Change." In *Non-State Actors and Authority in the Global System*, edited by Richard A. Higgott, Geoffrey R. D. Underhill, and Andreas Bieler, 274–290. London: Routledge.

Jervis, Robert, L. 1970. *The Logic of Images in International Relations*. Princeton, NJ: Princeton University Press.

Jetschke, A. 2000. "International Norms, Transnational Human Rights Networks and Domestic Political Change in Indonesia and the Philippines." EUI PhD thesis. http://hdl.handle.net/1814/5324.

Johnston, Alastair I. 2001. "Treating International Institutions as Social Environments." *International Studies Quarterly* 45(4): 487–515.

———. 2005. "Conclusions and Extensions: Toward Mid-Range Theorizing and Beyond Europe." *International Organization* 59(4): 1013–1044.

———. 2008. *Social States: China in International Institutions, 1980–2000*. Princeton, NJ: Princeton University Press.

Jordan, Lisa, and Peter Van Tuijl. 2000. "Political Responsibility in Transnational NGO Advocacy." *World Development* 28(12): 2051–2065.

Judd, Ashley. 2009. "Without Family Planning." *USA Today*, November 9.

Judge, Anthony. 1994. "NGOs and Civil Society: Some Realities and Distortions." http:// www.laetusinpraesens.org/docs90s/civpol.php.

Karnani, Aneel. 2007. "Microfinance Misses Its Mark." *Stanford Social Innovation Review* Summer: 34–40.

Katzenstein, Peter J., ed. 1996. *The Culture of National Security: Norms and Identity in World Politics*. New York: Columbia University Press.

Katzenstein, Peter J., Robert O. Keohane, and Stephen D. Krasner. 1998. "International Organization and the Study of World Politics." *International Organization* 52(4): 645–685.

Kaufmann, Daniel, Aart Kraay, and Massimo Mastruzzi. 2005. "Measuring Governance Using Cross-Country Perceptions Data." World Bank. http://siteresources.worldbank.org/DEC/Resources/MeasuringGovernancewithperceptionsdataFinalforPublisher.pdf.

———. 2006. "Measuring Corruption: Myths and Realities." *Development Outreach* 8(2): 124–137.

———. 2009. "Governance Matters VIII: Aggregate and Individual Governance Indicators, 1996–2008." World Bank Policy Research Working Paper 4978, World Bank, Washington, DC.

Keck, M. E., and K. Sikkink. 1998. *Activists Beyond Borders: Advocacy Networks in International Politics.* Ithaca, NY: Cornell University Press.

Kelly, Robert Edwin. 2005. "'A Lot More Than the NGOs Seem to Think': The Impact of Non-Governmental Organizations on the Bretton Woods Institutions." Dissertation, Ohio State University.

Kerner, Andrew. 2009. "Why Should I Believe You? The Costs and Consequences of Bilateral Investment Treaties." *International Studies Quarterly* 53(1): 73–102.

Khandker, Shahidur R. 2005. "Microfinance and Poverty: Evidence Using Panel Data from Bangladesh." *World Bank Economic Review* 19(2): 263–286.

Khidr, Mohammed. 2006. "Foreign NGOs Have Their Own Agenda." *Yemen Times*, October 5.

King, G., M. Tomz, and J. Wittenberg. 2000. "Making the Most of Statistical Analyses: Improving Interpretation and Presentation." *American Journal of Political Science* 44(2): 341–355.

King, Gary. 1989. "Variance Specification in Event Count Models: From Restrictive Assumptions to a Generalized Estimator." *American Journal of Political Science* 33(3): 762–784.

King, Gary, and Will Lowe. 2003. "An Analysis Automated Information Extraction Tool for International Conflict Data with Performance as Good as Human Coders: A Rare Events Evaluation Design." *International Organization* 57(3): 617–642.

Korey, William. 1998. *NGOs and the Universal Declaration of Human Rights.* New York: St. Martin's Press.

Kouzzi, Saida, and Stephanie Willman Bordat. 2012. "Promoting a Violence Against Women Law in Morocco." In *Self-Determination and Women's Rights in Muslim Societies*, edited by Chitra Raghavan and James P. Levine, 37–70. Waltham, MA: Brandeis University Press.

Krain, Matthew. 2012. "J'accuse! Does Naming and Shaming Perpetrators Reduce the Severity of Genocides or Politicides?" *International Studies Quarterly*. Online First.

Kreps, David M. 1990. *A Course in Microeconomic Theory.* New York: Harvester Wheatsheaf.

Kumar, Anant. 2012. "Minting Money in an NGO Way." *Global Journal.* http://theglobal journal.net/article/view/812/.

Kydd, Andrew. 2003. "Which Side Are You On? Bias, Credibility, and Mediation." *American Journal of Political Science* 47(October): 597–611.

Lacey, Marc. 2003. "Kenya Starts Crackdown on Fake Charity Groups." *New York Times,* July 9.

Lakatos, Imre, and Alan Musgrave, eds. 1970. *Criticism and the Growth of Knowledge.* Proceedings of the International Colloquium in the Philosophy of Science London, 1965. Cambridge: Cambridge University Press.

Lake, George. 2012. "Female Genital Mutilation: Cutting the Woman from the Girl." *International Political Review,* January 31. http://www.theinternationalpoliticalreview .com/female-genital-mutilation-cutting-the-woman-from-the-girl/.

Lake, David, and Christopher J. Fariss. 2012. "International Trusteeship: External Authority in Areas of Limited Statehood." Paper prepared for the Collaborative Research Center 700 Workshop "Governance in Areas of Limited Statehood," San Diego, March 30 and 31.

Lambsdorff, Johann Graf. 1999. "Corruption in Empirical Research: A Review." http:// gwdu05.gwdg.de/~uwvw/downloads/contribution05_lambsdorff.pdf.

Landman, Todd. 2005. *Protecting Human Rights: A Comparative Study.* Washington, DC: Georgetown University Press.

La Porta, Rafael, Florencio Lopez-de-Silanes, Andrei Shleifer, and Robert Vishny. 1999. "The Quality of Government." *Journal of Law, Economics, and Organization* 15(1): 222–279.

La Rue, Frank. 2011. "Report of the Special Rapporteur on the Promotion and Protection of the Right to Freedom of Opinion and Expression, Frank La Rue." UN General Assembly Human Rights Council. 17th Session. Agenda Item 3. GE.11-13201.

Lebovic, James H., and Erik Voeten. 2009. "The Cost of Shame: International Organizations and Foreign Aid in the Punishing of Human Rights Violators." *Journal of Peace Research* 46(1): 79–97.

Lee, Sunny. 2007. "Bad Apples Sour Relief in North Korea." *Asia Times Online,* November 1.

Li, Quan, and Rafael Reuveny. 2003. "Economic Globalization and Democracy: An Empirical Analysis." *British Journal of Political Science* 33(1): 29–54.

Lowe, Christian. 2006. "Russia NGOs Fear Trouble as Law Comes into Force." *Reuters News Service,* April 17.

Lucas, Robert E. 1988. "On the Mechanics of Economic Development." *Journal of Monetary Economics* 22(1): 3–42.

Lyon, Thomas P. 2010. *Good Cop/Bad Cop: Environmental NGOs and Their Strategies Toward Business.* Abingdon, UK: RFF Press.

Macan-Markar, Marwaan. 2004. "Govt-NGO Partnership, the Key to Millennium Development Goals." *Inter Press Service*, November 24.

Maddala, G. S., and Shaowen Wu. 1999. "A Comparative Study of Unit Root Tests with Panel Data and a New Simple Test." *Oxford Bulletin of Economics and Statistics* 61(S1): 631–652.

Makoba, J. Wagona. 2002. "Nongovernmental Organizations (NGOs) and Third World Development: An Alternative Approach to Development." *Journal of Third World Studies* 19(1): 53–64.

Manji, Firoze, and Carl O'Coill. 2002. "The Missionary Position: NGOs and Development in Africa." *International Affairs* 78(3): 567–583.

Mankiw, N. Gregory, David Romer, and David N. Weil. 1992. "A Contribution to the Empirics of Economic Growth." *Quarterly Journal of Economics* 107(2): 407–437.

Mansfield, E. D., H. V. Milner, and B. P. Rosendorff. 2003. "Why Democracies Cooperate More: Electoral Control and International Trade Agreements." *International Organization* 56(3): 477–513.

Marshall, Monty, and Keith Jaggers. 2010. Polity IV Project. Center for Systemic Peace. http://www.systemicpeace.org/polity/polity4.htm.

Martens, Kerstin. 2002. "Mission Impossible? Defining Nongovernmental Organizations." *Voluntas* 13(3): 271–285.

Martimort, David. 1996. "Exclusive Dealing, Common Agency, and Multiprincipals Incentive Theory." *Rand Journal of Economics* 27(1): 1–31.

Masud, Nadia, and Borina Yontcheva. 2005. "Does Foreign Aid Reduce Poverty? Empirical Evidence from Nongovernmental and Bilateral Aid." IMF Working Paper 01/100, International Monetary Fund, Washington, DC.

Matlosa, Khabele. 1999. "Aid, Development and Democracy in Lesotho, 1966–1996." Paper presented at a Workshop Organized by the Centre for Southern African Studies on "Aid, Development and Democracy in Southern Africa," University of the Western Cape, Cape Town, South Africa, November 21–22.

Matos, Noquel A. 2009. "Recession Mixed Blessing for NGOs." http://bgia.bard.edu/userfiles/file/Recession.pdf.

Matthews, Jessica T. "Power Shift." *Foreign Affairs* (January–February): 50–66.

Mayer, Ann Elizabeth. 1995. "Cultural Particularism as a Bar to Women's Rights." In *Women's Rights, Human Rights: International Feminist Perspectives*, edited by Julie Stone Peters and Andrew Wolper, 176–188. New York: Routledge.

McBeath, Gerald A., and Tse-Kang Leng. 2006. *Governance of Biodiversity Conservation in China and Taiwan.* Cheltenham, UK: Edward Elgar.

McCarty, Nolan M., and Adam Meirowitz. 2007. *Political Game Theory: An Introduction.* Cambridge: Cambridge University Press.

McCormick, John. 1999. "The Role of Environmental NGOs in International Regimes." In *The Global Environment: Institutions, Law, and Policy*, edited by Norman J. Vig and Regina S. Axelrod, 52–71. London: Earthscan.

McCoy, Kevin, and Oren Dorell. 2008. "It's a Hard Time to Be a Charity." *USA Today*, October 27.

McGann, James, and Mary Johnstone. 2005. "The Power Shift and the NGO Credibility Crisis." *International Journal of Not-for-Profit Law* 8(2): 65–77.

Meernik, James, Rosa Aloisi, Marsha Sowell, and Angela Nichols. 2012. "The Impact of Human Rights Organizations on Naming and Shaming Campaigns." *Journal of Conflict Resolution* 56(2): 233–256.

Mercer, Jonathan. 1995. "Anarchy and Identity." *International Organization* 49(2): 229–252.

Miguel, Edward, Shanker Satyanath, and Ernest Sergenti. 2004. "Economic Shocks and Civil Conflict: An Instrumental Variables Approach." *Journal of Political Economy* 112(4): 725–753.

Miller, Gary J. 2005. "The Political Evolution of Principal-Agent Models." *Annual Review of Political Science* 8: 203–225.

Ministry of Health (MoH) of Ghana. 2011. "Ghana MDG Acceleration Framework and Country Action Plan Maternal Health." http://www.undp.org/content/dam/undp/library/MDG/MDG%20Acceleration%20Framework/MAF%20Reports/RBA/MAF%20Ghana_MDG5_Low_Web%20(2).pdf.

Mitchell, George. 2010. "Reframing Nonprofit Effectiveness." http://www.maxwell.syr.edu/uploadedFiles/moynihan/tngo/TRANSNATIONAL_NGO_INITIATIVE/Watchdogs%2024_AUG_2010.pdf.

Mitchell, Neal J., and James M. McCormick. 1988. "Economic and Political Explanations of Human Rights Violations." *World Politics* 40(4): 476–498.

Moe, Terry M. 1985. "Control and Feedback in Economic Regulation: The Case of the NLRB." *American Political Science Review* 79(4): 1094–1116.

———. 1987. "Interests, Institutions, and Positive Theory: The Politics of the NLRB." *Studies in American Political Development* 2(2): 236–299.

Mohammed, Arshad. 2007. "US Sends Firmer Signal to Pakistan on Democracy." Reuters. http://www.reuters.com/article/2007/06/14/us-pakistan-usa-democracy-idUSN1416211720070614.

Mohan, Saumitra. 1998. "Genuine NGOs Struggle with Credibility." *Indian Express*, January 29.

Mohanty, Mritiunjoy. 2006. "Microcredit, NGOs, and Poverty Alleviation." *The Hindu*, November 15. www.hinduonnet.com/2006/11/15/stories/2006111506441200.html.

Mojumdar, Aunohita. 2006. "Fighting NGOism." *Hindu Business Line*, January 13.

Mokhtari, Shadi. 2012. "The Middle East and Human Rights: Inroads Towards Charting Its Own Path." *Northwestern University Journal of International Human Rights* 10: 194–212.

Moore, J. F. 2003. "The Second Superpower Rears Its Beautiful Head." Berkman Center for Internet and Society, Harvard University. http://www.fresnik.com/stuff/secondsuperpower.pdf.

Morrow, J. D. 1994. *Game Theory for Political Scientists*. Princeton, NJ: Princeton University Press.

Mudingu, Joseph. 2006. "How Genuine Are NGOs?" *New York Times*, August 7.

Mundy, Karen, and Lynn Murphy. 2001. "Transnational Advocacy, Global Civil Society? Emerging Evidence from the Field of Education." *Comparative Education Review* 45(1): 85–126.

Murdie, Amanda. 2009. "The Impact of Human Rights INGOs on Human Rights Practices." *International NGO Journal* 4(10): 421–440.

———. 2014. "The Ties That Bind: A Network Analysis of Human Rights INGOs." *British Journal of Political Science* 44(1): 1–27.

Murdie, Amanda, and Tavishi Bhasin. 2011. "Aiding and Abetting? Human Rights INGOs and Domestic Anti-Government Protest." *Journal of Conflict Resolution* 55(2): 163–191.

Murdie, Amanda, and David R. Davis. 2010. "Problematic Potential: The Human Rights Consequences of Peacekeeping Interventions in Civil Wars." *Human Rights Quarterly* 32(1): 50–73.

———. 2012a. "Shaming and Blaming: Using Events Data to Assess the Impact of Human Rights INGOs." *International Studies Quarterly* 56(1): 1–16.

———. 2012b. "Looking in the Mirror: Comparing INGO Networks Across Issue Areas." *Review of International Organizations* 7(2): 177–202.

Murdie, Amanda, and Alex Hicks. 2013. "Can International NGOs Boost Government Services? The Case of Health." *International Organization* 67(3): 541–573.

Murdie, Amanda, and Jakub Kakietek. 2012. "Do NGOs Really Work? The Impact of International Development NGOs on Economic Growth." *Journal of Sustainable Society* 1(1): 1–10.

Murdie, Amanda, and Dursun Peksen. 2013. "The Impact of Human Rights INGO Shaming on Sanctions." *Review of International Organizations* 8(1): 33–53.

———. 2014. "The Impact of Human Rights INGO Shaming on Humanitarian Interventions." *Journal of Politics* 76(1): 215–228.

Naím, Moisés. 2007. "Democracy's Dangerous Impostors." *Washington Post*, April 21.

Najam, Adil. 1996. "NGO Accountability: A Conceptual Framework." *Development Policy Review* 14(4): 339–354.

Nancy, Gilles, and Borina Yontcheva. 2006. "Does NGO Aid Go to the Poor? Empirical Evidence from Europe." IMF Working Paper 06/39, International Monetary Fund, Washington, DC.

National Democratic Institute (NDI). 2012. "In Burkina Faso, Legislators Emphasize Mining Oversight." http://www.ndi.org/burkina-faso-mining-oversight.

Neba, Ndenecho Emmanuel. 2009. "NGO Input and Stakeholder Participation in Natural Resource Management: Example of Northwest Cameroon." *International NGO Journal* 4(3): 50–56.

Nelson, Paul J. 2007. "Human Rights, the Millennium Development Goals, and the Future of Development Cooperation." *World Development* 35(12): 2041–2055.

Nelson, Paul J., and Ellen Dorsey. 2008. *New Rights Advocacy: Changing Strategies of Development and Human Rights NGOs.* Washington, DC: Georgetown University Press.

Neumayer, Eric. 2005. "Do International Human Rights Treaties Improve Respect for Human Rights?" *Journal of Conflict Resolution* 49(6): 925.

"NGOs: Achievers or Deceivers?" 2004. BBC News. http://news.bbc.co.uk/2/hi/africa/3502733.stm.

NGO Statement on US IDP Policy. 2008. http://www.refugeesinternational.org/policy/letter/ngo-statement-us-idp-Policy.

Nicholson, Zara. 2012. "Idasa, Black Sash Lose Millions in Funding." *Cape Times*, February 2.

Nur-Tegin, Kanybek, and Hans J. Czap. 2012. "Corruption: Democracy, Autocracy, and Political Stability." *Economic Analysis and Policy* 42(1): 51–66.

Ojukwu, Chris C., and J. O. Shopeju. 2010. "Elite Corruption and the Culture of Primitive Accumulation in 21st-Century Nigeria." *International Journal of Peace and Development Studies* 1(2): 15–24.

Okafor, Obiora Chinedu. 2006. *Legitimizing Human Rights NGOs: Lessons from Nigeria.* Trenton, NJ: Africa World Press.

Olzak, Susan, and Kiyoteru Tsutsui. 1998. "Status in the World System and Ethnic Mobilization." *Journal of Conflict Resolution* 42(6): 691–720.

Omara-Otunnu, Amii. 2007. "Western Humanitarianism or Neo-Slavery." *Black Star News*, November 7.

OneWorldSouthAsia.2009."EconomicCrisisLeavingMillionsHungry,SaysStudy."http://southasia.oneworld.net/archive/globalheadlines/economic-crisis-leaving-millions-hungry-says-study#.UNCQ5m88B8E.

Otto, Dianne. 1996. "Nongovernmental Organizations in the United Nations System: The Emerging Role of International Civil Society." *Human Rights Quarterly* 18: 107.

Oweyegha-Afunaduula, F. C., Isaac Afunaduula, and Mahiri Balunywa. 2003. "NGOnising the Nile Basin Initiative: A Myth or Reality?" Paper presented at the Third World Water Forum, Japan, March.

Oxfam.2011."RiskofAnotherForgottenEmergencyinAfricaasThousandsFleeIvoryCoast Violence." March 7. http://www.oxfam.org/en/pressroom/pressrelease/2011-03-07/risk-another-forgotten-emergency-africa-thousands-flee-ivory-coast.

Paine, Harold, and Birgit Gratzer. 2001. "Rev. Moon and the United Nations: A Challenge for the NGO Community." *Weed*, November.

Paris, Roland. 2001. "Human Security: Paradigm Shift or Hot Air?" *International Security* 26(2): 87–102.

Parker, Melissa. 1995. "Rethinking Female Circumcision." *Africa* 65: 506–524.

Pasipanodya, Tafadzwa. 2008. "A Deeper Justice: Economic and Social Justice as Transitional Justice in Nepal." *International Journal of Transitional Justice* 2: 378–397.

Peksen, Dursun. 2009. "Better or Worse? The Effect of Economic Sanctions on Human Rights." *Journal of Peace Research* 46(1): 59–77.

———. 2012. "Does Foreign Military Intervention Help Human Rights?" *Political Research Quarterly* 65(3): 558–571.

Peksen, Dursun, and A. Cooper Drury. 2009. "Economic Sanctions and Political Repression: Assessing the Impact of Coercive Diplomacy on Political Freedoms." *Human Rights Review* 10(3): 393–411.

Peters, Melanie. 2008. "Charities, NGOs Funds 'Drying Up.'" *IOL News*, November 9.

Peters, Toni. 2011. "Colombia Has Improved Under Santos: Human Rights Watch." *Colombia Reports*, October 12.

Petras, James. 1997. "Imperialism and NGOs in Latin America." *Monthly Review* 49: 10–27.

———. 1999. "NGOs: In the Service of Imperialism." *Journal of Contemporary Asia* 29(4): 429–440.

Petras, James, and Henry Veltmeyer. 2001. *Globalization Unmasked: Imperialism in the 21st Century*. London: Zed Books.

Pevehouse, Jon C. 2005. *Democracy from Above: Regional Organizations and Democratization*. Cambridge: Cambridge University Press.

Pitner, Julia. 2000. "NGOs' Dilemmas." *Middle East Report* 30(1): 34–37.

Poe, Steven. 1990. "Human Rights and US Foreign Aid: A Review of Quantitative Studies and Suggestions for Future Research." *Human Rights Quarterly* 12(4): 499–512.

Poe, Steven, and C. Neal Tate. 1994. "Repression of Human Rights to Personal Integrity in the 1980s: A Global Analysis." *American Political Science Review* 88(4): 853–872.

Poe, Steven C., C. Neil Tate, and Linda C. Keith. 1999. "Repression of the Human Right to Personal Integrity Revisited: A Global Cross-National Study Covering the Years 1976–1993." *International Studies Quarterly* 43(2): 291–313.

Poskitt, Adele. 2012. "CSO Accountability and the International NGO Accountability Charter." http://foundationforfuture.org/en/Portals/0/Conferences/Accountability/Presentations/Session%201/Pres-4-CIVICUS_INGO_English.pdf.

Pottinger, Lori. 2000. "Scandal in Lesotho: Caught Wet-Handed." Africa Files. http://knowmore.org/wiki/index.php?title=SCANDAL_IN_LESOTHO:_CAUGHT_WET-HANDED.

Power, Jonathan. 2001. *Like Water on Stone: The Story of Amnesty International*. New York: Allen Lane / The Penguin Press.

Prakash, Aseem, and Mary Kay Gugerty, eds. 2010. *Advocacy Organizations and Collective Action*. Cambridge: Cambridge University Press.

Price, Richard. 2003. "Transnational Civil Society and Advocacy in World Politics." *World Politics* 55(4): 579–606.

Princen, Thomas. 1995. "Ivory, Conservation, and Environmental Transnational Coalitions." In *Bringing Transnational Relations Back In: Non-State Actors, Domestic Structures and International Institutions*, edited by Thomas Risse-Kappen, 227–253. Cambridge: Cambridge University Press.

Provost, Claire. 2011. "Aid from OECD Countries—Who Gives the Most and How Has It Changed?" *Data Blog—The Guardian*. http://www.guardian.co.uk/news/datablog/2011/apr/06/aid-oecd-given#data.

Pruthi, Priyanka. 2012. "Marking Its First Year Without Any Polio Cases, India Takes a Giant Leap Toward Wiping Out the Disease." http://www.unicef.org/infobycountry/india_61293.html.

Przeworski, Adam. 2004. "Democracy and Economic Development." In *The Evolution of Political Knowledge: Democracy, Autonomy, and Conflict in Comparative and International Politics*, edited by Edward D. Mansfield and Richard Sisson, 300–324. Columbus: Ohio State University Press.

Quackenbush, Stephen. 2004. "The Rationality of Rational Choice Theory." *International Interactions* 30(2): 87–107.

Ranis, G., F. Stewart, and A. Ramirez. 2000. "Economic Growth and Human Development." *World Development* 28(2): 197–219.

Reinhardt, Gina Yannitell. 2006. "Shortcuts and Signals: An Analysis of the Microlevel Determinants of Aid Allocation, with Case Study Evidence from Brazil." *Review of Development Economics* 10(2): 297–312.

———. 2009. "Matching Donors and Nonprofits: The Importance of Signaling in Funding Awards." *Journal of Theoretical Politics* 21(3): 283–309.

Reitan, Ruth. 2007. *Global Activism*. London: Routledge.

Reiter, Dan. 2001. "Does Peace Nurture Democracy?" *Journal of Politics* 63(3): 935–948.

Reuveny, Rafael, and Quan Li. 2003. "Economic Openness, Democracy, and Income Inequality: An Empirical Analysis." *Comparative Political Studies* 36(5): 575.

Richards, David L., Ronald D. Gelleny, and David H. Sacko. 2001. "Money with a Mean Streak? Foreign Economic Penetration and Government Respect for Human Rights in Developing Countries." *International Studies Quarterly* 45(2): 219–239.

Risse, Thomas. 2010. "Rethinking Advocacy Organizations? A Critical Comment." In *Advocacy Organizations and Collective Action*, edited by Aseem Prakash and Mary Kay Gugerty, 283–294. Cambridge: Cambridge University Press.

———. 1999. "The Power of Norms Versus the Norms of Power: Transnational Civil Society and Human Rights." In *The Third Force: The Rise of Transnational Civil Society*, edited by Ann M. Florini, 177–209. Washington, DC: Carnegie Endowment for International Peace.

————. 2002. "Transnational Actors and World Politics." In *Handbook of International Relations*, edited by Walter Carlsnaes, Thomas Risse, and Beth A. Simmons, 255–274. London: Sage.

Risse, Thomas, and Stephen C. Ropp. 1999. "International Human Rights Norms and Domestic Change." In *The Power of Human Rights: International Norms and Domestic Change*, edited by Thomas Risse, Stephen Ropp, and Kathryn Sikkink, 234–278. Cambridge: Cambridge University Press.

Risse, Thomas, Stephen C. Ropp, and Kathryn Sikkink, eds. 1999. *The Power of Human Rights: International Norms and Domestic Change*. Cambridge: Cambridge University Press.

Robinson, Piers. 2011. "The CNN Effect Reconsidered: Mapping a Research Agenda for the Future." *Media, War and Conflict* 4(1): 3–11.

Rodrik, Dani. 1989. "Promises, Promises: Credible Policy Reform via Signaling." *Economic Journal* 99(397): 756–772.

Roelofs, Joan. 2006. "The NED, NGOs, and the Imperial Uses of Philanthropy: Why They Hate Our Kind Hearts, Too." *Counter Punch*, May 13.

Romankov, Leonid. 2000. "Opening Totalitarian Societies to the Outside World: A View from Russia." In *Realizing Human Rights: Moving from Inspiration to Impact*, edited by Samantha Power and Graham Allison, 63–76. London: Palgrave Macmillan.

Ron, James, Howard Ramos, and Kathleen Rodgers. 2005. "Transnational Information Politics: NGO Human Rights Reporting, 1986–2000." *International Studies Quarterly* 49(3): 557–588.

Ropp, Stephen C., and Kathryn Sikkink. 1999. "International Norms and Domestic Politics in Chile and Guatemala." In *The Power of Human Rights: International Norms and Domestic Change*, edited by Thomas Risse, Stephen Ropp, and Kathryn Sikkink, 172–204. Cambridge: Cambridge University Press.

Rose, Pauline. 2009. "NGO Provision of Basic Education: Alternative or Complementary Service Delivery to Support Access to the Excluded?" *Compare* 39(2): 219–233.

Rose-Ackerman, Susan. 1996. "Altruism, Nonprofits, and Economic Theory." *Journal of Economic Literature* 32(2): 701–728.

Roth, Elana. ND. "Where Abortion Is Illegal, Trying to Ease the Pain." *NYU Live Wire.* http://journalism.nyu.edu/publishing/archives/livewire/global/abortions/.

Roth, Kenneth. 2004. "Defending Economic, Social and Cultural Rights: Practical Issues Faced by an International Human Rights Organization." *Human Rights Quarterly* 26(1): 63–73.

Roy, Arundhati. 2004. "Help That Hinders." *Le Monde Diplomatique*, November.

Russett, Bruce, John Oneal, and David R. Davis. 1998. "The Third Leg of the Kantian Tripod for Peace: International Organizations and Militarized Disputes, 1950–1985." *International Organization* 52: 441–468.

Salamon, Lester M., and Helmut K. Anheier. 1992. "In Search of the Non-Profit Sector: The Question of Definitions." *Voluntas* 3(2): 125–151.

Sartori, A. E. 2003. "The Might of the Pen: A Reputational Theory of Communication in International Disputes." *International Organization* 56(1): 121–149.

Sawitri, Adisti Sukma. 2006. "For Some NGOs, Another Disaster Means New Flashy Cars." *Jakarta Post*, August 24.

Schafer, Mark J. 1999. "International Nongovernmental Organizations and Third World Education in 1990: A Cross-National Study." *Sociology of Education* 72(2): 69–88.

Scharpf, Fritz W. 1999. *Governing in Europe: Effective and Democratic?* New York: Oxford University Press.

Schepers, D. H. 2006. "The Impact of NGO Network Conflict on the Corporate Social Responsibility Strategies of Multinational Corporations." *Business and Society* 45(3): 282.

Schmitz, Hans Peter. 2002. "From Lobbying to Shaming: The Evolution of Human Rights Activism Since the 1940s." Paper presented at the International Studies Association Meeting, New Orleans, March 24–27.

Schmitz, Hans Peter, and Kathryn Sikkink. 2001. "International Relations Theory and Human Rights." http://kiosk.polisci.umn.edu/courses/spring2001/4485/ir2.pdf.

Schock, Kurt. 2005. *Unarmed Insurrections: People Power Movements in Nondemocracies.* Minneapolis: University of Minnesota Press.

Schofer, Evan, and Ann Hironaka. 2005. "The Effects of World Society on Environmental Protection Outcomes." *Social Forces* 84(1): 25–47.

Schuller, Mark. 2007. "Invasion or Infusion? Understanding the Role of NGOs in Contemporary Haiti." *Journal of Haitian Studies* 12(2): 96–119.

Schulz, William. 2001. *In Our Own Best Interest: How Defending Human Rights Benefits All Americans.* Boston: Beacon Press.

Sen, Gita, and Caren Grown. 1988. *Development, Crises and Alternative Visions: Third World Women's Perspectives.* London: Earthscan.

Shandra, John M., Carrie Shandra, and Bruce London. 2010. "Do Non-Governmental Organizations Impact Health?" *International Journal of Comparative Sociology* 51(1–2): 137–164.

Shaw, Randy. 1999. *Reclaiming America: Nike, Clean Air, and the New National Activism.* Berkeley: University of California Press.

Shigetomi, Shinichi. 2002. *The State and NGOs: Perspective from Asia.* Singapore: Institute of Southeast Asian Studies.

Shircliff, Eric J., and John M. Shandra. 2011. "Non·Governmental Organizations, Democracy, and HIV Prevalence: A Cross·National Analysis." *Sociological Inquiry* 81(2): 143–173.

Sievers, Eric W. 2003. *Post-Soviet Decline of Central Asia: Sustainable Development and Comprehensive Capital.* Abingdon, UK: RoutledgeCurzon.

Sikkink, Kathryn. 1993. "Human Rights, Principled Issue-Networks, and Sovereignty in Latin America." *International Organization* 47(3): 411–441.

———. 2002. *Restructuring World Politics: Transnational Social Movements, Networks, and Norms.* Minneapolis: University of Minnesota Press.

Simmons, Beth A. 2009. *Mobilizing for Human Rights: International Law in Domestic Politics.* Cambridge: Cambridge University Press.

Sinclair, Hugh, and David C. Korten. 2012. *Confessions of a Microfinance Heretic: How Microlending Lost Its Way and Betrayed the Poor.* San Francisco: Berrett-Koehler.

Smith, Daniel Jordan. 2008. *A Culture of Corruption: Everyday Deception and Popular Discontent in Nigeria.* Princeton, NJ: Princeton University Press.

———. 2010. "Corruption, NGOs, and Development in Nigeria." *Third World Quarterly* 31(2): 243–258.

———. 2012. "AIDS NGOS and Corruption in Nigeria." *Health and Place* 18(3): 475–480.

Smith, Jackie. 1998. "Global Civil Society? Transnational Social Movement Organizations and Social Capital." *American Behavioral Scientist* 42(1): 93.

———. 2005. "Building Bridges or Building Walls? Explaining Regionalization Among Transnational Social Movement Organizations." *Mobilization: An International Quarterly* 10(2): 251–269.

Smith, Jackie, and Dawn Wiest. 2005. "The Uneven Geography of Global Civil Society: National and Global Influences on Transnational Association." *Social Forces* 84: 621.

———. 2012. *Social Movements in the World-System: The Politics of Crisis and Transformation.* New York: Russell Sage Foundation.

Smith, Stephanie. 2012. "Melinda Gates Responds to Contraception Program Controversy." *CNN Health,* July 6. http://www.cnn.com/2012/07/06/health/melinda-gates -contraception/index.html.

Soto, Alvaro. 1991–1992. "The Global Environment: A Southern Perspective." *International Journal* 47(4): 679–705.

SP. 2008. "NGOs Gone Bad." Strategy Page. February 17. http://www.strategypage.com/ htmw/htun/articles/20080217.aspx.

Spar, Debora L., and Lane T. LaMure. 2003. "The Power of Activism: Assessing the Impact of NGOs on Global Business." *California Management Review* 45(3): 78–101.

Sparr, Pamela, and Caroline Moser. 2007. "International NGOs and Poverty Reduction Strategies: The Contribution of an Asset-Based Approach." Brookings Global Economy and Development Working Paper 8, Brookings Institution, Washington, DC.

Spilker, Gabriele, and Tobias Böhmelt. 2013. "The Impact of Preferential Trade Agreements on Governmental Repression Revisited." *Review of International Organizations* 8(3): 343–361.

Stavins, Robert N. 2008. "Addressing Global Climate Change with a Comprehensive US Cap-and-Trade System." Discussion Paper 2008-2, Belfer Center for Science and International Affairs, Cambridge, MA.

Steinberg, Natalie. 2001. "Background Paper on GONGOs and QUANGOS and Wild NGOs." World Federalist Movement. December. http://www.globalpolicy.org/ngos/intro/defining/2001/0112wild.htm.

Steinberg, Paul F. 2002. "Civic Environmentalism in Developing Countries: Opportunities for Innovation in State-Society Relations." World Development Report 2003 Dynamic Development in a Sustainable World.

———. 2005. "From Public Concern to Policy Effectiveness: Civic Conservation in Developing Countries." *Journal of International Wildlife Law and Policy* 8(4): 341–365.

Stole, Lars A. 1991. *Mechanism Design Under Common Agency*. Program in Law and Economics, Harvard Law School.

Streeten, Paul. 1997. "Nongovernmental Organizations and Development." *Annals of the American Academy of Political and Social Science* 554(1): 193.

Stroup, Sarah S. 2012. *Borders Among Activists: International NGOs in the United States, Britain, and France*. Ithaca, NY: Cornell University Press.

Stroup, Sarah S., and Amanda Murdie. 2012. "There's No Place like Home: Explaining International NGO Advocacy." *Review of International Organizations* 7(4): 425–448.

Sundstrom, Lisa McIntosh. 2005. "Foreign Assistance, International Norms, and NGO Development: Lessons from the Russian Campaign." *International Organization* 59(2): 419–449.

———. 2006. *Funding Civil Society: Foreign Assistance and NGO Development in Russia*. Stanford, CA: Stanford University Press.

Svensson, Isak. 2007. "Bargaining, Bias and Peace Brokers: How Rebels Commit to Peace." *Journal of Peace Research* 44(2): 177.

Tarrow, Sidney G. 2005. *The New Transnational Activism*. Cambridge: Cambridge University Press.

Teegen, Hildy, Jonathan P. Doh, and Sushil Vachani. 2004. "The Importance of Nongovernmental Organizations (NGOs) in Global Governance and Value Creation: An International Business Research Agenda." *Journal of International Business Studies* 35(6): 463–483.

Thomas, Daniel C. 2001. *The Helsinki Effect: International Norms, Human Rights, and the Demise of Communism*. Princeton, NJ: Princeton University Press.

Tibet Truth. 2012. "Boycott China." http://tibettruth.com/boycott-china/.

Tomz, M., J. Wittenberg, and G. King. 2003. "CLARIFY: Software for Interpreting and Presenting Statistical Results." *Journal of Statistical Software* 8(1): 1–30.

Transformation Resource Centre. 2003. Annual Report 2003. http://trc.org.ls/.

Tschirhart, Mary. 2010. "Self-Regulation at the State Level: Nonprofit Membership Association and Club Emergence." In *Voluntary Regulation of NGOs and Nonprofits: An Accountability Club Framework*, edited by Mary Kay Gugerty and Aseem Prakash, 85–100. Cambridge: Cambridge University Press.

Tsikoane, Tumelo, Tefetso H. Mothibe, 'Mamoeketsi E. N. Ntho, and David Maleleka. 2007. "Consolidating Democratic Governance in Southern Africa: Lesotho." EISA Research Report No. 32. http://www.eisa.org.za/PDF/rr32.pdf.

Tsutsui, Kiyoteru, and Christine M. Wotipka. 2004. "Global Civil Society and the International Human Rights Movement: Citizen Participation in Human Rights International Nongovernmental Organizations." *Social Forces* 83: 587.

Tvedt, Terje. 1998. *Angels of Mercy or Development Diplomats? NGOs and Foreign Aid.* Trenton, NJ: Africa World Press.

UCDP/PRIO. 2008. "UCDP/PRIO Armed Conflict Program." http://www.prio.no/CSCW/Datasets/Armed-Conflict/UCDP-PRIO/.

UIA. 2008/2009. *Yearbook of International Organizations.* Vols. 1–4. 45th ed. Brussels: Union of International Associations.

————. 2012. "2.2 International non-governmental organizations (NGOs)." http://www.uia.be/22-international-non-governmental-organizations-ngos.

UK House of Commons International Development Committee (UKIDC). 2006. *Humanitarian Response to Natural Disasters: Seventh Report of Session 2005–2006.* Vol. 1. London: Stationery Office Limited.

Ullah, A. N. Zafar, James N. Newell, Jalal Uddin Ahmed, M. K. A. Hyder, and Akramul Islam. 2006. "Government-NGO Collaboration: The Case of Tuberculosis Control in Bangladesh." *Health Policy and Planning* 21(2): 143–155.

UN. 1990. *Human Development Report.* New York: Oxford University Press.

————. 2005. *The Millennium Development Goals Report.* New York: UN.

————. 2008. "Consultative Status with the UN." http://www.un.org/esa/coordination/ngo/.

————. 2011. "Working with ECOSOC: An NGOs Guide to Consultative Status." http://csonet.org/content/documents/Brochure.pdf.

UNAIDS. 2003. "UNAIDS-AFRICASO Human Rights and HIV/AIDS Project in Tanzania." http://data.unaids.org/Topics/Human-Rights/tanzania_needs_assessment_en.pdf.

UN ECOSOC. 2009. "Report of the Committee of Non-Governmental Organizations on Its 2009 Regular Session." E/2009/32, March 4.

UNICEF and World Health Organization (WHO). 2012. *Progress on Drinking Water and Sanitation: 2012 Update.* UNICEF and the World Health Organization. http://www.unicef.org/media/files/JMPreport2012.pdf.

United Nations Development Programme (UNDP). 1994. "New Dimensions of Human Security." Human Development Report 1994.

————. 2006. "Human Development Report 2006 Beyond Scarcity: Power, Poverty and the Global Water Crisis." http://hdr.undp.org/en/media/HDR06-complete.pdf.

————. 2012. "2011 Millennium Development Goals in Lesotho." http://www.undp.org.ls/millennium/default.php.

UNODC. 2010. "Corruption Widespread in Afghanistan, UNODC Survey Says." http://www.unodc.org/unodc/en/frontpage/2010/January/corruption-widespread-in-afghanistan-unodc-survey-says.html.

UN Office of the High Commissioner for Human Rights (OHCHR). 2012. "New Restrictions on NGOs Are Undermining Human Rights: Pillay." http://www.ohchr.org/EN/NewsEvents/Pages/DisplayNews.aspx?NewsID=12081.

USAID. 2006. "Success Story: Improved Water Access Reduces Conflict." http://www.usaid.gov/stories/sudan/water.html.

———. 2012. "USAID Implementing Mechanisms an Additional Help for ADS Chapters 200–203." http://transition.usaid.gov/policy/ads/200/200sbo.pdf.

US Department of State (USDoS). 2007. "Burkina Faso: Bureau of Democracy, Human Rights, and Labor 2006." March 6. http://www.state.gov/j/drl/rls/hrrpt/2006/78721.htm.

———. 2012. "2011 Human Rights Reports: Introduction." Bureau of Democracy, Human Rights, and Labor. http://www.state.gov/j/drl/rls/hrrpt/2011/frontmatter/186157.htm.

US House of Representatives. 1990. "Hearing Before the Subcommittees on Human Rights and International Organizations, and on Western Hemisphere Affairs of the Committee on Foreign Affairs." Second Session. September 12. US Printing Office. 35-697.

Vakil, Anna C. 1997. "Confronting The Classification Problem: Toward a Taxonomy of NGOs." *World Development* 25(12): 2057–2070.Vaknin, Sam. 2005. *NGOs—The Self-Appointed Altruists.* London: United Press International.

Valbrun, Marjorie. 2012. "Amid a Slow Recovery, Haitians Question the Work of Aid Groups." http://www.publicintegrity.org/2012/01/10/7838/after-quake-praise-becomes-resentment-haiti.

Van Tuijl, Peter. 1999. "NGOs and Human Rights: Sources of Justice and Democracy." *Journal of International Affairs* 52(2): 493–512.

Vivanco, José Miguel. 2011. "Anti-Union Violence, Human Rights, and the US-Colombia Free Trade Agreement." Written Testimony to the United States House of Representatives Committee on Ways and Means Subcommittee on Trade. March 17. http://waysandmeans.house.gov/uploadedfiles/human_rights_watch.pdf.

Volk, Yevgeny. 2006. "Russia's NGO Law: An Attack on Freedom and Civil Society." Heritage Foundation Web Memo 1090. May 24.

Vreeland, James Raymond. 2008. "Political Institutions and Human Rights: Why Dictatorships Enter into the United Nations Convention Against Torture." *International Organization* 62(1): 65–101.

Wagner, Natascha. 2011. "Why Female Genital Cutting Persists." Working Paper, Graduate Institute of International and Development Studies, Geneva. http://www.natascha-wagner.com/uploads/9/0/1/5/9015445/job_market_paper_fgc.pdf.

Wallace, Tina. 2004. "NGO Dilemmas: Trojan Horses for Global Neoliberalism?" *Socialist Register* 40: 202–219.

Wallander, Celeste A. 2005. "Ukraine's Election: The Role of One International NGO." CSIS, REP. March 1. http://www.csis.org.

Waltz, Kenneth. 1979. *Theory of International Politics.* New York: McGraw-Hill.

Wapner, Paul. 1995. "Politics Beyond the State Environmental Activism and World Civic Politics." *World Politics* 47(3): 311–340.

Ward, Carol, Yodit Solomon, Bonnie Ballif-Spanvill, and Addie Furhriman. 2008. "Framing Development: Community and NGO Perspectives in Mali." *Community Development Journal* 1–18.

Warkentin, Craig. 2001. *Reshaping World Politics: NGOs, the Internet, and Global Civil Society.* Lanham, MD: Rowman & Littlefield.

WDI. 2008. "World Development Indicators." World Bank. CD-ROM.

———. 2012. "World Development Indicators." World Bank. http://data.worldbank .org/data-catalog/world-development-indicators.

Weeks, Jessica L. 2008. "Autocratic Audience Costs: Regime Type and Signaling Resolve." *International Organization* 62(1): 35–64.

Weiss, Thomas George, and Leon Gordenker, eds. 1996. *NGOs, the UN, and Global Governance.* Boulder, CO: Lynne Rienner.

Welch, Claude E., Jr. 1995. *Protecting Human Rights in Africa: Strategies and Roles of Nongovernmental Organizations.* Philadelphia: University of Pennsylvania Press.

———, ed. 2001. *NGOs and Human Rights: Promise and Performance.* Philadelphia: University of Pennsylvania Press.

Wenzel, Andrea. 2006. "NGO Neo-imperialism." Andrea in Afghanistan. November 25. http://andreawenzel.blogspot.com/2006/11/ngo-neo-imperialism.html.

Wieczorek-Zeul, Heidemarie, ed. 2005. *UN System Engagement with NGOs, Civil Society, the Private Sector, and Other Actors.* UN Non-Governmental Liaison Service.

Wilcke, Christopher. 2008. "Precarious Justice: Arbitrary Detention and Unfair Trials in the Deficient Criminal Justice System of Saudi Arabia." Human Rights Watch. 20(3E). March.

Willetts, Peter. 2000. "From 'Consultative Arrangements' to 'Partnership': The Changing Status of NGOs in Diplomacy at the UN." *Global Governance* 6(2): 191–212.

———. 2002. "What Is a Non-Governmental Organization?" UNESCO Encyclopedia of Life Support Systems. Article 1.44.3.7 Non-Governmental Organizations. http:// www.staff.city.ac.uk/p.willetts/CS-NTWKS/NGO-ART.HTM.

Wilson, Tamar Diana. 2002. "Pharaonic Circumcision Under Patriarchy and Breast Augmentation Under Phallocentric Capitalism Similarities and Differences." *Violence Against Women* 8(4): 495–521.

Women's Commission for Refugee Women and Children. 2007. "We Want Birth Control: Reproductive Health Findings in Northern Uganda." February. http://www.women srefugeecommission.org/docs/ug_rhaidp.pdf.

Wood, Reed M. 2008. "'A Hand upon the Throat of the Nation': Economic Sanctions and State Repression, 1976–2001." *International Studies Quarterly* 52(3): 489–513.

Wooldridge, J. M. 2006. *Introductory Econometrics: A Modern Approach.* 4th ed. Mason, OH: Thomson/South-Western.

World Bank. 2012. "Involving Nongovernmental Organizations in Bank-Supported Activities." http://web.worldbank.org/WBSITE/EXTERNAL/TOPICS/CSO/0,,content MDK:22511723~pagePK:220503~piPK:220476~theSitePK:228717,00.html.

World Health Organization. 2010. "Global Strategy to Stop Health-Care Providers from Performing Female Genital Mutilation." Geneva: WHO, in Partnership with FIGO, ICN, MWIA, UNFPA, UNHCR, UNICEF, UNIFEM, WCPA, and WMA.

Wotipka, Christine Min, and Francisco O. Ramirez. 2007. "World Society and Human Rights: An Event History Analysis of the Convention on the Elimination of All Forms of Discrimination Against Women." In *The Global Diffusion of Markets and Democracy*, edited by Beth Simmons, Frank Dobbin, and Geoffrey Garrett, 303–343. Cambridge: Cambridge University Press.

WRC. 2001. "Policy Statements: NGO Statement on Children and Armed Conflict." Watchlist on Children and Armed Conflict. http://www.watchlist.org/advocacy/ policystatements/2001nov.php.

Yaziji, Michael. 2004. "Turning Gadflies into Allies." *Harvard Business Review* 82(2): 110–115.

Zinnes, C., and S. Bell. 2002. "The Relationship Between Legal Reform, Donor Aid and International NGO Development in Transition Economies." IRIS Discussion Papers.

INDEX

Italic page numbers indicate material in figures and tables.